Nothing Sexier Than Freedom

Helen Edwards

Published in 2017 by
Sexy Freedom LLC

Arizona USA

www.sexyfreedom.com

This is a work of creative nonfiction. The events are portrayed to the best of Helen Edwards's memory. While all the stories in this book are true, the names and identifying details have been changed to protect the privacy of the people involved.

Cover Art: Designed by Kristyn McQuiggan of Drop Dead Designs & Tiffany Moule with Moule Designs

This book contains explicit language - readers discretion is advised.

*I dedicate this to those who walk this Earth
in emotions made of every unturned sacred
stone.*

*Thank you, Mom, my soul sisters, my son, my amazing
editors, the men, and those who believed in me and
made this possible!*

Rich, this achievement is for you.

I love you all.

Before the Beginning, There Were My Thoughts

MY NAME IS HELEN. There is nothing about me that fascinates the world or sets me above anyone else I know. To many, I'm considered your average thirty-something American woman. I have some college under my belt, have worked a multitude of random jobs, have been an active citizen, and — for my own logical reasons — still don't feel the need to skydive.

If you were to see me at the gym, I would be *that girl...* the one dancing off the beat from the music you can hear. You would most likely consider me someone that is ugh, weird. I look normal from a distance, fancy when dressed up, but without any makeup on, I could totally be stereotyped to fit in with everyone waiting in line at the welfare office.

I read a ton of books, practice yoga, meditate, and volunteer when I can to help those in need. All my closest friends and family would agree that I have a very giving heart and have done a lot to contribute to my community.

5

I don't curse around my mother. I've been to many personal development workshops, and have changed my life for the better in many ways because of what I've learned. I believe love is the most powerful force in the whole wide world and consider myself a spiritual person. Everything about me sounds wonderful and kind. (I'm pretty much a fuckin' saint).

However, that is not *everything* about me. See, as I mentioned before, Love is the most powerful force in the whole wide world, which also includes loving yourself, every part of you that is YOU. To understand what loving YOU is all about (from my perspective), you would need a vast open mind and an eccentric imagination.

The reason I wrote this book is because I have a radical mindset with the wildest perspectives on sex, love, science, and spirituality that must be shared with the world. Here's the thing: I love that I live an adventurous life with an ever-changing open mind. I don't deny myself that which I feel is normal to a human's existence such as: Sex, Lust, Fun, Attraction... And I can't leave out the most important...*Desire*. The fuel for every human's mind, body, and spirit.

I believe that anything that sounds so bad but feels so good (especially if scientists somehow prove it's good for your well being in some beautifully demented scientific way) is good for you! I have a feeling that I am not alone in my way of thinking or behaving. In fact, I know there are women out there who are struggling to break free from the chains of judgment society has locked onto their sexuality.

I was that woman who once felt ashamed for my dreams, fantasies, and desires until I realized this is my one and only conscious experience to feel and breathe life and everything that is included. My sisters... I am breaking free, because I'm a fucking bird! (I've also claimed to be a lion, lioness, cat, kitty, snake, wolf, a beautiful free running horse, and many other random exotic animals).

Right now, I believe I'm a free source of energy whipped into a spiritual being having a human experience. The key word here is: *Experience*; not *Experienced*.

There is no '*d*' at the end of that word. You weren't born into the world and told, "Okay, baby, now here's the deal: you are a free spirit about to embark on a human experienced." Even as a baby you would probably say to yourself, "Goo-goo what the Goo? You're telling me that Life is boring, and everything has already been done and I was just born to be a statue? I'm going back inside the womb where I can be like water!"

I don't think so! You are here, and Life is here too! We were given four bad-ass powerful action tools, and those gifts are basically what every super woman needs to turn every situation in life into a fantastic and memorable *EXPERIENCE*. The powerful action tools are as follows: See the book, read the book, learn the gifts, and play with the gifts. That's the way we love it, slickity slick!

This book is for the timid, the outcasts, the average, the overachievers, the underachievers, the believers, the saints, the deceivers, the dreamers, the dirty girls, the classy girls, the bitches, the housewives, and all the women who dare to step out of their comfortable gym shoes and try on a pair of hot black knee-high hooker boots.

Ladies, it's time to stop beating yourselves up with what everyone else thinks about you for at least a few minutes. OMG! The exhale you can take when you let go of the suffocation of everyone else's overwhelming opinions about every little move you make is uhh...*LIBERATING*!

We are constantly on this search for happiness, every goddamn day; it's a circus of daily emotions. You want to know what will make you happy and healthy in this one small moment of life you have? Falling in fucking love with your amazing self and every beautiful moment throughout the day despite what anyone else thinks! Also, not a bad idea to throw in hot passionate sex! Is this a book about sex? Yes. However, it is also about our human life and the mind games we all have to deal with. It's about success and failure, feeling lost and feeling found.

Most of all this book is about connecting and realizing we all have minds that are distorted... but also how empowered we can be when we stop resisting ourselves and utilize our minds for our happiness instead. This is a book about acceptance of yourself-flaws, your self-image, your self-actions, and most importantly your self-emotions!

Is it based on a true story? Yes. However, all names have been changed to protect those who think they are innocent. LMVT! – *(Laughing my vagina tight)*

If by now, you have decided to give this book a chance, then two things. One: You can relate and together we will celebrate our release from guilt and dance on mountains of hot bodies with a glass of red wine in our hands. Two: No matter who you are or what you have been through, there is no moment like this moment and there will never be again.

Therefore, breathe... Everything will be okay... I say that confidently because only the brave can get through an emotionally empowering, seductively filthy, courageously vulgar, and fucking incredibly awesome mind-bending (not to mention enlightening) book as this!

There is an unsettling belief that once you are of a certain age, or reach a certain point in your life, you *should* be at a certain place, or *should* portray a certain image that is acceptable by all of society within a million-mile radius.

You should pay attention and get good grades in your teens because you're going to eventually party in your twenties and start maturing by your thirties and have your shit together by your forties, so you can retire by your fifties and play golf in your sixties and hope you live to see seventy, so your kids can take care of you in your eighties.

Every living being is but a blink of an eye in a history page that no one will remember in another blink of an eye. So why the hell do we care so much about what everyone thinks about how we choose to live our one beautiful gift of life?

The funny thing is when you ask a question there will be a ton of people who would love to jump in your face with a million answers based on their own understanding of a philosophy, life blueprint, or belief, or give an answer they themselves were told. It's remarkable how many people think they have 'It' figured out. Whatever 'It' is. Maybe they have, maybe I just don't like their answer, so I continue to search for something that makes more sense to me, for whatever I feel is acceptable in the moment.

Maybe I've figured it out and it just hasn't hit me yet that I'm a freaking genius! Maybe just maybe…I've subconsciously been following in many great and successful people's footsteps and have not yet come to realize it.

There are days when I want to sink down into a hole and hide away from everyone's opinions that linger in my own head. There are days when I find myself bawling in the parking lot right before work because I feel like I'm wasting my life working for someone else's dream instead of my own. There are days when I am screaming from within because I look up and see a plane and I feel very strongly that I should be on that plane soaring through the heavens to my next great adventure!

Then reality sets in and I go back to work. I go back to fucking work! Work for someone else, making them more money and holding my hand out when I'm done for a couple coins, so I can pay my bills, maybe go have a beer with friends and do it all again the next day… And the next, and the next… And the next.

I watched Joe Rogan's YouTube video, Rethink Your Life, where he said, "Do what you want to do! What the fuck is it that you want to do?" All I could hear in my head was, "Travel, Feel Love, Fly, Have Incredible Sex, and Dance." I could see images of dancing free through the night with friends, having hot passionate sex, and standing on top of mountain peaks with my arms spread wide open.

I once believed you had to be somewhere at a certain age or be something by a certain time in your life. I once strongly believed there was a heaven and there was a hell. I once believed certain things or beliefs other than mine were wrong and only mine were right. Let's just say my original Crayola box was missing a ton of colors and the world I once lived in was pretty dull.

Now the world has opened a universe to me with many galaxies. Sounds funny and a bit cuckoo to people who fear thinking outside of what they know. We don't have to be somewhere, or have something, or have it all figured out by a certain age. We don't have to have our minds made up and stick with that for the rest of our lives if we desire to try something or someone new. Why should we? Because our parents or society taught us that?

I believe in the wise, but I also believe there are a lot of people who have put their own twist on the oldest and wisest of lessons passed down, only because they fear losing control of us. People are afraid of people because each of us is a creative being. Do you understand how powerful creativity is? It's imagination on crack! In other words, every single person you see is capable of creating his or her own separate world in this world — which would be crazy wild!

Money is an illusion...a vehicle that seems to disrupt many hearts, relationships, and beliefs. Don't feel bad for working hard and making lots of it. Don't feel bad for saving it, getting smart about it, or learning to use it wisely. Money is awesome!

Like money, sex also tends to be a teeter—totter subject. Sex is awesome! Don't feel bad about loving it! Because one day your hip bone is going to hurt bad enough that all you can do is watch it on a screen. Love is amazing! Don't let other people dictate your passion to love yourself or whom you choose to love.

Dancing is awesome! You don't have to stop because you turned thirty, forty, or eighty. Keep dancing and releasing that wild energy inside that desires to move in mysterious motions.

Wear whatever the fuck you want! Express yourself at any age, and if you want to change your mind one day and change it back the next for reasons you feel strongly within your gut but can't quite explain, do it!

If you're unsure of what kind of job you want to retire from or are unsure of what your passion in life is yet, you don't have to stress about it. Here's a concept for you: cut the imaginary ropes tied to everyone else's opinions and your brain, and just... breathe... in... life. Try on some new jobs and find out what you enjoy.

It's like Life itself is saying, "Hey, I know you don't have much time, so, you want to go outside and play?" Life is not defined as being an adult — there is no way possible it is that easy. Life is a spirited child, for sure. No one ever grows up. Maybe old, but not up. So why be somewhere at a certain time when time could end at any given moment?

I had this vision once where I could see every human born and they were born with invisible wings to fly. As soon as they tried to use their wings to soar with pizzazz and great imagination, those who were full-grown and "grounded" by society and all of its ideologies, ingrained the newly born with a belief that there are limits to everything, and that all must abide by these limits and labels because that is the order of life. Then the grown people placed an invisible chain on the newly born and said to their young brains, "You can go far, but not too far because you belong to our circle now."

I could see that the grown people were also in chains and they themselves were told the same thing when they were born. It's as if *Life* once again was showing me that this is not what *Life* had intended for our species or for any species! This vision reappears all throughout my life. I can't be the only one Life speaks to. There must be others out there who feel this way, in fact I'm sure of it!

Get ready, my darlings.
This book is for you!

ॐ

Chapter 1

Endings and New Beginnings

"The pain is horrendous."

THE DAY I DIVORCE Raymond is the worst and the best day of my life. The chains of commitment echo as they hit the floor. Even though tears drizzle down my sweet young face, the heavens open up and the sunlight beams through the clouds enough to reveal to me a pathway to a journey of abundance and freedom. All of Raymond's and my closest religious friends turn their backs on our decision to part ways; we are shunned and left out to the wolves of the world. *The pain is horrendous*, yet we know our marriage has run its course. We both are certain of our choice to go our separate ways.

The only Good Samaritan to clothe my lonely heart-broken ass is my full-blown free-thinking friend, Lana. She takes me in and allows me a shoulder to cry on and reveals to me the ancient ways. No religion needed, no saving needed, no right, no wrong, just life: Breathe, Exist, Live, Strive, Evolve, and Die. OMFV!! (Oh my fucking vagina.) Are you kidding me? Why have I been living in a bubble for years? I've been blaming and beating myself up for my true human nature, or lack of it, for most of my life. Even suicide was an everyday purposeful thought. That is, until Lana introduces me to a mystical world of Mother Earth's greatest human gifts: Dancing under the moonlight, laughing a lot out loud, and connecting with a multitude of other random people everywhere, every day. All I had to do was set myself free. So how did I get here? Well, let me show you…

Chapter 2

Pain and Pleasure of Passion

"I did not see this coming."

MY EYES CAN BARELY stay open, as I muster the last of my energy to gaze upon the miracle in front of me. He's small, scrunched up, and pasty all over. "A healthy little boy, do you want to hold him?" the nurse asks.

"I... I..." I drift asleep.

Once awake with some energy back in my body I glance at Life itself in a newly birthed form. He's the most amazing creation I've ever seen. There is nothing like the overwhelming feeling of unconditional love for another human being. I had witnessed love from different perspectives in my eighteen years of life; however, nothing could prepare me for the love and nurturing I feel for a child I gave birth to. I swear to protect this child from any harm from this world.

In the evenings I sing sweet hymnal

lullabies and pray over his tiny body. "Dear God, protect my son always. Please don't ever leave his side and if anything should happen, take me instead."

Every night I watch my son fall asleep and kiss on his fluffy cheeks "goodnight." Raymond and I look at each other with a tender glance as if we were in agreement that we both had "done it;" we made Love, our son Keme was born.

But that feeling of tenderness between Raymond and I doesn't last.

A few days after Keme's first birthday, Raymond drops this on me: "I'm not in love with you anymore."

Did I just hear what I think I heard coming out of my husband's mouth?

"I don't understand. What do you mean, you don't love me?" My young 20-year-old voice shakes as I wait for a reply. He stands six feet tall in the doorway, wearing a plain white tank top and black khaki pants and even after two years Raymond's green eyes still have a way of dominating my soul. However, something isn't right on his face. He looks like a young man confused about which direction to turn at a four-way intersection of a dirt road in the middle of the Kentucky plains. I scrounge around everywhere in my mind for the words to say that will keep him from walking out that door.

"You don't mean that, Raymond," I plead. "You just told me I was your 'Heart' last night! I think you're confused. We're both confused. We can get through this together."

"I'm sorry. I just don't... I'll be back for my things later." He turns and walks away.

I did not see this coming. The man I swore my life to, the man I would take a bullet for, the man I pampered every night with my love, the man I left my friends and my family for, the man I bore a child for; walking out of my life at the drop of a dime.

I can feel my heart beating at an unprecedented speed about to detonate in a matter of seconds.

"OMG," I whisper as he disappears out of the front door.

The shock is physically crawling through my body; I can't breathe or stand. Despair is the name of the cloud that hangs over my head as I search for something to cling onto. Paralyzed by sudden confusion, I can't create a sound, but I can hear my screaming voice bleeding from the pain in my stomach. Anger fills my heart with questions — just questions. I am alone; I am betrayed; I am broken.

With the little strength I have left, I call my sister for help. "He left me! He left me! Come please come," I scream to my sister.

"I'm coming. Everything is going to be okay. I'm coming," she assures me.

Everything is moving in slow motion; my veins are flowing with grief. I fall to the kitchen floor into a fetal position, wishing this were all just a bad dream. With unstoppable flowing tears I shut my eyes, and when I open them, five years have passed and the young fragile girl who once thought she couldn't live without a man is now becoming a woman to be reckoned with.

Chapter 3

A Devilish Grin and a Secret

"What seems like hours are only minutes of an intimate gaze of our eyes meeting with lots of mind fucking."

"DID YOU SLEEP WITH HIM?" my husband demands. I glare into Raymond's eyes and can see straight into his anguished soul as he anticipates my answer.

A memory suddenly flashes into my mind of Shane's hands all over my breasts as he threw my body into a universe of sexual ecstasy the week before.

"No, I did not sleep with him!" I snap. "I love you, Raymond… I would not hurt you like that." I devilishly grin.

Raymond weaseled his way back into my life a month after he left me the first time, leaving a total of three times in our first five years of marriage. I was devastated that first time, but each time he left and returned, I became a little less emotional. After the third time Raymond left and returned, I possessed a very beautiful yet naïve attribute. See, no matter how many times Raymond hurts me, I will only continue to take him back because I possess a heart of compassion. I love Raymond more than anyone or anything, so I devised a plan going against one of my greatest attributes to protect myself from falling into Raymond's trap over and over again.

Raymond has a way of manipulating me. He's too young at the time to realize he's hurting me with his ever-changing mind of wanting to be both single and married year after year. I never can stand my ground with Raymond because he's the one who provides the larger financial contribution to our household.

I always dread that he will leave me abruptly like he did the first time, so I fear speaking up or fighting too much for my own way. Whatever Raymond says, I try to go with to make him happy. He has a heart of gold and a strong passion to pursue his goals no matter the cost, even if it means leaving my son and me for months at a time.

It's very difficult being naïve year after year hoping that he means what he says when he says he's going to stay with me forever. It soon becomes such bullshit that I can't wait for him to leave so I can hang out with friends and do my own thang.

While Raymond and I were separated during the third time, I leave to stay with my cousin and her family. She is seeing a Marine and keeps raving about all the fun they're having.

Shane couldn't have come at a better time. He's young, tall, and muscular and an active Marine for the United States. My cousin has convinced me to go on a blind date with him to the Marine Ball. I instantly fall for Shane's east coast accent and dorky demeanor, which means he is easily persuaded by my command.

Our first night together I ask Shane to hold me and do nothing more; I want to see if he's the gentleman I presume him to be. He is. Shane gives me the excitement and the attention I need and am not receiving from my husband. I can talk dirty and play just as dirty with him; Shane possesses all the perfect ingredients for my cake on the side.

"Take off your panties!" Shane demands as he looks at me as I walk into the hotel room where we meet in Carlsbad, California. Immediately I feel the rush of heat throughout my body, my nipples plump like juicy grapes.

"Who the fuck do you think you're talking to... Shane?" I say in a monotone and low sexual voice.

He slowly approaches me until he's a few

inches from my face. What seems like hours are only minutes of an intimate gaze of our eyes meeting with lots of mind fucking. My breathing becomes louder, and I can hear myself moaning softly before any physical touch has taken place. His eyes undress me as we remain frozen in a standoff.

"I said, take your panties off woman!" he repeats lower and more powerfully.

I gulp. Holy fuck, I'm so turned on right now, how does he do this? Somehow the seducer within me manages to say, "If you want them off so bad, maybe you should remove them yourself... Man!"

Shane loses all control. He grabs my new beautiful floral shirt and rips the cloth in two! His lips meet my skin like a blade to its prey for an untimely death. His hands grasp my body, pulling me closer. Shane lifts me off the ground and pushes me harder up against the wall. My legs straddle his waist and I place one hand around his neck and with the other I yank his hair back.

"Is this all you've got?" I whisper alluringly.

The fire in Shane's eyes grows more intense; he rapidly undoes my pants until he rips them off. I remember I am on my period and maybe it isn't a good idea for me to get him this excited.

"Shane," I laugh. "Ummm, we can't do

this."

"Oh no you don't, we're doing this!" he rebukes.

"Uh, yeah, so… I'm actually on my period and I have a tampon in."

He looks at me as if nothing, not even a woman's menstruation was going to stop him from having what he animally hungers for. I am thankful my pussy is clean— shaven even though there is a plug in it. It's time to exhale and see what Shane is made of as he lays me down and aggressively spreads my legs open, kissing my body with hard luxurious pressure all the way down to my inside thighs.

The next day we wake up, and it looks as though a murder scene has taken place. Dry blood is all over the sheets, and clothes. We both stare at each other and smile; a night like that is going to set the bar for many to come and we both know it.

<hr>

I WISH I COULD tell you my husband, Raymond, comes to his senses and begs me back after I lit his shit on fire, but that's not what happens. No, actually what happens is we both decide to play the Hokey Pokey game for a few years. You know the game I'm talking about, the one where we are both one foot in and one foot out of the relationship the whole time. It's a very popular game! Some people play the game for years and become professionals at it. I become that professional.

Chapter 4

My Walking Heart

"What the fuck am I supposed to do?"

KEME GROWS AND FLOURISHES with a heart of champions; he is full of energy and laughter. Raymond and I realize our youthful commitment to each other has started to take different roads and the both of us are no longer on the same path. A few days after Keme's first birthday, Raymond leaves us.

After Raymond and I officially separate, each time he visits my house to see Keme, is heart wrenching. Keme cries for his father as he watches him walk away every time, "Dad... Dad... No..."

It tears me to pieces seeing Keme's heart break at such a young age. I want to do anything to repair our family and see Kemes happiness with his father remain permanent.

Raymond manages to beg his way back into my bed and back into our lives on a few separate occasions. The anger and resentment I feel toward Raymond for leaving us over and over again is one small step away from wishing he would just die rather than hurt us once again.

When Keme is six years young, Raymond files for a divorce and demands our son remain within his custody. Raymond is the sole provider for our family and I am a complete chaotic mess with no job.

I cannot bear the thought of taking my son out of a good school, a good home, a warm bed, and mostly away from his dad whom Keme adores more than anything. Flashbacks of my own childhood go through my mind; leaving with Mom and staying in random place after place, I can't put my own son through this. I promise Keme that everything will be okay no matter what happens, and then I leave my home to stay with a cousin.

Words from my close friend, JJ ring in my ears, "You don't want to take your son out of his home with nowhere to go. Don't do that to him. Let him stay with his dad. Let a man raise a man."

My Mother and my sisters beg me to fight for my son, but all I can see is the heartbreaking sorrow on my son's face when his father visited and left again.

"What do you mean you are going to *let a man raise a man?*" Olivia snaps. "You're his mom! He needs his mom!" she cries.

"Helen, are you seriously going to let Raymond have sole custody?" Margaret asks, repulsed.

"Oh Helen, you are going to regret it if you don't get sole custody," Mom sadly predicts.

My heart sinks. I wish they knew how shameful I feel for making such a horrendous decision. I wish they understood the confusion and conflict I feel within myself about the whole situation. Am I making the best motherly decision? Of course, I'm not... but what the fuck am I supposed to do? Drag my son out of his home and away from his father who actually wants to have a relationship with him and care for him? My dad wasn't in our lives very much, but what if he had been? Maybe our lives would have been a lot better. Who knows?

The courts favor that Raymond gets sole custody but everything else will be joint custody and I don't rebuke the decision. I am appointed to pay child support every month. My family is ashamed and appalled that I didn't fight for my son. I have never felt so alone and disgraceful in my entire life.

It is devastating to say the least that I could have let something like this happen to my family who I swore an oath to love and protect. Time and memories of the divorce and the court visits seem to blur as if it's all a bad dream. Working hard and playing harder help keep my mind off the deep wound of this awful conscious decision I managed to make.

***

"Is everything okay at home, Keme?" I smile as I help put Keme's coat on. He's growing so beautifully, thirteen already. Time flies!

"Yeah, I just always worry about my Dad," he says.

"Why do you worry about your dad?" I am a bit confused.

"Well I just don't want him to stress about me or his job." Keme always pronounces a heart of compassion and care. He really astounds me by the things he says and the intuition he feels at such a young age.

"Keme, you don't need to worry about your Dad. He's a good man and is always in control." We both smile.

"Do you worry about me?" I wonder.

"No" ... Well that was a quick answer...

"Oh." I jump back.

"Mom, it's just that I know you are strong and I always know you can handle anything. The only thing is I think you need a boyfriend, so you aren't alone. I don't want you to be alone."

My son, my walking and talking heart he moves me effortlessly. Hmm. He doesn't worry about me? He believes I am strong? He's worried about his Dad, whom he's with every day? This has me concerned for his well-being at his Dad's house.

One day, Keme will confide in me that he is glad he lived with his Dad and that I didn't try to take him because he felt his Dad needed him more.

<hr />

A hot shower is exactly what I need this evening. I shut my eyes and allow the water to wash over my body. "Breathe." I remind myself. The tears flow simultaneously with the drops pouring over my face. Words of my sister echo in my ears from the conversation we ended a few minutes earlier.

"Helen, you have a teenager! You can't be playing around with all these guys and daydreaming about your life anymore. You need to figure it out because you're a mom. Don't you want to set a good example for your son?" Olivia voiced.

"I'm not playing around with 'all of these guys," I rushed to my defense.

"Look, all I'm saying is don't forget about

your son."

I want to die over and over again every time someone thinks I have to be reminded of my son. Do my sisters not realize I am a mother no matter if my son is in my presence or not?

"Olivia, I never forget about Keme. I know you have your kids with you all the time, but this is the way it is in my life and I'm keeping my personal dating life away from my son."

"Yeah sure you are," she mocked. "You had a good man who wanted to take care of you and help you see your son more. Then you just break up with him, why, because the sex wasn't good? Helen, that's shallow! How many guys are you going to introduce to Keme as your *new boyfriend*?" Olivia isn't the type to hold back anything that's on her mind.

When she wants to say something to you, all emotions aside, you're going to hear everything that needs to be said. I love my sister and respect her opinion, but sometimes I can't help but want to throw a football at her face.

"For records sake, Olivia, for the past seven years, I have only introduced three different men to Keme and after each break-up, I have a truthful conversation with him. He's old enough to understand that life is going to have some unpredictable things happen and he doesn't judge me for it," Once again, defending myself.

"You need to go to church, Helen. Seriously, you need God in your life."

Oh great, here we go again. All I called her for was to see how she is doing and BAM now I need God. "Okay, Olivia, I'm on it!" I poke.

"You know, I feel bad for you, Helen. One day you are going to end up all alone and you aren't going to have your son or any man around to take care of you." A rush of anger fills my body, signaling to me that this is the final hit. "Thanks Olivia, I gotta go, I have to be up early for work tomorrow. Love you. Bye." My whole body and mind go numb.

As I allow the water to flow across my back, I rest my arms on the wall and weep. The memories of my son from birth to teen flood my mind. Each great memory is a trigger for an anguished cry of regret. There have been nights when I specifically set a small amount of time just to spend on one shared memory with myself; in a secret place alone where no one can see or hear me cry. It's like watching a short one-minute video and grieving over a life you once had that you can never get back ever again. Being the observer of a sorrowful memory, you can't touch, redo, or take back is a hellish place to be.

There are many things I could have said to my sister to defend myself. I'm angry, but not with her... with myself. Memories of different moments with random women questioning my mother- hood overwhelms me.

"*You*... pay child support?" asked with the looks of disgust and disbelief on their faces.

"Wait, your son doesn't live with you?" said with their surprised eyes and jaw dropping questions.

"Why does your son live with his Dad?"

Then there are the magic trick questions, "OMG, you have a son?"

Or my personal un-favorite question of them all, "How do you do it?"

The answer is... I don't know how I do it. Maybe it's the fact that I spend each day living in the present moment, and do my best not to think of the past, or the future, because one seems painful and the other seems scary. To be honest, I could go to therapy or counseling for the rest of my life and never feel "healed" from deciding to leave my unhappy marriage and say goodbye to my son that day many years ago. There is no cure for a mother who separates from her walking heart. However, there is forgiveness, and that is a prescription that must be taken two to fourteen times a day for life.

Yes, I've been viewed as the party girl, the fun friend, the adventurer, as well as many other spectacular kinds of people, and it's a wonderful life. But when my son is around, I switch to Mom mode real quick. It's natural and it feels normal no matter the length of time my son and I have previously spent apart.

HE'S TALLER than me now; I can't believe it. I just keep thinking back on a fond memory of Raymond and me cradling his tiny body, singing church songs to rock him to sleep. Keme was the cutest little monster, drooling all over his tiny T-shirts; now his face is forming so handsomely, everyone is always saying, "He looks just like his momma. He's gonna be a heartbreaker, Helen." I glance over at my son and smile. What an amazing young human being.

"Hey, son, do you believe in God? I'm just curious about your thoughts," I ask him.

"Not really. I mean, I don't know. I haven't really thought much about it. Why, do you?"

There are moments when you want to say all the right things to your child to lead him on the path of righteousness, hoping that whatever you tell him is going to give him wings to fly through any unhappy situations in life.

I pause, "You know, Keme, I don't know either. Sometimes I do and sometimes I don't. I want you to know whatever you choose to believe in life, just remember to be kind and loving to yourself and everyone around you as much as you humanly can be."

"I just think that it doesn't matter if you believe there is or not. Everyone is going to die at some point. Bad things happen to everyone. I don't see why everyone wants you to believe in God."

"Yeah, it can get confusing when people try to force their beliefs on you. It's like they want to scare you into believing what they believe," I laugh and Keme agrees.

"Look, my Love, you are going to go through many changes and experiences in life. I want you to know you can talk to me about anything. I will do my best not to judge you."

"Why did you and my Dad not work out anyways?" Keme abruptly asks.

The day I wondered about was finally here. He's fifteen with a young desire to know everything. What should I say? How much should I tell? How much can my son handle? What is appropriate and what can I still protect him from? I take a deep breath. "I loved your Dad more than anything, Keme. He was my best friend and we tried for many years to make our marriage work. We were teenagers, like you now, just a few years older. We didn't know what we were doing and instead of hurting each other for the rest of our lives we let go of one another. It never stopped us from loving you together though. You know that right?"

"Yeah, I know."

"Why? Do you think I should try and get back with your Dad?" I goof.

Keme laughs, "Nooo! You are way more fun without my dad. Do you think you would ever get married again, Mom?"

"I don't know, baby. I am not sure if I believe in marriage anymore. It's weird. Marriage is a legal paper and it almost makes you feel trapped a little. Well, that's the way I felt anyways. I am not sure if I will feel differently about it in the future, you know, anything could happen. But, I do believe in having a best friend, partner, or companion for life. It's nice to have someone you can spend your life with who makes you feel good and happy and you can make him feel great too."

Keme nods his head. He's able to understand and agree; it's amazing to see your child reach this point of intellect.

We get to the airport and it's time for Keme to catch his flight back home to California.

"It was such a fun time with you here, Keme. I can't wait to see you again and I am going to miss you. I love you *so much*, my son." I give him the biggest bear hug ever.

"I love you too, Mom. I'll call you when I get home." Keme smiles.

The drive back to my apartment without the presence of my son next to me feels empty. There is always this depressed cloud hanging over my head every single time I say goodbye to Keme. I use every self-help tool I can think of to protect myself from badgering my Self to complete nonsense.

He's on a plane back to California and I live in Arizona. It breaks me that I can't get myself to move to California and be with him because I don't see myself happy in that state. It eats at my soul that I am choosing my own happiness instead of having a life near my only son. I want to scream and physically hurt myself for being a coward, for hiding behind parties, and pretending that I am content with being a mom who does not get to see her baby boy daily.

Tears flood down my face and I scramble to think of things to stop the pain before I wreck on the freeway because I can't see the damn road from the waterfalls pouring from my eyes.

"Fuck you, Universe! Fuck you, God! Fuck Me!" I scream!

I am raging from opinions and judgment on myself and from others. I hate life in this very moment. Everything seems unfair, life seems cruel, and I feel like the worst person alive on the planet. I start to wonder what the hell I am doing with my life… for the trillionth time.

"Why the hell am I so scared to live life the way I want? I have nothing to lose! I've already lost it!" I scream at myself as I hit the steering wheel.

Dang, that hurt my hand. Probably shouldn't do that again. I sigh. "Okay, calm down. I am not a bad mom; I am a damn good mom." I reassure myself. Breathe and release. God, he is such a good kid! I release, I forgive, and I exhale.

My thoughts are broken from an incoming text:

HEY DUDE, I KNOW YOUR SON JUST LEFT. I'M HERE FOR YOU. WANT TO GO SEE A MOVIE TODAY?

I wipe my eyes and pull myself back together as much as I can. It's Lana, my only girlfriend I know who has a very similar situation with her own child. I feel comforted and my mind refocuses. I reply:

YEAH DUDE, I COULD REALLY USE A COMEDY RIGHT NOW.

Let's Go There:

A lot of emotion with this. You better believe it! If I didn't know who this woman was or knew the way she felt, my conclusion would be that all the sex and wild desires she has in her life are there to mask her bigger issue, her relationship with her son. The problem with that conclusion is that the wild desires began long before her son appeared in her life. I might also have a lot of opinions and judgments to say about everything I just read. Trust me; if I haven't heard it from someone else, I've heard it from myself. Don't worry; I have all opinions and judgments covered by now. Wink!

This chapter was not an easy chapter to write. In fact, it was my most challenging chapter to write. Everyone is given a path and a few partners to wander through the maze of life beside. Along the path you tend to lose, trade, and even circle back to your maze partners; once a new life springs onto your path it's a game changer for everyone.

I once had a counselor ask me, "How do you feel about your relationship with your son right now?"

Visions of beautiful fields of flowers, kids playing in the park, puppies jumping around came to mind. Right after that, a new vision of me breaking a chair and crying endlessly on the ground appeared. Talk about pleasure and pain in an instant!

"It can always be better," I responded.

Just like any relationship, no matter who it's with, it can always be better. My son is truly my walking heart and for the rest of my life I may have to do a lot of forgiving of myself, but I have found a great source of information and strength from the decision I made. I can only hope my son forgives me and can come to understand everything one day even if it doesn't come easily.

A man has raised a man and we are both profoundly proud of our son. His father was able to raise his son and I had a very large part in that whether anyone sees it or not. Paying child support is not the worst thing in the world nor is it the easiest to do. I've met women who complain to me about their exes not paying child support and how they won't allow their children to see them. They are more than surprised to hear my devil's advocate opinions about the situation. I've been able to open women's eyes to situations they wouldn't have been able to see before, had I not been through this ordeal of my own. Through this personal experience Life has revealed to me what inside-out strength looks like. Understanding and compassion have taken on new forms throughout the years; growth was undeniably at work each day within my soul.

Here is the thing you must remind yourself: There are going to always be people with their own opinions about what a mother should be and what she "should look like." It is okay for each of us to have our own opinions and judgments about one another. I say it is okay because sometimes that is the only way to be authentic with one another; even when the opinions come off overwhelmingly negative. The question is, do you plan to wear it; to allow those opinions and judgments about you become your gown for the evening? People change. Period. Some change day to day. We are all growing and sometimes once we realize that and are aware of it, everything in that moment changes for you. Compassion and understanding flourish and it's a magnificent place to be and witness for yourself.

Yes, there are going to be many women who are mothers, or will become mothers, who may go through some difficult challenges in the journey called Life. Whatever may come, whatever may go, I deeply desire that each of us women can embrace any challenge with strength and support, especially from one another. I can't tell you to be positive when you are in pain or "let it go" when you feel like you are carrying a weight as heavy as love (which is infinity heavy) but I can suggest a good cry, a good wine, and some great friends to help hold you up; this could make all the difference in the next few steps you take.

Please be kind and try to understand one another, we are all trying to make it.

Chapter 5

We Are All Trying To Figure It out

"Life in my apartment with myself is a California gangsta party."

"**FUCK! WHAT AM I** going to do with my life?!" I shout out loud to myself. I flop down on the bed and lay back to cozy up with my pillow. It's 10:30 a.m. I've already completed my morning workout and breakfast is over.

Ring! Now what? "Ugh!" I sigh. I work from the luxury of my own home. You would think I would be very happy; however, I damn near hate my job. The phone is constantly ringing and every single time I answer it's a different voice with the same freaking questions and problems. The repetition is getting on my last nerve.

"I understand, Ma'am. Do you mind if I put you on a brief hold while I populate my system? Thank you."

Populate was a genius word that my best friend, Veronica, said when she worked for the same company. Basically, it gives us a five-minute window while the customer goes on hold to chat, cook, shower, make a personal cell phone call, catch our breath, or have quick sex. During this particular "populate" window I am simply trying to catch my breath, hoping time will fly by so I can log out and be done with my workday faster. I glance around my room for little notes and affirmations I have left in random places for moments like this.

"This fucking job! Arrrgh!" Here I go. The battle begins between good Helen and bad Helen. My thoughts are raging war within my head and it's annoying... not to mention exhausting.

There is no one around, just little me in a big one- bedroom apartment all by my lonesome. My office desk sits up against the white wall in my bedroom. My king-size bed is only a foot away from my desk. Perfect for when I place someone on hold. That way I can jump on my bed and cozy up with my pillow for a quick second or two. Luckily, I have a balcony I can gaze out of and allow my dreams to pour out of my head while working endlessly to get through my day without quitting on the spot. I inhale all the beauty Phoenix, Arizona has to offer in the beginning of spring, wishing I could stay outside longer.

I'm in my thirties; I thought by now I would have it all figured out. I feel like I have wasted the past five years of my life trying to figure it out. I feel my body sinking down as I wonder what exactly I am trying to figure out all the time. I sigh. It feels good to exhale a portion of the built-up stress in my head.

Dammit! The affirmations and positive thoughts are not working fast enough. I'm about to start doubting and bashing myself. I'm fully aware of this part of my inner chick; the part of me that feels like I am not meeting the requirements of society's infrastructure, and the part of me that feels I am falling behind everyone else my age because I don't have a solid career.

"What am I going to do?" I whisper. There are tons of options running through my head. I mean I can do anything, so why is it so fuckin' hard to figure it out?! Okay, I am smart. I can figure it out. Let's see, I have mad skills, I can type 65 wpm — fuck, that's fast!

"Ah ha! I love people!"

Wait, actually, I don't always love people. There are times when people get on my nerves and I can't stand to be around the species.

"Damn, I sound mean," I tell myself. "Well, it's not like I have to tell people that."

I chuckle to myself and laugh louder at the fact that I'm having a conversation with the chick inside my head. Hmm, maybe I should masturbate really fast — I will probably feel better.

"Oh shit!" I quickly remember my call. "Ma'am, thank you so much for holding, my system is going a little slower than normal today. Can you hold for a few more minutes? Thank you."

I have to admit, working from home has its upsides. There are no coworkers to snitch for putting a customer on hold for ten minutes — a really messed up thing to do, but at the same time, I just don't care anymore. This is a job I don't want anyways, I think to myself.

Suddenly, I hear an electronic beat come on my Pandora radio station. "Ooh that is the jam!" I run over to my computer and turn up the volume. The music strikes my ears and pulses through my veins straight into my heart. It's almost like a mystical creature has opened her eyes within my soul. I can feel and SEE my visions clearly!

Life, beautiful life, transcending into glorious adventures outside of my body. I can see myself traveling around the world, meeting smiling faces from all walks of life; best of all, I am smiling, and I can FEEL happy energy all around. Oh, that vision touches my soul! I jump up and start dancing to the song. My hands are in the air, I'm waving them like I don't care, and my body is losing control. Dancing solo all over my apartment, I let my hair down and I am completely unstoppable.

Do I have a clue to the answer of what I'm going to do with my life? I don't have an ounce of an answer to that question. All I know is I hear a bumpin' beat that wakes up my pumpin' heart and I see a vision of who I believe I can be and BAM life changes instantly in this moment. I like to call these bursts of sudden "feel good" combustions, "Woooh and Whoa" moments. As quickly as they come, sometimes that's as quickly as they go. However, I love having these explosions of electronic energy bursts because I feel hopeful and that's when I'm most creative and active toward my larger goals.

The song is coming to an end and my body calms. I glance at myself in the mirror and for a moment. She, Helen, remembers me again. Strong, bold, beautiful, fearless, and capable, I am... I Am! My eyes shut and for a minute I remember myself this morning on my hike up the mountain trail. There is a most rewarding and breathtaking phenomenon when reaching the top — it feels amazing. I had taken off my shoes and felt the natural dirt beneath my feet. I had felt as if time and reality were all an illusion, as if I were alive inside an art piece. My most mesmerizing revelations come to me when I am on top of the mountain. I exhale as if I'm letting the dream go in hopelessness.

I open my eyes and remember the customer on hold. Back to work, I jump back on my workout ball because a regular chair puts me to sleep. "Thank you for holding, Ma'am. My system is still slow. Let me get you to an agent who can better assist you."

Let's Go There

IF THIS WASN'T me and I had my shit together, then I would have probably judged the girl in this chapter as irresponsible and very unprofessional. I admit I was unprofessional and didn't respect the people or businesses I worked for when   I was in a state of "I hate this job." There are a gazillion of us who have been in this same situation, or are still in this same hellish place in life. And I get it — people should be lucky or thankful they even have a job, right? Look, when anyone is in a mindset of: I don't really care, I don't give a fudge sickle, or who gives a shit, gratitude rarely makes an appearance.

Since I was a little girl I have been daydreaming about the life I wanted to live and the great adventures I was going to take. Isn't that what we all do when we are young? Dream about a more magnificent life, doing what we want, taking adventures without anyone telling us what to do? Having, feeling, and being total freedom! It's never been my normal to settle down in one place for too long, and when I would try to settle down, I felt as if invisible chains were on me and I freaked out! I attended a Tony Robbins seminar and learned there are six basic human needs: Certainty, Uncertainty, Significance, Connection, Growth, and Contribution.

Everyone is different, and these basic needs are listed in different orders based on the individual's habitual priorities. Veronica said she heard all it takes is for someone to fulfill your top three basic needs and BAM you will become addicted to that person. For a long time, I thought that Contribution was my most important need. The more I became aware of my life habits, I realized Uncertainty was my numero uno.

No wonder jobs, men, and places never stick; I am addicted to variety. At first, when I became aware of this addiction and habit to Uncertainty, I wanted to change it because I thought it was bad. But once I embraced the part of me that thrived and felt most alive with Uncertainty, it was like the heavens parted and the sun washed over me with glorious light rays. I felt the taste of freedom and only desire more of that feeling.

Funny how once you become aware of your deepest clarities about yourself, and you stop resisting, the coolest connections happen within your soul. My clarity is about to open up a freedom for me that not only brings pleasure, but also, for the first time, will allow me to experience truth. A truth so beautiful it has no beginning, no end, no box, no altar, just is, just is, and I will love every minute I get to experience it in this lifetime.

Chapter 6

I Got It Under Control

"I've never had a problem getting a man to meet with me when I am assertive and direct with confidence."

MAILBOX ALMOST FULL! There is no way I am going to respond to all of these guys! I'm not about to feel bad for deleting without reading what they wrote. If there is an attraction, then I will see what they have to say. If they don't have a photo, then "Delete." If they write something lame in the first two sentences, "Delete." And if they carry on low energy emails with me, "Delete." Online dating, here I cum! This is going to be fun!

Stop the press! There is a face that makes me speak five orgasmic words.

"Holy-Shit-I-Want-Him!"

I instantly send this gorgeous man a message getting straight to the point, that I need to meet him. I type...

WHAT'S YOUR NAME AND NUMBER SO WE CAN MEET, AND SEE IF WE HAVE A CONNECTION SO NO ONE IS WASTING ANYONE'S TIME.

He agrees and types back.

I'M KYLE, AND I WOULD LOVE TO MEET YOU TOO.

I have to admit, it's that easy! I've never had a problem getting a man to meet with me when I am assertive and oozing with confidence. This man looks perfect and I have to have him somehow. A place is set to meet and before I know it, I'm on my way.

Kyle is beautifully built. He's 6'4" tall with chocolate- almond skin. His face is smooth and his eyes are dark but his smile is what turns me into a melting pot of paralyzed desire. At first glance, he looks like an older and more mature Chris Brown. He has muscular arms with a few tattoos on his left bicep. Hot! It's the first time I have an instant connection with someone. In that moment I'm ready and willing to go all in and all out for Kyle. I know Kyle will be mine because every part of me feels that he's the one I have been waiting for my whole life. Our first date is the best date I have ever been on and the only date I've felt 100% in sync with a man. Kyle is effortless, fun, and open—minded to whatever I suggest. The instant physical attraction is mutual. In my gut and in my heart, I feel sure Kyle is the one for me. My hearts on fire and love is sure to be the culprit. The relationship moves quickly; Kyle and I are already professing our love to one another.

We continue to see each other almost every day for two weeks before the night comes. I can no longer adhere to Kyle's wishes of holding off on sex. I want him and can't wait. I have to seduce him and spread my legs far enough that he sees the drought can no longer persist. I've got him hooked! He quickly jumps up to grab a condom and rushes back to me; there I imagine fireworks and magic beanstalks sprouting from all around me. I am built up on the expectation that everything else is perfect and our sex promises to be the same.

Then reality strikes and bursts my giant bubble into a million little pieces. Something isn't aligned; there's no sexual chemistry. I try to get into it and remember how hot he is, but all I can hear is his girlish high-pitched moaning. "What the hell is this!" screams my inner voice. He is humping me like a teenage boy searching for his manhood. "No! No! No! This can't be happening!"

He's too fine and too mine for this to be true. "Fuck! Now I have to fake this orgasm, so he can get off me and I can return to our perfect world and hope the next time is better."

FAKING AN ORGASM: A false sexual moan that is used as a secret weapon to make the other person feel he or she has satisfied you, so the other person cums and gets the fuck off you!

It's said that babies are super cute so when they cry adults won't go totally insane. Some of those babies grow up to be super fine-ass men, and in moments when sex isn't explosive, a woman can fall back on all the other nice things her man has to offer. Where Kyle lacks in the bedroom, he makes up for in his attentiveness and in his love for me. He's great at surprising me with gifts, and I always have fun with him wherever we go. I'm in love and willing to do pretty much anything with Kyle.

For four months he's the rock star of my world. I introduce him to my family, my friends, and I even disconnect all engagements from all other men. I'm so in love with this man and do everything I can for our sexual chemistry to intensify each and every time. Kyle shows his love by giving me the undivided attention he knows I crave when we are together.

His interest in self-improvement I can rely

on, knowing he respects my drive when he sees me suddenly changing jobs. He encourages me when I feel I have failed, like the time I miss the plane to a retreat I am looking forward to. Kyle makes me a card, dinner, and looks in my eyes and assures me there are more retreats to come.

Kyle also flies us to New York to meet his family. I am the first woman he has ever introduced to his mother. I am not ready to meet her, but I want to make him happy, therefore I agree to it. I know this man loves me despite our challenges with intimacy because he keeps moving forward with me.

I wish I could say that the sex becomes better over time, but it doesn't. In fact, everything starts to fade, especially his tenderness for me. I don't think men realize how much women value "Tenderness." It's like receiving pure honey straight from a honeycomb. Kyle's attitude changes along with his desire to touch me. Now, I may feel damn guilty for faking orgasms and lying to save some souls from untimely catastrophes, but I won't say "no" to pleasure the man who steals my heart away.

It's one of those *should we go out* nights. You know the kind of night when the relationship is feeling faint, and you're desperate to keep it exciting even though you know you will be making all the effort. My best friend, Veronica, is having a birthday dinner and I believe it's a great opportunity for Kyle and me to enjoy life together. The night's going super-great and everyone is having a marvelous time. I made a superb decision by going out.

We make it back to Kyle's house; I am drunk and Kyle is a little thrown off by it. I am giving him drop-dead head as fast as the speed of lightning. I don't feel like it, or want to keep going but he insists that I am performing like no one else. Fucking men! Not only am I drunk but my ego is flying high as a kite. I have to keep going to verify everything he's saying is true. OMG! Here it comes, Blaurrrrgh! I run to the bathroom in disbelief that this is actually happening. Did this just happen? Yes, this did just happen. I totally puked all over Kyle's hard dick! I can't help but laugh in the bathroom as I grab as much toilet paper in one hand as possible.

"Don't move!" I shout to him.

I can hear him saying, "Sorry it got everywhere." I don't think he realizes what happened until I rush over and clean him. "Oh shit! I thought that was my cum that was all over me," he says.

I am so embarrassed, but I can't hold back my laughter. "No, I uh, actually, your dick choked me and I accidentally puked all over you. This has never happened to me before.

You're just so big!" This is classic and a tale to be told to the girls immediately (Although, I had to wait until the next day).

I truly believe I love Kyle with all my heart and all my soul but it's my flesh that feels dissatisfied. No matter how I plead with Kyle to please me more, touch me more, and love on me more, he fails to meet the requirements of a Dominatrix like me. Every woman knows when she has reached her limit of dealing with the ongoing bullshit of a partner. Especially when it's a partner she loves; it's an intuitive feeling inside as if time has fast-forwarded and we can vividly see that nothing has changed. In those few seconds of our psychic abilities, we not only see the past, present, and future, but we feel it too.

I realize my journey with Kyle is certain to end when I ask him to go down on me and he is "too tired." I'm fuming over the fact that we have only been in our new relationship for four months and Kyle is already turning me down. My anger rises because earlier that day, I went through Kyle's laptop and found a shit ton of porn sites he had been taking care of himself with. This whole time he had me believing he was "too tired" or "not that sexual" or "I'm too much of a sex fiend." Bullshit!

I turn over to go to sleep, feeling ugly, denied, and stupid for having to ask for a simple pleasure from a man I placed on a pedestal. Soon I feel my body cave in, my breathing slows down, and a tear slides down my cheek. Kyle has turned the course of our relationship toward rough seas. I can easily steer us back on course, but my alter ego has other plans. Oh she-devil, how I love thee.

The next day on my lunch break at work, I call the one person I know who I'm hoping to count on for an ego boost. It has been four months since I have spoken with Ross; I don't know what to expect.

"Hi, I'm just calling to see if you have the photos you stole from me," I say.

"What do you really want, Helen?" Ross asks.

"Well if you have my photos, I'd really like them back. I can meet you at that bar we always liked to go to up on North Black Road at 7-ish tonight?" I wait for a response.

"Okay, see you there."

Am I really going to do this? I have been completely faithful for four months to Kyle and I love him so much. Is meeting up with Ross wrong? We have only been broken up for six months and I swore I would never see his cheating ass again. We spoke briefly four months ago when Ross tried to beg me back, which he does every time we break up. Even though I was notorious for cheating, I am not solely driven by my vagina to cheat. Lack of intimacy, communication, and emotion are what drive me to cheat. I had met Ross shortly after my divorce from Raymond in 2006 on a blind double date. He was fun, energetic, playful, adventurous, and super affectionate. He had supposedly just gotten out of a relationship the same time that we met. Although he had many positives to him, he also had a crazy hot temper. I both feared him and passionately loved him. Somehow, the intensity of our ever-changing relationship kept our fires burning for one another year after year.

Ross was my best sexual lover of all time with orgasms guaranteed every single day — even on days when I was on my period. He was dirty — dirty and supremely affectionate, yet he just wasn't satisfied with one lover. It broke me to find out that I was the faithful one while Ross still begged his ex-girlfriend of nine years back via text message. I found out while seeing a late-night text come through from "Wells Fargo." I mean, what bank texts you at ten o'clock...

WHY HAVEN'T YOU RESPONDED YET?

Oh, hell no! I ended up talking to the girl and finding out that Ross had been carrying on a relationship with her simultaneously with me. It was fascinating. I really loved Ross and thought my cheating days were over only to find out his weren't. I broke it off with Ross four months after we met only to reunite and break it off again two more times before meeting Kyle.

Six months later, here I am wanting to meet up with my own personal copy in a devilish male form.

Although, this time I have a legitimate reason to see him. It's only so I can get my professional nude pictures back from him and then I won't ever talk to Ross' punk ass again. I am really good at talking myself into thinking that what I'm doing is pure logic without any discrepancies.

It's a good thing Kyle and I don't live together. Tonight, I tell Kyle I need some "me" time and he is more than happy to give me my space and not blow my phone up. This allows me to do what I need to do without any worries.

I walk in the bar and see Ross sitting there with his hat on. Instantly, I feel a sexual energy pulsating through my vagina, as if there's some invisible string attached from my clit to his cock, pulling us into each other's realm. I sit next to him at the bar. "Hi, where are my pictures?"

He looks at me with his spellbinding blue eyes and smiles, "What can I get you to drink?"

Damn, I knew I shouldn't have come to meet with him. Then again, I know exactly what I'm really doing here. How the fuck does Ross do this!? He is average, pudgy, basically as tall as me, works in the construction field, and isn't even as fine as Kyle! Not even two drinks in and I can feel Ross' sexual hunger as his eyes are fixed upon me. I know we both want the same thing and it will guarantee a most delightful evening.

Fuck it! I lose all control. "Let's get out of here!" I grab Ross' hand and lead him out of the bar. We jump into the back seat of his SUV in the parking lot behind the bar. Ross wastes no time and becomes a hungry beast, yearning to place his lips on every part of me. I can feel spirits moving all around me and through me as if the magic leading up to sex has taken us both to another steamy dimension of life. My shirt and pants are practically ripped off my body and Ross is tonguing the shit out of my pussy lips. Holy hell, I am about to cum right in his mouth. He doesn't stop until he can taste the juice dripping into the back of his throat.

The orgasm is too much for me to bear. I try to push his head away, but he sucks my pussy even harder — he loves the struggle. My eyes roll to the back of my head, OMG, I am about to faint. Now that is a fucking orgasm!!

Ross doesn't let me get off that easy. His dick is hard and ready to enter the floodgates. He pounds me just the way I like it, gripping my ass harder and harder. The windows of the

SUV are fogged up and the vehicle is rocking. Anybody walking by can totally hear my moans. Ross pulls out quickly and cums all over my back. We both need a second to breathe. The high of our altered experience is slowly fading as reality sets in.

I cannot believe I just made this happen. A range of emotions comes to the surface: Uncertainty, confusion, excitement, fear, pleasure, and sadness. I'm in a relationship! Okay, don't panic, I really needed this release; it's well worth it. Get your shit together and go. As I drive home I replay everything in my head as if to remind myself that I had full control, so I could stop doubting my decisions of the night. I'm going to be fine; I won't see Ross or Kyle for a few days because both men have high demanding jobs. This gives me time to shake it all off and keep moving forward. I love Kyle. I just needed a quick sexual fix from Ross. Thank you, Ross, thank you SUV, and thank you me, but this is not to happen again.

It does happen again. And again. And a whole lot of fucking... again. Ross and I realize we are two peas in a weird science pod. We both are mirrors into each other's secret lives. Ross is a good liar, I'm a cheater, and we both hate each other for lying and cheating on each other but insanely love our heat and passion.

Confusing right? Tell me about it. I explain to Ross I can't go back to him since I have a

63

serious relationship with a good man and I don't want to fuck it up. Ross and I agree we will just be friends with benefits and to keep it on the low—low. This is a turning point in our relationship. We accept the idea that to remain in each other's lives we have to abide by the "friends only" title, meaning if anyone asks why we still talk to each other we respond with, "We are only friends, nothing more."

Veronica and I live in apartments a few doors down from each other and when I need some time with Ross, I let Kyle know I won't be home because I'm hanging out with Veronica. It's a perfect cover-up just in case Kyle drives by and sees my car home. It's also perfect for Veronica and me to hang out every day and talk about all of this craziness going on in our lives. None of my girlfriends took a liking to Kyle when they first met him, so my continuous "playing around" is an excitement for everyone. It's like all of my closest girlfriends love the soap opera stories of my life and are waiting for the peak point to unfold. And oh my word — does the shit hit the fan with this soap opera!

Two months into my cheating escapade with Ross, I visit the clinic because I'm not sure if I have a urinary tract infection or an STD. God Dammit! I'm smarter than this; how could I put anyone at risk, especially myself? I tell Kyle I have to go to the clinic for my yearly pap. I call Ross and yell at him for possibly giving me chlamydia. Ross is always the culprit because he's just as untrustworthy as me. Ross is pissed that I would even suspect him of sleeping with anyone else. I probably should have waited for the results before accusing Ross of anything, but this reveals to me that I have become very careless, sloppy, and emotionally destructive.

Somehow, Ross had gone through my phone on one of his many nights over and found Kyle's phone number. (Note to amateurs: Set display lock code on phone.) This is the kind of morning where everything feels chaotic until the doctor says, "Oh looks like it's just a urinary tract infection... Here, take this prescription. It should be gone in a few days."

I head straight to Veronica's apartment to give her the good news! For some reason Kyle is blowing my phone up. I text him that I will call him back later. The return text from Kyle numbs my whole body for a few seconds.

"Holy shit! Veronica! Kyle just texted me..."

A GUY NAMED ROSS JUST CALLED ME AND TOLD ME YOU AND HIM HAVE BEEN SLEEPING WITH EACH OTHER FOR A FEW MONTHS. CALL ME NOW!

Veronica's mouth drops wide open. "No way! What are you going to do? Are you going to call him? What are you going to say!?" I feel my alter ego step up and save me from losing face.

"I'm going to call him right now. I need you to call all the girls and get everyone here tonight. I think I'm going to need a drink!" I shockingly surprise myself with a chuckle. My five-minute walk to my apartment from Veronica's seems like hours. My heart races. OMG, Kyle knows. I walk in the private space of my studio apartment and glance over at our "cute couple" picture pinned on my refrigerator. Oh god help me. My fingers shake dialing Kyle's phone number. Take a deep breath, Helen, here I go.

"Hey Kyle," I wait.

"Uh, Helen, do you want to tell me why some guy named Ross just called me telling me that you and him have been fucking for the past four months? Is this true?!"

I know I can deny everything and probably convince Kyle that Ross lied. It's my chance to save our relationship. Flashbacks of our romantic beginning zip through my mind followed by memories of crying myself to sleep.

"It's true."

"OH YOU FUCKED UP. WE ARE DONE!" Kyle snaps...He instantly hangs up.

I gulp. Silence... I thought for sure I was going to weep and regret my answer but instead I feel like the chains of attachment are instantly broken. I can breathe! I cry out loud, "YES!"

I had tried breaking up with Kyle earlier in our relationship after I realized our sex sucked and before I had done any cheating. He had begged me back, swearing he would show me his desire even more strongly than before. I knew once I jumped back into the relationship that if things didn't change it would be very difficult for me to get out. The thing is, I trust too quickly and love too strongly. It's coded in my blueprint to forgive and believe in a multitude of second chances, especially if the person begging me back cries. Done! He instantly wins!

A part of me longs to cry but the conversation in my head leads me to the CD player to blast some man—hating music. Fuck Ross! Fuck Kyle! Getting caught couldn't have happened at a more perfect time. In two months Veronica and I leave the country on a backpacking adventure through Europe. I am strong! Life moves on. Drop a tear or two, Helen and then move on. Time to celebrate. Exhale, I am free again! I put on my best pair of sexy shoes and black tights to relish in my own curves. My red lipstick is in full bloom and my eyes are staring back into the mirror, looking at the Ms. New Hot & Single Thang! I walk back over to Veronica's apartment where she is freaking out waiting to hear, "What happened!?"

Yup! All the girls show up! As if we all

belong to the Queen Warriors of the Round Table, it is truly a room of camaraderie. Queen Veronica, Queen Lana, Queen Dotty, Queen Viv, and Queen Sonia — everyone's eyes watch as I enter the apartment dressed to represent my bad-ass self at the table. Clapping and laughter break the silence.

"Okay, okay, settle down you guys... I'll tell you all what happened... but first..."

Veronica interrupts holding up what looks to be a pipe of pot.

"Oh no she didn't," Lana laughs, pointing at Veronica.

"What?" Veronica bursts out laughing.

"I'm just sayin', this is a night worth celebrating, ladies! How often does Helen get caught and we all get to hear about it all together!? Puff puff pass ladies! Woooh!"

Veronica lights the pipe, passes, runs to the kitchen to make some vodka sodas for everyone and races back to hear the story. Veronica is not just a good host, she's a great host!

This is a night to be remembered for the rest of our lives. We drink, we laugh, we smoke, we laugh harder, and we open up to each other and share our own personal stories of "getting caught." I am not alone. The Queens of my Round Table are my sisters and as the smoke clears I realize everything that led up to this moment was worth it. It has been months since I have felt this free, this alive, and this happy. I promise myself that I will learn a few lessons from this. And I do. Don't be careless with yourself and cherish thy sisters!

Thank you, Universe!

Chapter 7

Beautiful Danger

"I am feeling powerful."

HE IS TALL, DARK, AND HANDSOME. Cliché for sure! God damn... I have not laid my brown eyes on someone this fine since Kyle. The music is loud, everyone in the club is sippin' on a bottle full of bub — some drunk, some dancing, and the music is bumpin' all around me but suddenly I can't hear or see anything but this mouth—watering 6'4", sexy skyscraper-built man a few feet in front of me.

Tonight, I am feeling powerful and I'm wearing the perfect outfit to prove my persona. Nothing like picking the applause-winning black and white checkered skirt that compliments my tight breast—boosting tank along with knee-high hooker black boots for this moment. I watch like a hawk as he orders a drink at the bar; his right hand is signaling to pay his bill so he can carry on his night. I'm lost in gratitude to the Gods of Lust for placing this gorgeous piece of walking art right in my path.

Suddenly, I can feel her, my alter ego silently but confidently whispering, "Go get what you desire." I look over to my two girls, Lana and Dotty, shouting as loudly as I can, "I'm going after him!"

They follow me as I pounce like a tigress around the bar and hunt him down. I give my lips one last lick to make sure they have the glossy you want me look and I go in for the goal.

"Hi, I just wanted to cum up to you and tell you that you're very handsome." In this moment, I feel confident, sexy, and determined to make him mine.

My eyes narrow seductively. My smile is heightened by the way I lick my lips and bite the lower one. I remain vibrant, energetic, and bold when I speak. I have said enough for him to catch my drift - that I'm diggin' his style. Now I allow the man to play his part in the game. I walk away into the crowd.

He comes after me. "Hey! You threw me off by coming up to me like that. Normally I'm the one going up to people. You're confident — I like that! My name's David... I'd like to talk where it's quieter sometime." David's voice is deep with an accent, definitely not from the States. "I'm originally from North Africa," he explains.

"Is that right?" I smirk. I view him up and down, inhaling every manly part of him.

Holy guac; his lips are sexy! My mind drifts to different scenes of the two of us falling in love and living happily ever after. Focus, Helen, one step at a time.

We exchange numbers. Mission accomplished. Lana and Dotty are waiting for the famous 'signal' I give when I have scored a connection with a beautiful man. Thumbs up and a wink! There it is! The girls raise their glasses and we all shout,

"To a fuckin' good night! Woooh!"

The night continues with glances and flirtatious small touches. Soon the night comes to an end and my girls and I part ways with the good-looking men we have circled ourselves with.

The cab drops me at home at 2:30 a.m. Once I open the door I quickly take off my shirt and throw it to the side of the living room, making my way to the bathroom where I can wash up and brush my teeth. I'm exhausted. I take off my boots and skirt, throw them into the laundry basket and climb into bed to snuggle up with my eight-year on-and-off-

again boyfriend, Ross. Mmmm... Ross. My...
Always there for me lover.

"Hi, Baby. I'm home," I whisper.

"What time is it?" Ross grumbles as he lifts the covers, so I can crawl in to snuggle with him. "Did you have a good night out with the girls?" He gently kisses me.

"Lover, you know me, I always have fun with the girls! I'm tired now, hold me." I have one last thought before I fall asleep and enter my dream state:

"Life is great! It really is."

<hr />

IT'S THE NEXT DAY, and the girls and I recap the night, the fun moments, and the men. The conclusions are in, and it turns out the fine piece of ass I so diligently praised all night, David, doesn't seem that "into" me. Thanks to the award- winning book, *He's Just Not That Into You*, my girls and I are equipped to know when a man is into us and when to give it a rest and walk away from the fucker.

David's night before clues included wandering eyes, short attention span to the conversation at hand, and his one-word responses through text. I wish I could tell you I am okay with leaving David behind and moving on to the next "potential" man;

however, I've learned I'm wired in a different kind of fashionable, fun way. There's no way I'm going to let David go... Yet, that is. This man is too fine! I've got to at least give him the pleasure of taking me to dinner, so I can gaze upon his masculine physique one last time.

I can hear a voice inside of me say, "I've got plans for David. I will see him again for sure!" I'm excited.

And I do see him again. In fact, there is much I learn about David over a four-week period: He is young, he is reserved, and his maturity level is not quite up to par with mine. -MUST BE THIS TALL TO RIDE- Believe me, he is tall enough to ride physically but not tall enough to ride my timeline any longer.

The sex with David is a two-trial term and both times with the same result: He cums, I don't, and I want to leave his presence immediately after it's over. He fails miserably the second time and can't even eat me out longer than a minute. I'm very disappointed in his performance and as soon as I get home I have already signed a mental agreement that David is no longer going to be needed for my pleasure. He's a great man and I can see him going far professionally, but he's not ready for a woman like me, and I'm not in the mood to train a baby how to run.

I realize it's not that David isn't into me... it's that I'm not that into him, and I have already subconsciously come to this conclusion on our last night out together in the Green River House Bar just two hours before our last physical encounter.

There are signals I tend to perform when I find myself getting bored with a man. Like flirting with another man without any hidden agenda. And boy do I ever flirt on my last night with David — with a much older man. This new catch holds an interesting conversation, stares at me as if I am the only woman in the bar, and possesses the keys to a sexy black 2017 Maserati GT. Now how do I get Maserati's number without making it conspicuous? Very easily.

While David runs to the restroom, I ask Maserati and his friend what they do for a living. Maserati's friend owns his own company and I make it sound like I could use that kind of service in my own life, so they give me the website to learn more information, and BAM! Like, I said, it's that easy. Websites and emails are the new digits, ladies. Suddenly bored with David, I am excited about my new potential Maserati, and keeping Ross at arm's length while we are once again off in our on-again-off-again relationship. You would think I'd be exhausted.

Seems like I'm playing a game doesn't it? Aren't we all? Honestly, I don't believe I'm playing a game with anything or anyone I mentioned previously. Or am I?

<hr />

MANY FEELINGS and voices are in my head right now. I can hear so many wise words of wisdom from all of these famous people swirling in my mind. "Be in the present moment," "Let the past go," "The future will worry about itself," "Accept who you are, flaws and all," "When you stop resisting, that is when the tension releases," "Be true to yourself," and so many more.

I question myself, "Am I a cheater? Am I a liar? Am I doing something bad? How come I don't feel bad? How come I don't feel guilty? Is there something wrong with me? If it is so wrong, why does it feel so right?"

Breathe. Take a step back and observe. There once was a time I heard this voice in my head, "I am a bad person for cheating and lying. I am hurting someone and it's not right." I beat myself up with words of unkindness, "I am a slut and I'm so going to hell for this."

My confidence disappeared and beating myself up only made me want to be "bad" all the more, because I just didn't care. "I will drink more and be bad more because I am a bad-ass bitch!" is what I proclaimed! That's what I thought, felt, and manifested.

Breathe again. Take a step back and observe. Now, I feel different about what I do. I don't think cheating is always a bad thing. I don't think lying is always a bad thing either. Hear me out for a second. If I don't live in the past and I'm not yet in the future, then isn't it more than okay to believe that the present moment might be all you have and the only universe that exists is all who are in it at that very moment? If we live in the present and literally are in the present moment, emotions and all, then why not allow ourselves to feel dramatically amazing around others we are attracted to? Why not allow lust to move our bodies into a powerful state of fucking feel-good orgasmic vibration?

Oh, is it the word "lust" that has your mouth dropped to the ground? What was that? I can't believe she thinks it's good to lust? Fuck yeah! Let me put it in another beautiful way. All of your emotions and feelings are like colors. Some colors are vibrant and bright while others are dark and dull. Let's pretend the color for lust is the color rusty plat. (Okay, yes I made that color up, but it sounds cool.) My point is that we are all creators and artists designing masterpieces out of our lives.

Do you want to paint your life using two colors (good and bad) or do you want to paint the best piece of your life with colors beyond your wildest imagination? I'm talking about the kind of colors that when you combine (lust, fragrance, confidence, power, sex, authority, demands, beauty, cunningness, elegance, posture, gratitude, etc.), you create a passion so wild that fire doesn't even know what to call it! BOOOM!

Now for those of you who are married, or for those of you who believe in monogamous relationships, I get it! I believe in that, too! Oh no, did I throw you off? Oh I see, you thought I was one of those "open relationship" people. Sure, I agree with that, too!

What!? I know, I know. Am I blowing your mind yet? How do you think I felt when I realized how I was in resistance to both ways, all ways, and everything and everyone? There must be boundaries and limits to my beliefs, right? Yes! Of course, there are boundaries and limits to all of this openness. This is about to get really hypocritical! So, stop for just a minute and go pour yourself a glass of wine at once because this shit is only about to get crazy. I'm about to pour one and join you!

Chapter 8

Organic or Processed?

"I am a raging chaotic mess."

"**WHAT IS WRONG WITH ME?**" I say aloud as I prepare to lie down in bed. What am I thinking? I'm only seventeen. How did I get myself emotionally tied to a few different boys — all of them in different area codes? I crack a small mischievous smile. The next day I go to school and head straight to the cafeteria to meet up with one of my besties, Penelope. We are both in the last semester of our senior year of high school and she's just as crazy and wild as me. I know she has to understand what I'm about to tell her.

"Penelope, I need to tell you something and you have to promise to keep this between us. Promise?"

"I promise! What the fuck is it? Helen, what did you do now?" She laughs.

"Okay, so this is serious..." I insist, "you

have to promise you won't say anything and just hear everything I have to say before you say anything, okay!"

"Okay, okay! I promise," she agrees.

I sit back and take a deep breath. "So I have this friend and she's like the coolest and sweetest chick you would ever know. She would never hurt anyone and totally respects everyone especially the people she loves..."

I pause to be interrupted by the unstoppable gestures from Penelope, "This friend is you, isn't it, Helen!"

"No! It's not me, I swear, just listen." I laugh and continue, "So my friend, she kinda' slept with three guys who live in three different area codes in a twenty-four-hour period, and all of them are in love with her, and they all think she is basically their only girl. What should she do?" I wait for her response.

She busts up laughing, "She's a hoe! Three guys! Damn, Helen, where did you find this friend?"

I laugh too and wonder if I should reveal the truth. Is Penelope right? Am I a hoe? I don't feel like a hoe. Then again, what is a hoe supposed to feel like? When I was in my single-digit childhood I had heard my aunt's call each other "hoe" or sometimes even me. But I never did anything bad, never saw my aunts or mother do anything bad, therefore, hoe had no reflection of wrongness to it. However, I knew everyone else's understanding of hoe was not good. Now I think, well, if I'm a hoe, then so be it. That doesn't mean it has to be a bad meaning to me just because it is to others.

At a very young age, my mother had taught all of her five children, four girls and a boy, that this world can be a very cruel and dark place.

"Everyone is going to voice his opinion about who you are and what your life is supposed to be like, but only you can decide who you are and what you want to be true in your life," Mom repeated.

I watched Mom constantly trying to find her way in this world with five of us attached to her. She would leave us with our drunk dad a lot and my dad's family would tell us how my mother was a stripper and running off with numerous men. We didn't care what was said about our mother. She was the most gorgeous, strong, and determined human we knew. I wanted to be like Mom when I was little. I used to try on all of her sexy clothes and wish I could go with her on all of her wild adventures.

I grew up watching my mom being torn down by men's demeaning words and physical abuse only to rise stronger and more powerful despite it. She taught us there wasn't much of a difference in what a man and a woman can do. My mother did what she had to do to get us out of many dark places in our younger years. I now see and understand why she did what she did and how hard it was for her to break the chains of her own programming.

Ten years have passed and again I am screaming into the mirror, staring at a hideous drunk monster. "Why! What is wrong with me? Why can't I stop!? This beauty is my curse!" I shout at myself in my one-bedroom apartment building.

I am a raging chaotic mess. I snap and hit the mirror only to crack it and realize I will have to pay for the damage tomorrow with money I don't have. "Fuck men! Those bastards! I don't care about them, they never cared about me!" I scream.

"Get it together, Helen," I hear a voice say inside my head. I need to take my drunk ass to bed before I break something else; bad enough I've already broken my marriage. I really need to go to bed.

Knock! Knock! Knock!

"Helen! Wake your ass up! Open the door, hahaha, crazy night but we got to go to work!" I hear my awesome saucer friend, Lana, shout outside my apartment window.

I jump up out of bed! "Ugh. I feel like shit," I moan, feeling the effects of the night before as if a party bus had collided with a ball of rubber bands; I must be the rubber bands. I let Lana in and turn on the radio. Ahh, music, the love of my life; I instantaneously feel better about the day.

"What happened last night?" I laugh.

"You don't remember? You were fucked up!" Lana pokes. "No shit, Sherlock!" I snap.

"You were dancing all wild like you always do and then you left with that one guy, Gino. Then I get a text from you that says you ditched Gino and got a ride home from Larry. So, which one got to stay over last night?" She laughs.

All of a sudden everything comes back to memory, "Oh shit! Hahaha, I know what happened. Gino is really cool, but Larry... he is fine! Larry brought me home, went down on me, made me cum and then I told him I was tired and that I would call him tomorrow. Basically, I was like, 'please me' muther fucker and then get the fuck out!'" We both laugh hysterically.

Lana pauses for a quick second, "What about your boyfriend, Will?" I have to think for a minute to remember Will's face. I had started seeing him about a month after my breakup with another miscellaneous boyfriend, Justin. I tend to lose track with all of these games I run simultaneously.

"Oh yeah, Will, I forgot about him." I appear slightly bewildered. "He's just a boyfriend, doesn't mean anything." I shrug.

"What do you mean he doesn't mean

anything? He's your boyfriend!"

I shake my head and think about that for a second, wait a bit more, and feel nothing. "Lana, there's something you need to understand about me. 'Boyfriend' is just a label to me, just like peanut butter is a label for all different types of mashed up peanuts. They are all the same flavor... so why not try as many as you like until you find which one you like the best? He ain't my husband and I'm not even sure he'll last. I live for the moment and I don't feel guilty about it."

Lana's face is surprised and content at the same time as if I've said something that allows her to release her own held-down demons and set her mind free.

"Now let's go to work before we both have to beg for our jobs back."

ॐ

Pause for a Thought

THERE WAS OBVIOUSLY some twisted shit I was going through in my earlier years of life. Let's take a moment to examine what professionals might say about this:

A psychiatrist might say I have multiple personalities. I don't disagree with this statement. I think everyone has multiple personalities. If we didn't, then we wouldn't have multiple interests in hobbies, enjoy different genres of music, or have a diversity of friends.

A psychologist might say that my behavior came from programming I learned from my mother at a very young age and that I had a subconscious desire to become just like her. I don't disagree with this statement either. It's probably true. Why wouldn't I want to be like the most amazing person who chose life for me, who also showed me how to be strong through any adversity?

A priest might say that the devil was living inside of me and I needed to be saved. I don't disagree with this statement either because technically I am a cute little devil on the rampage who needed to be saved, financially — because my three jobs were really weighing on my shoulders.

A therapist might say I need counseling because it looks like I have "daddy issues" and I'm filling a void with pleasures from all of these men. You know, I don't disagree with that either because the fucking therapist probably knows what he or she is talking about. My dad popped in and out my whole life, so this might be exactly the way I want to keep it with all men. It is my 'normal.'

Fuck it! All of the professionals are right in their ways of thinking, or should I say "learning," about human behavior. Should I feel bad for what a professional or expert has to say about my life? Why? Because what I am feeling or doing is "bad?" Who doesn't experience emotions of feeling "bad" or "good" in this life? There is no escaping some kind of suffering in this world. Why beat myself up for what is normal to me just because it is not normal to others?

Then again, what is normal?

Chapter 9

The Forbidden Fruit

*"There is something very magical
about releasing all of your guilt,
anger, shame, and pretty much all
the negativity in your life into a
higher spiritual guru's hands."*

TIME TRAVEL TO THE PAST when I was in the
dawn of my early twenties, married to my only
spouse – Raymond - whom I loved but also
resented quite a bit.

Holy shit, he is good - looking! OMG, I just
said, "shit" in church. OMG, I just said, "Oh
my god" in church. Good thing no one can hear
my thoughts. I mean, God can hear me but I'm
sure I'm not the only one in here who's
thinking sinful thoughts. I'm sure someone in
this building is thinking of murdering her boss
or boyfriend right now.

Focus, Helen, listen to what the pastor is

saying as he leads the opening prayer. I can't stop thinking about the lead singer of the worship band that just performed. Not only is he handsome; he is a 'Man of God.' I bet if he has a wife he treats her like she is the only woman on the face of the planet.

He probably never fails to please his woman or ever looks at any other woman with lust in his heart. I wonder if he is a virgin. Damn, he is only getting hotter in my mind. Fuck! Okay, enough cussing in my head. God can hear you Helen! Jesus! I mean that in a good way. Lord, help me clean my thoughts from impurities.

"Amen" the crowd voices together. All heads lift up to focus on the pastor; it's time to get fed the message that will help keep each of us from the temptations of the world in the coming week. My eyes return to the lead singer of the worship band; he has blonde hair and hazel eyes. He is rockin' a contemporary modern look and his smile is already filling every woman's heart in the room with temptation. I am fantasizing up a storm of different ways he falls madly in love with me. I'm interrupted by the deep voice next to me.

"Whoa, Helen, that was pretty deep... what the pastor just said, huh?" my husband says in his lowered voice. Now I'm totally taken out of my trance.

I reply, "Yeah, babe! We are seriously

going to start praying as a family every night."
My shoulders droop lower and I'm suddenly
feeling more lost than when I first entered
church. My excitement is gone, the fantasy
disintegrated, and now I must repent. I'm
married, what am I doing thinking about this
other man?

"And Jesus will forgive you if you confess
your sins and accept Him in your heart! Come
to the front and you will be saved now," the
pastor shouts.

I should definitely go up there. But how
many times do I need to be saved? Seriously, I
have been baptized more than five times, saved
fifteen times, and confess my sins a gazillion
times a day. I'm no idiot; this definitely cannot
be what the real Jesus had in mind for future
generations. Fuck it! I go up to the front to
accept Jesus yet again and start bawling like a
baby 'cause I feel like the worst person on the
planet.

There is something very magical about
releasing all of your guilt, anger, shame, and
pretty much all the negativity in your life into
a higher spiritual guru's hands. When I return
to my seat, my husband gives me a big hug. I
feel clean and whole again. Everything is going
to be better from now on - I can feel it!

Boy do I feel it that night, fucking the shit
out of my husband while fantasizing about the
lead singer of the worship band. The more I

fantasize about the singer's face instead of my husband's face, staring back at me, lusting after my body, touching me for the very first time, I shiver and scream, "Yes! Yes! Oh hallelujah, yes!"

During the course of my eight-year marriage, I manage to claim six different religions and faiths, mentor many women during these years to better their own marriages, eventually lose count of how many times I get saved, sleep with a ton of worship leaders, pastors, deacons, and other hot men from church (through extreme lustful fantasizing), and have some of the best and naughtiest orgasms I've ever had with my now ex-husband.

Not even our church is a place where I can leave my fantasies at the door. I try many times, but it's like saying to my brain, "Hey, you wait outside while I go inside, get washed of my filth, and then come back out and put your dirty ass back in my head." There is something very profound when you start to listen to the questions in your head. Why is my mind filthy or dirty? Why does everyone care? Why do I put such a demand on my husband to be the man to meet every one of my gazillion needs? I mean, I caught Raymond watching porn several times. Is he fantasizing in church or fantasizing while having sex with me too? He's just a man and I'm just a woman and we are just fuckin' human! Here today, gone tomorrow, therefore why the pressure?

Chapter 10

Confidence in Confusion

"There is nothing sexier than getting glammed up only to sweat it out by circling our hips and throwing our hands in the air for the world to witness our playfulness."

"OMG YOU GUYS, we just walked in looking like the United Nations," Sonia laughs. We all wonder what the hell she's talking about.

"Look," she points, "Lumi is peach-fuzz Asian with full luscious lips and curvy hips, Viv is a tapioca salt-white sensation with a J Lo booty, Veronica is a hoola-hooping goddess with country white girl roots, Dotty is a sultry mix of Egyptian and black cocoa beauty, Lana is a fantasy model straight from the reservation, Helen is a year-round tanned brown queen. We look like an international soup bowl." Sonia laughs aloud again.

We all look at each other as if we have been

enlightened about our colorful differences for the first time. We're on a girls' beach trip to San Diego, California.

It has been a while since the seven of us girls have had the chance to get together to reminisce, share some laughs, and catch up. The live music has all of us jamming out in our seats at the River Rusty Bar Restaurant. Damn, we are a powerhouse of confident women!

I lift my glass into the air, "Ladies, let us cheer to this moment. We are amazing women and we are loving and accepting of each other. Thank you for all of you, because of each of you, life has been ridiculously fun, and memories will be cherished forever!"

We all raise our glasses and Veronica shouts, "I love you bitches! Woooh!"

I have a feeling this night's about to get very loud and very creative.

There comes a time in every woman's life when she must take a look around and realize that without a glass of wine in hand, without her most sophisticated, dirty bitches around, and the perfect playlist calling the wild child out of her, life would cease to exist, and the world could seriously become a state of perfect bullshit. Yikes! Don't get me wrong, nothing against bullshit but too much of it gets   old, real fuckin' fast! Now we all know there is no escaping bullshit, and everyone has some kind of bullshit in her life; however, the less bullshit I have on my plate... the better. I would like to stay as far away from the perfect bullshit as possible.

As I move my upper torso to the beat of the music, Dotty leans over and says, "I'll be right over there," she points to the bar flocked with men. The girl's got swag!

"Ask him to buy us all a drink!" I shout back as I watch Dotty head to the bar. I'm not referring to any man in particular but I know whomever she chooses to talk to is about to win a chance to meet one of the most talented seductresses of the night.

Five minutes later the drinks pour in from all directions around the bar. The table quickly becomes an alcohol display: Coronas, margaritas, wine, Bud Lights, Tequila shots, and don't forget all the fun breakable glassware. I think it's a nice display and a nice gesture; although by now all of us ladies are diva'n it out on the dance floor.

There is nothing sexier than getting glammed up only to sweat it out by circling our hips and throwing our hands in the air for the world to witness our playfulness. As the night progresses so do our wicked desires for a night of audacious climax. The moment is perfect; everything seems to glisten with feminine magic. Lumi's prowess is devouring a white knight's tongue; Dotty has the eyes of   a handsome titan glued to her as he cradles her ass in his hands; Viv is nuzzled in the corner by a sexy professional basketball player; Sonia has two men fighting for her attention when she's clearly eyeing another man across the bar; and Veronica and I, as the unity believers we strive to be anywhere we go, are saving a horse, and riding two cowboys on the dance floor. The night couldn't be more spectacular. Or that's what we so diligently lead our most beloved partners at home to believe.

The night continues like that, but finally, exhausted, we decide to call it quits. We climb into two taxis and head back to the hotel. I don't pay much attention to my girlfriends, as I quickly snatch off my heels and fall into a bed. I am asleep within seconds.

The next morning, I wake up with a headache.

"Holy shit, last night was fun!" I say as I sit up with hair like a tumbleweed. I glance around to see who made it in last night. "One, two, three, okay... four, five, six um, where's Lumi?"

"I'm right here!" Lumi laughs from the bathroom.

"Oh good. We all made it home safe. So who fucked last night?" We all laugh and grunt, still sleepy.

We lounge a bit longer. After about an hour we rise to get ready for another amazing day out on the Southern California beach on our girls' trip. We are determined to make every single moment count as something spontaneous and glorious.

"Let's go rent bikes!"

Veronica shouts "Fuck yeah!" I woohoo!!

There's something wonderful about a group of friends with a multitude of interests and open minds to try anything. There is never a dull moment in our shared adventures. Each of my beautiful girlfriends has an essence to her character that has glued us together throughout the years. As we ride through the wind along the California coast I can't help but smile with gratitude. I have known all of these amazing women for almost ten years now. We have witnessed each other cry over numerous heartbreaks and we have celebrated many successes. Let's stop here and have some lunch, girls!" Veronica shouts.

Over lunch I slip back into my observing mind, watching the interaction between the seven of us. Time has gone by quickly over the years, but we still find opportunities to connect and share our lives. The moment is slow—motion as my mind jumps back in time when I first moved from California to Arizona. Some years back I didn't foresee my life this way; I thought I had it all figured out. No, in fact, what seems like a lifetime ago I was nuzzled on my husband, Raymond's chest, talking about how great our life would be when our son was older, and we would finally have enough money to buy the house we had always dreamed of together. Later that same year my life had fallen completely apart during an awful divorce. In a new city and state, there were no friends or family to support me through that horrendous time. Until I met these amazing women who now sit in front of me. They are a group of fantastic goddesses.

I met Viv in a Sprint store. Viv is a bad-ass district manager for many stores. She is vibrant, positive, and an action-taker for sure. She introduced me to many of the other amazing women in my life by employing us at Sprint. I was at a club when I met Lana. A bathroom attendant introduced us inside the ladies' room because I was complaining I didn't have any friends. Lana and I exchanged phone numbers. She was engaged when I first met her and protected me through many crazy nights I could have seriously hurt myself. Lana is the cynical type; she is sarcastic, cautious, and evaluates most situations before taking a risk.

Sonia and Dotty were at one of Viv's famous theme parties. Dotty was in a dance group and I swear she looked just like Alicia Keys. She is flirty, ambitious, and super uber smart. Sonia is viciously sexy, and she can seduce any man to give her anything. I wanted to learn Sonia's skills and try them out myself. Sonia is secretive, adventurous, and always has a plan.

I also met Veronica thanks to Viv and the Sprint store. When I first met Veronica, I thought she was butch because she wore her sleeves rolled up and her hair in a pompadour. Veronica thought I was mean and always giving her dirty looks because my eyebrows were usually arched. Then we realized we both like to take long lunch breaks to the movie theatre and the bar and quickly became good friends. Veronica is social, spontaneous, and very enthusiastic.

Veronica and I met Lumi at a bar. At the time, Lumi was engaged and had just moved to Phoenix straight from China. She is beautiful and very fun to hang out with and we just knew she would fit right in with our group of awesome ladies. Lumi is wise, honorable, and wild when you least expect it.

These fantastic women have all been through their own ordeals throughout the last ten years. We have watched each other survive some mean breakups, some big thumbs- ups, and some wicked hang-ups. Anytime one of my soul sisters felt like life was crashing in on them and they started to question their purpose or when they found themselves depressed beating themselves up harshly, they knew they could come to me.

It didn't matter if they sounded crazy or cried over spilt milk, I acknowledged their pain and let them vent until they got it ...all the bullshit... out of their system. If they were having money problems and I had anything in my bank account, I would offer it, even if it was my last twenty dollars. I drove hundreds of miles to see my girls who lived out of state to keep a close bond with them. Nothing made me feel more alive and happier than seeing my soul sisters living with smiles and experiencing life the way I knew we all truly desired to live... Free.

I remember growing up meeting many girls who would say, "I don't really get along with girls...most of my friends are guys," or "Girls don't like me, that's why I hang out with boys," or my favorite, "I'm more like a guy... that's why most of my friends are guys."

I would respond with, "Oh that's cool. We should hang out!" It's as if I could see right through a woman's tough persona and make a *go* at letting her know she could be fragile around me.

When my sisters and I were little, my mother planned an escape from my physically abusive father to hide away in a women's shelter. During our time in the shelter I watched women put their differences aside and be each other's rock. I was eight years old when I first witnessed women come together.

It left a powerful mark on my life. Mom would tell my older sister, Margaret, and me,

"Women can hate on each other all they want but if you ever need to protect someone, you better drop everything for her because that someone could be you one day."

The first ten years of my life, from what I can remember, I had been witnessing women covering up their bruises and making excuses for men who had hurt them. I will never forget a young woman in the shelter who had burns on her face that were inflicted by her boyfriend. Memories linger of my mother hugging this young girl and telling her to get out of the abusive relationship. These experiences from my childhood help keep me humble and remind me that women are tough but also very delicate. Why hate on other women when none of us knows what the hell any of us are really going through, ya know?

The most abusive relationship I had ever been in was the one I witnessed between my father and mother as a child. The sadness that painted my mother's face when my father would shamefully degrade her with foul language, the yelling and slamming I could hear from the bedroom, and the sobbing I could hear from my mother as my dad stormed out the door to find comfort at the bar was enough for me to wish the two had never met.

Fast forward the time to my first boyfriend

at sixteen slapping me across the face for laughing at him as he caught himself from tripping over a staircase to his room; the burn on my cheek. I'd never felt such instant rage until then. I snapped, grabbing onto the collar of his T-shirt with both hands, slamming him up against the wall, clocking him straight in the face with a powerful fist three times like a straight bat out of hell.

"What the fuck is your problem!" My puppy love boyfriend, Al shouted. "I lightly smacked you!" He cried.

Lightly, my ass! To me it didn't matter. He put his hands on me and that was a big no-no. It was at that moment I realized I had the same capacity to react and physically harm someone I loved with the same disregard to his humanity. I never wanted to be like my abusive father and hurt anyone I loved, and at the time didn't know how to defend myself without getting cray—cray.

Speed up to the age of twenty during the second time my husband had left me. I was living with my oldest sister, Margaret, and one of my childhood friends, Domino, drove me home after a night drinking at his house. As I stumbled into my room, motioning him to be quiet because my infant son was asleep in the crib right next to my bed, I thanked him for taking me home. Domino started taking off my clothes, saying I was too drunk to do it on my own. Too drunk and trusting his friendship, I agreed. Domino lay me down on my bed and began kissing me. I laughed, thinking he was out of his mind. He knew I was still married and that Raymond was coming in two days to reconnect with me, so we could get our marriage back on track. I pushed Domino away as he kept saying,

"You know you want this, girl." I wondered what the hell was wrong with Domino. He wasn't like this.

"No. Domino. I'm still married. My son is right here. Stop." I tried to roll out from under him, but Domino pulled me back.

Domino shoved my legs apart and forced his dick into me. I tried to push him away, but his weight was too much.

"Domino!""Yeah, you like that?" he said in a raspy voice.

I began to sob silently as he grunted over me, his sweat falling to my face, mixing with my tears.

Finally, after what felt like ages, he stiffened and then fell down next to me. He let out a huge sigh and turned his head to look at me, smiling. He noticed my tears and his smile immediately disappeared.

"What's wrong?"

"Just forget it," I said, turning my back to him.

"No, what's wrong with you?" he tries to

make me look at him, but I refuse.

"Go to sleep and don't worry about it," I said, wiping tears from the side of my face.

Am I crazy to think one of my best friends just raped me? I wondered.

I shook my head. "No way. That's impossible. I let that happen." We had been friends for years. There was no way I could think he raped me. I sucked up my tears and lay awake all night, staring at the wall and ceiling, replaying in my mind what happened.

I finally heard Domino's soft breathing, which turned into loud snoring. It must have been somewhere before dawn that I fell asleep, as I awakened to find him sitting on the side of the bed looking at me.

I gave him a tight, stiff smile and got up. He followed my lead and we both dressed in awkward silence. He gathered his keys and looked at me again. I could tell he wanted to say something, but I was in no mood to hear it.

I walked to the door and opened it. He hesitated, then walked toward it. I touched his arm. "Domino. You gave me your virginity last night didn't you?"

He nodded. I could tell he was feeling shameful.

"Look, let's pretend last night never happened and never tell a soul, okay." I firmly said. He nodded in agreement.

I closed the door behind him, knowing our

friendship was over. I never spoke of it. Close friends and family asked about the abrupt ending of my friendship with Domino; I played it off as if we both had suddenly gotten busy in our lives. That was the first time I had committed adultery in my marriage and I had twenty-four hours to shake it off. The stench, guilt, and anger that flooded my body from what Domino and I had done sickened me. The idea of rape or him entering me against my will fucked with my mind for years. How could I let it happen? How could he do such a thing? How did I put myself in that situation? How could I lose a best friend? How could I never tell anyone? How would anyone ever believe me?

Domino was such a good person. I couldn't destroy his reputation. I was too drunk and maybe I didn't say no and it was all in my head. After knowing one of my family members was brutally raped there was no way I could say I was or even think I was. I got off easy and I probably could have done more to stop it. I just couldn't play the victim — no way, no how. I was determined to let this go somehow.

I shake my head to bring me back to the present. Damn that was tough to write about! I haven't looked back at that moment in my life for many years. I can still see it in my mind no matter how well I've trained myself to pretend that certain events didn't happen. It does fire up some emotions in me such as anger and sadness. I was alone and did what I thought was best for my son and myself at that time, which was to conceal it all. I believe this is one of the many reasons I gravitate toward compassion for women. Even though women tend to spiral out of control with our emotions, we also are strong with them too.

Jealousy over other women has also been a big hurdle to overcome in my life. I often compared myself to other beautiful women and criticized myself for not having larger breasts or a big sexy plump booty and six—pack abs. Sometimes I would sabotage my relationships with good men because I couldn't get over being jealous of stories in my mind of these men wanting others more than me. I've come to realize that most of women's biggest battles are not with others but within their own minds.

I'm sure you are thinking, well, if she is such a believer in women empowering women, then why does she think it's okay to cheat and lie too? I respect this question.

There are so many jealous and insecure women in this world. Everyone is questioning if his or her partner is being faithful these days, especially knowing that there are women out there like me. I get it! Here's the thing: I am not saying that the answer to everything is cheating and lying. I'm also not okay with being with a man who is married or in a relationship (unless it's an open relationship).

My girls and I have been through waterfalls and lakes of tears created by men who think with their dicks instead of their hearts. All I'm saying is we are women! Women! Haller for a mutha-effin dollar! Women are more powerful than most of us give ourselves credit for. When we actually decide to stop the jealousy and the finger pointing, and band together to laugh with one another and understand one another, it's like a beautiful firework display on the Fourth of July in Vegas, baby!

Women are fierce, courageous, unstoppable creations of the planet! It's said that women live longer than men. I'm okay with that because I usually have more fun with my female friends than any boyfriends I've ever had. If you don't have a group of women in your life, start making friends today. If you hear a voice in your head say, "I'm not good at this or that..." Stop it! Let's make this easier; the first woman you need to make friends with is yourself. Start there... the rest of your posse will show up.

Trust me women, you don't have to compare yourself to me or any other women, we've all got mad issues. Wink!

Chapter 11

Je T'aime Mon Amour

"This is the day I give birth to my liberation."

THE FIRST TIME I LAY EYES on her there is this enchanting feeling, a sensation from my scalp to my pink zone down into my toes. Her dark brown chocolate-covered cranberry eyes grab my attention. It's a moment straight out of the movies as if everything around us has gone into slow motion. I am locked in by her devilish smile and seductive eyes. Her beautiful long dark hair, flowing over the almond skin of her shoulders, has me in complete awe.

Who is she? Why is she staring at me? I turn around to see if anyone else can see this magnificent glory staring at me, but they seem to be lost in another dimension. Or maybe it's the other way around — am I in another dimension? Damn, she is fucking smoking hot in that long red and black silk dress. I smile and wait to see what sign she will give me next; there is definitely something sultry about this woman. She nods at me as if she's getting ready to do something fierce, as if she's signaling she's about to do something mischievously bad. I'm about to have a fucking orgasm right now!

I observe her as she walks around the room, totally aware of all the men and women lusting after her sugar sauce. Every part of her screams mighty goddess on the prowl! How did she get here and with whom? This gala is a private event for members only. Who invited this chick?

I suddenly feel myself becoming judgmental; my body is tensing up and I am uncomfortable in my own skin. I lost her! I look around. Where did she go? Why am I so uptight! I've got to get the fuck out of my head. "Bartender, another glass of your sweetest red... please."

I recognize this song, it's Cher, This is a Woman's World. I am more relaxed, flirty, and my body is starting to move from side to side. Why do I let anything get to me? Why do I judge myself or others so harshly? My conversation with myself is suddenly broken by a familiar face looking at me from across the room. There she is again, what the fuck! She charmingly signals to me with her pointed finger, "Come to me."

It's as if she has put an imaginary spell on me; abruptly I lose all resistance and feel my body floating through the air across the room toward her. Without any words I can feel her energy soaring into my body through the windows of my heart. A force of heat skyrockets out of my root chakra, shooting through my temple. My breathing is stronger and desire fills my lungs; I can hear myself shouting, "Yes!"

I reach out to touch her, the goddess beholding me. "Thank you for coming." I shout with gratitude. "Now let's go create a night to remember!"

I lean in and bring my hand up to stroke back her luscious hair to feel her smooth face; slowly moving my hands down, I devilishly say, "Let's go!"

Magnetically, we move our bodies as one - as if we are the only people flowing between the waves of the music's vibration. Voices mesh into one voice, the sound of the music is the only language that speaks in volumes, and everyone in the building becomes one energy, together praising the universal light in harmony. It is magnificent! She's truly an enchantment and has embodied my spirit with her divinity. I revel in her essence and my body moves in spirals I never thought possible. I can feel eyes staring at our performance like bees swarming around the queen in control of her honey throne.

THERE ARE MANY NAMES I like to call what some refer to as my alter ego, sometimes I call her my inner goddess, my queen self, my true being, my animal spirit, or sometimes I think of her as my god—like free spirited guru from within. On this day, the day I meet my other amazing self from within is the first day I realize I can be whoever I want to be in this world. This is the day I give birth to my liberation. At first I don't understand who she is, but do understand I am responsible for her creation. I called her into existence and didn't see her fully come alive until this night at the gala. Every ounce of her is strikingly majestic and powerful.

When I became aware she and I were one, I felt different, more alive and awakened to higher possibilities. Now I know when I allow my alter ego to come out, I am transcended into a state of paramount consciousness. My eyes feel like they see differently, my confidence increases, my body language changes, and even the way I speak is much different. I feel fearless, empowered, and most of all safe with my alter ego. She's a beast, a bird, an exotic creature for sure! When I am her, there is no wrong, there is no right, there is just a playground of illusions and dimensions of energy floating around. I can shift into anything and be like a kid, or be like a queen, for that moment. She's fucking incredible!

Let's Go There

This is a chance for everyone to label me as crazy, bipolar, having multiple personalities, or being possessed — whatever labels he or she may have. I don't mind the labels. Its research at research's finest to label me. If that is what people must do to feel they have accomplished something... then go for it. This was a profound experience for me. I wasn't on any drugs or medications during this experience. To be honest, I believe I only played a part in the creation of my alter ego because the other part is natural and developed out of pure existence. The part I helped create was to help me get through a life of struggle and pain at a very young age. I just didn't realize an alter ego could actually happen, until the weird science project in my mind actually came alive, revealing herself in manifested form where I could see the proof. If you ask me — that's pretty bad ass!

Chapter 12

My Little Girl

*"Labels can be defining
moments in each of our
lives."*

IF MY KINDERGARTEN TEACHERS would have prepared me to be strong and hold my composure in the adult world, would my life and the world have turned out better? If only I was taught that adults eat small children, yell at each other on the freeways, and are scared to talk to one another in the checkout lines at the supermarket; I would have begged God to keep me a child forever. It's tough being an adult!

Instead I was taught to color, paint, and build blocks; then I was sent out to play at recess with other kids and learn to be social. Awww... to be a kid again; they say the funniest things at all the wrong times, don't they? The funnier part is as adults, we still do that. The child lives within each of us and is still growing up. Our inner child is still asking "Why?" and still open to influences from those around us.

It's a rude awakening to find out everything you believe in, everything you know as truth, and everything that controls your next move in life is a contribution from thousands, if not millions of people from all over the world. Some you know as Mom or Dad, family and friends, our ancestors and even the media and entertainment world. Hell, if dinosaurs had talked, you could have beliefs implanted in your blueprint from them too! Maybe this   is why some people are considered to be snakes. I'm just saying... you never know. No one knows. Which brings me to the point of this chapter. *You can place whatever label you want on yourself if that is what makes you feel more comfort at the end of the day.*

Labels are a bizarre characteristic stamp to which we find ourselves emotionally and physically attached. I was aware at a very young age that something bigger than all of us connected each of us together. I wasn't sold on the idea that it was God or religion even though I was raised Catholic. Racism and gangs drew my attention because I couldn't figure out how these adults were once children who played at recess with a ton of different other kids and grew to separate themselves so harshly. What happened to them along the way to adulthood? During the time I went to live with my dad in California, while I was attending high school, I had another glorious label-learning experience. I was in English class and sat diagonal from a funny-looking white boy who had his wrists taped up in gauze. He always carried around a large book with a star on it. I had been taught that the star with a circle was satanic. This made me very curious.

"Hi, I'm Helen. Whatcha reading?" I asked.

"Oh. Hi. I'm Rocky. It's a book about witchcraft and satanic rituals. Are you into that?" he asked.

I wasn't into it but I wanted to know what it was and why he was into it. So I did what any curious kid would do. I lied. "Uh yeah! I'm totally satanic. We should be friends." I smiled.

Over the next few months we learned a lot about each other. We even found out that we took the same route from home to school and lived only a block away from each other. Rocky confessed that he would cut his wrists and hated life because in his words, "People sucked." His older brother was a white supremacist and his mom worked at a high-class car dealership down the street from the school.

I often told Rocky that I felt like cutting

myself, but I didn't even like getting shots at the doctors and I was too chicken. He said it made him feel good and you get used to the pain. He explained how satanic ritual made him feel like he belonged and wasn't an outcast. I realized that people just want to be accepted into the circle; whatever circle they felt most drawn to that made them feel as if they belonged. One-day Rocky didn't show up at school and I never saw him again. I often wondered if it was because his mom sought help for him. I was just sad for him because I could feel his pain. I was glad I had lied and broken through the label rope that had kept us apart, because even if I had made him smile and feel like he had a friend for a small amount of time on his journey... that was worth it for me.

Labels can be defining moments in each of our lives. People ask me all the time, "What are you?" That answer can be an ethnicity, a job or entrepreneur title, a religion, a doctor's prescription, a serious illness, an achievement, a relationship, I mean anything! I have enjoyed trying on different labels throughout my lifetime. I don't go around telling compulsive lies and labeling myself to fit in. Before I read, Total Freedom by J. Krishnamurti and listened to Joe Rogan's Experience Podcast or learned about all of these far-out philosophical ideas about labels and attachments, I was a kid thinking: Can't we all just get along?

If you want to be crazy and wild, then be crazy and wild. If you want to accept a certain label as you, then go for it. I won't fight you on what label you place on yourself. What I do care about is what you do with that label, and what kind of person you become from having that imaginary label taped over your forehead.

My mother had taken me to a child therapist when I was nine because my anger was out of control and depression was taking over my well-being. I remember my siblings asking my Mom, "What's wrong with her? Why does she have to go to a counselor?"

My mom replied, "Oh because she is depressed and it can be manic." At that young age I didn't understand what manic meant, but the day my Mom discontinued my therapy, she explained manic depression. That it's not a good label, and that I could change it, or any label for that matter, and I had the power to take any situation and turn it around. Later on, at seventeen, I was diagnosed as being severely manic. I can still remember slamming my bedroom door and screaming at the top of my lungs, "Whyyyy! I hate myself! I hate this life! I just want to die!" I would fall to the floor with tears streaming down my face as I curled into a ball. My mother would rush in and demand me to pick myself up off the ground.

"You don't slam doors in my house!" She would sternly say.

I would stop crying and shut off all emotions in that instant as if I was a human capsule with no life. Mom would come over to hug and rock me.

"Listen baby girl, I know you don't understand everything that goes on in life or in that head of yours but one day you will. You're gonna be fine," she assured.

I was just an angry little girl for a list of issues I didn't know how to handle like Dad hitting Mom, Mom leaving Dad, getting beat up at school by bullies, getting called ugly and monkey girl, being called nasty names by aunts and uncles, puberty and body changes, sexual wrongs, and the constant voices in my head feeding me lies.

Mom refused to put me on the medications that any therapist prescribed, and scared me straight by telling me that if I didn't choose to be happy when things were bad then worse things could happen in life. Mom was my protector, and when I look back at that moment, it was brave of Mom to scare me straight, because she gave me the gift of one of my greatest truths... a choice to choose happiness. Do I always choose happiness?

Nope, not all the time. In fact, being unhappy can sometimes feel natural, comfortable, and effortless. This is why I nurtured my alter ego. After a time mom was not around to protect me or to scare me straight, therefore I had to learn to protect myself. Now I have to stand up for what I believe to be true today. I've got to say "no" to labels that don't serve my happiness.

I just can't get myself to fall back on the idea of being a manic or bipolar diagnosed person. It's too wild to think that I could be placed on medication because I was slapped with a manic label when I was young. I don't think I was manic or should have been told that I was at 17. I was a young girl who had some bad things happen to her at an innocent age. I was also going through puberty, and I had no idea how to handle the anger that developed.

Now, I am a grown woman who experiences a ton of different emotions - including depression, and I have the tools to work through them. Does this mean I'm a saint who whips out her tools when my emotions go from zero to one hundred on the "She's lost it scale?" No. My whole life I've had to push through my own death threats. I'm a woman with fluctuating hormones and emotions. Period. I'm not saying that everyone who says he or she is bipolar is not or shouldn't take meds. Hell no, I'm not saying that. Don't get it twisted! Believe me, there are people who need the label to get their meds, to get help because it positively serves them and that's the best way. No judgments, relax. This is about my journey with my belief about labels.

Oftentimes, I've come across people who tell me their '*Story*,' and quite often they are stories of the victims they once were, or still are. I've met many women who have told me their stories of being molested, raped, physically and emotionally abused, and so on. In fact, my whole entire life I've grown up not only hearing these stories but witnessing these tragedies. This breaks my heart because I understand these stories all too well. I've been a victim of things I don't like to look back on, experiences I was too young to control and take responsibility for. This is why self-improvement appealed to me.

It was right after my divorce that my amazing friend, Viv, offered me a free ticket to an Anthony Robbins' four- day, Unleash the Power event in Los Angeles. I wanted to go, but I didn't want to spend money on a plane ticket and tried to get out of going. Viv wasn't having it. I called my good friend, Penelope, who I learned moved to L.A. after high school with her new husband. I figured I would go to the four-day event for only one day and spend the rest of my time catching up with Penelope. That would make both of my friends happy; which in turn would make me happy. I went to the four-day event very closed-minded, with crossed arms, sitting in the back row huffing and puffing, wondering why I even came. I'll never forget when Mr. Tony Robbins said I could create a new story and quit telling my old one. There must have been thousands of people in that convention room, and yet I must have been the only one he meant to offer that advice to — I mean, duh, I only flew three hundred miles to get there.

It's not like this was the first time I had heard those directions given about creating a new story. I had heard this before from my school teachers, from random books, pastors, my mom and my step—dad. But when Tony repeated these familiar words, I was mesmerized like, Damn, now there is a man who can lead.

That, my friends, was the moment I decided to work on a new story for my life. It was a defining moment to look myself in the eyes and say to the nine—year old girl inside of me, "There will be more storms to come, more depression to work through but I will take care of us now. Everything will be okay."

I flew back to my apartment in Phoenix and turned up my stereo and danced all over the place. I rejoiced because I knew my victim story had just found its hero to see us through to the end. I consciously helped create and manifest my alter ego, my animal spirits, my inner true self, and so much more. I decided cheating wasn't always wrong and wasn't always right. I decided I was going to find a way to lift myself up higher than ever before. I also decided, since I don't know the day my life is to end, I am going to live, forgive, and love myself the best way I know how by choosing happiness in the forms I know best.

I promised the little girl inside me that I was going to protect her no matter the cost. After I got back home from my time in LA at the event, I went into my bathroom with some sticky notes and a pen. I wrote on one sticky note, "I will survive this game of life with a smile." I wrote on another sticky note, "I AM the change I wish to see in this world." I stuck them on my mirror and demanded myself to look in my dark "unsure of herself" eyes and believe I can do it, that I could keep the promise to be something great.

SOME MAY THINK people like me are broken based on what I have confessed. I get it. I've got overused balled up tissues next to my big bag of expired issues. I've got poison oak and pityriasis rosea right now and I still get up every day and say to myself, "Game on!" I'm no less beautiful with a rash nor am I going to stay in bed all day and give way to sulking because of it. This is life. Survival skills are inevitable if you want to make it to see your next birthday.

Broken? As the saying goes, the good thing about broken is it can be fixed. I am completely aware that along this journey in life, just like the journey through the supermarket, labels end up in your grocery cart and such is life. The body, the mind, the soul is a high energy attraction for labels and I only think it is fair to accept the titles and labels that one wishes for herself. Who's got the right to tell you what YOU ARE when everyone is still trying to figure his or her own life out? Doctors? Okay, major props to the docs. Most, not all, that is. Hey! I'm entitled to my own opinion as you are too. Damn, skippy!

Fast forward nine years later from my Anthony Robbins experience, I was able to take my son when he was twelve to one of Tony's events. I went against Raymond's wishes of not taking Keme out of school, but I took him out anyway to get to the event early. Keme had been going through emotional tantrums, slamming doors, and shutting down a lot trying to cope with the divorce. I knew my son was in pain and I had to do something. Taking my son to a Tony Robbins event was the best thing I ever did for him. I watched him transform and learn to apply the best tools to control his emotions. I have seen my son at his highest peak and have held his hands as he walked over burning coals — feeling the fear and allowing his courage to shine through was magnificent. My son changed and kept that change going, despite Raymond's disbelief that the event helped. Not only did it help Keme, it also strengthened our mother and son bond.

When it was time for me to drop Keme back to his dad's house, I informed Keme that no matter what people say, no matter what labels are thrown at him; believe the true power and choice is always within.

Chapter 13

Operation Fuck 'Em All

*"All rules and regulations
about what other people think
fly out the window."*

"DUDE, I CAN'T DO THIS. I don't even recognize myself.   I have anxiety through the roof and I am so unhappy in this relationship. What the fuck am I doing here? Helen, I need to get the fuck out of here, like now... today!" Hearing Veronica's voice over the phone stirs up past traps I have fallen into and makes my soul cry.

"Veronica, do you want me to come get you? If you want to get away for a few days, I can leave now and come get you." I wait for Veronica's reply. I can sense her tension from miles away, as if she's right next to me.

"Yes, Helen, come get me. I'm ready!" Veronica assures me. "Okay, I will be there in three hours!" I laugh.

I had left my home in Phoenix, Arizona in the summer of 2011 to stay with Mom at her country style house in Mohave Valley, Arizona for a few weeks to clear my head and find some peace outside of the city life.

I grab my shoes and feel my heart pounding with excitement as if we have both planned a crazy undercover escape plan. Veronica is in the kind of relationship that is constantly making her second-guess her true desires.

She's always boasting about how happy she is but secretly fighting with her true self who desperately longs to be free and out of her relationship. Nick is a great guy, everyone likes him, and he loves Veronica like no one has ever loved her before. To everyone around Nick, he is the best kind of person anyone could ever meet. Veronica loves him with all of her heart, her mind, and even her soul. But even with all of the love, something inside her burns like a fire to get out of the relationship. This burning feeling regarding Nick never goes away no matter how hard Veronica tries to convince herself.

I realize all the beautiful Goddesses in my life possess this powerful and imaginary arrow inside their souls. It is intuition. As women we have more emotional flow, so we tend to recognize our intuition through our true internal voices, sooner than a man can recognize a foul ball in left field on a sunny day.

However, even having a super—power as astonishing as intuition, we tend to question our inner wisdom because the short-term feeling is as cheap as a happy hour glass of wine, instantly feeling great. Nothing wrong with that until we actually wake the hell up from years of what was I thinking? Then step into the meanest hangovers of our lives!

The way I see it is we have a ridonkulous list of needs that we expect our men, who are simple creatures, to meet; then we wonder why our simple men can't meet our constantly changing needs. Look, if you are happy to settle with one man who will not meet all of your needs, or you are happy with one man who does his best to meet them... then more power to you, honey! But if you are unhappy and don't want to settle, find a few men to meet your list of needs. It's that easy. Oh shit! Did I just speak English to you? Why, yes, I did and you understood it as if English were your first language, didn't you? As I drive up to Veronica's pad, I text her.

I'M HERE.

She runs down with a backpack in hand crammed with clothes to last her a week. Veronica's serious about getting away from Nick for a while.

She jumps in the car. "Go! Just drive!" She

shuts her eyes and lets out the biggest exhale. "Awww, Helen, I swear as soon as I left the house I felt like I could fucking breathe! Dude, I can't do this! I mean, I love Nick, but fuck! I feel like I have to always make him happy and help him see the positive side of life. It takes SO much of my energy! I feel like my energy is being sucked dry!!!"

Veronica needs some pick-me-up energy at this very moment. As I drive up the freeway ramp back toward where I just came from, Mom's home, I hit number four on the CD player, dubstep blasts out of my speakers and Veronica's whole body (and mine) instantly transform as her fist flies in the air. She yells, "Fuck yeah! Turn it up! Woooh!"

Veronica's call lit up the spontaneity flame in my brain and I couldn't pass up rescuing my friend and taking on an adventure. The three hours' drive to my mother's house from Phoenix promised to be a full-on party in the car. Veronica and I lose ourselves to the seduction of every sound wave and electronic beat that flows into our ears. Three straight hours of free upper body movement, loud talking and laughing with one another are worth every minute of life in that moment. As soon as we reach our final destination, we agree: We are both in desperate need of one of our sacred nights. A Fuck It Night!

Now a Fuck It Night is no ordinary night.

In fact, it is known to the ancestors of our ancestors as an Anything Goes Night. Except to the new generation it's called a Fuck It Night because now cussing is almost acceptable — even on the radio. However, it's still sacred because you can't say "Fuck It" on family radio, so technically it's not acceptable.

(I know the dynamics, right! Pssshh!)

Let's Go There

A FUCK IT NIGHT (OR DAY) *is when anything goes. All rules and regulations about what other people think fly out the window. Your friends are not allowed to judge you because you are not allowed to judge them. Everyone watches everyone's back but no one is anyone's babysitter or shoulder angel. Oh, and there is always music — whether in the home, on the radio, in the garage, at the BBQ, by the pool, on your iPod, on your phone, in your car, or up in the club with a bottle full of bub. There is usually an enhancement vice to your Fuck It Night. The most important thing that makes it a Fuck It Night, or day, is the fact that you have fun and get away from all the bullshit that makes you feel stuck. It's not like an everyday go-to-the-bar night or get- drunk-and-shit-faced day or night. It's the kind of thing that you wake up and half remember and say to your friends or yourself, "Holy shit! Now that was a night to remember!" Even if you only remember bits and pieces.*

MOM REMARRIED WHEN I was in high school to a really good man, my step dad. They own two homes and decided to stay at their second home in Kingman, Arizona while I had Veronica visiting from Phoenix. We are grown women turned teens for a night. The music is sick loud all throughout the house. The goats and chickens outside are doing the backyard boogie. Even the moonlight is preparing for the birth of our Fuck It deliverance.

"Hey dude, should I wear the black heels or these sweet- ass flat boots?" Veronica holds up each pair with a look on her face like she is really asking, Which pair would I look cuter in when I'm drunk off my ass and fall in front of some hot guys tonight?

"Dude, the boots — all the way! I'm wearing flats too. I mean, c'mon, we are going to get *CRRAZZY*!!" I shout!

"Yeah!" Veronica high fives me. It's like we are teenage boys with mad testosterone ready to bang the shit out of some air guitars! We are taking shots and guzzling beers, just getting smashed. Clothes are flying and we are dancing all through out the bedroom, the living room, the bathroom, the kitchen, the hallway, the backyard, and finally the front yard. There in the moonlight we toast with our last drinks before our many more drinks, "To a night to remember! FUUUUCK IIIITT!" we shout! The cab rolls up. We jump inside, laughing over the idea that we are out of our minds and we love it!

Our cabbie loves us too! "Where to ladies?"

"To the casino, sir!" I say. The Laughlin, Nevada casino is the playground for the locals. It's like a mini Vegas strip. It is thirty minutes away and sure to be a blast!

At the casino, we high-five everyone we cross paths with as we enter through the front door. Veronica spots a succulent young man cruising a handicap scooter, and before I say a word, she grabs my hand and pulls us toward him. With a little batting of eyelashes and some candy-cane breath we quickly hijack the scooter.

Cut to next scene: Veronica and I are on the scooter doing donuts on the dance floor. After being kicked out for reckless driving, we find ourselves at the blackjack table playing with money we didn't know we had.

Four men surround us, gawking at our awesomeness and strangely our high-fives encourage them to keep handing us money.

"Where to next girls?" they ask.

Happens every time! Veronica and I look at each other like we are proud of collecting our own entourage in such a short time, not to mention they are hot and we have a few to choose from. Game on!

"Let's go to the next casino! FUCK IT!" I shout.

We high—five for the fifty-seventh time. Who's counting? I'm estimating here. We make our way to the second casino, taking photos with a cop who is as cute as a teddy bear (Veronica's idea). She thinks it's fun to ask the copper if it's okay that we have open drinks while we walk to the next casino... figuring it's an innocent question, considering this isn't Vegas. Snap! Picture taken, with copper in the middle and the two of us holding open beers on the side.

Cut to next scene: We are now in our second casino, our entourage following. The six of us are high-fiving everyone we come across. Veronica notices an elderly gray-haired woman wearing a beautiful red hat. There she goes!

"I love your hat, honey! You are sexy!"

The woman smiles, "Why thank you, dear."

We make our way to the casino bar. After a shit ton of drinks and shots, we both realize the music is controlling our every move. I jump on a random hot guy who probably came up to me just to ask for my phone number... but FUCK IT! I straddle the sexy bastard and our bodies are moving like sparks jumping out of the flames of a bonfire. Veronica is sucking face with two men at the same time. We are lost in lust and alcohol for the next few hours, dancing all over everyone and all over the floor.

We jump on chairs and scream out loud, "I'm a fucking bird!"

We share a table with random new friends — both men and women. Everyone is exchanging numbers and giving high—fives. The music slowly comes to an end but we don't.

"What should we do now?" Veronica laughs. "What time is it?" I ask.

"It's three am, girls" a random guy answers. "Want to come back to our room? We have more drinks."

Damn he's hot. By the time the music ends we realize we began with one set of men and have ended up with   two different hotties. Veronica and I glance at each other and then at the two men. We lift up our waters and shout, "FUCK IT!"

Later that morning, Veronica and I stumble in at mom's house at seven thirty a.m. with smiles on our faces, reminiscing about our whole night. We pull out numbers, random pieces of candy we had in our pockets, and shit we found stuck in our hair. We try to piece together our night and enjoy every minute of it. We look through the pictures and videos that I love to document our nights out and laugh our asses off.

"Oh my god, Helen, I can't believe we did that! A picture with a cop!" Veronica gasps as if she remembers something bad. "Oh shit and I kissed two guys!" We laugh and laugh and agree: We successfully achieved our Fuck It Night.

Chapter 14

Breathe Me Out

"What could be more valuable
than having sexual passion
with a partner?"

FAST FORWARD TO WHEN I FELL in love with Mark, whom I had met online in the summer of 2013 and moved in with after four months of dating in Phoenix, Arizona.

"Hi, babe, how was your day?" I can barely get the words out of my tired-ass mouth. I have just spent the whole day talking to customers at my new job and all I want to do is come home and get loved on by the one person I have in my life for that exact purpose.

"It was good," Mark quickly replies then returns to his main attention grabber, his cell phone.

I roll my eyes and go to the room to take a quick shower. The anger pulsates through my veins, moving throughout my body. I step into the shower, allowing myself to exhale and feel the water wash away my negativity from every part of my body. I sob. I wonder to myself, have I circled back again ten years later? It was just a decade ago I was in an unhappy marriage and had divorced a man I'd pushed my own dreams aside for so I could support his. As I shut the water off and get out of the shower to dry myself, I glance into the mirror. I hardly recognize myself. What have I gotten myself into? A year ago I was single, I was happy, I was having fucking sex for Christ sake!

Mark and I had fallen in love too quick. For some odd reason I couldn't sexually connect with Mark as I could with a few men from my past. For Mark, I was the cream of the crop; he would be very hurt if he knew I've faked almost every orgasm the past year. Oh my fucking God! I feel like I am going to eventually lose my cool with Mark and turn into a crazy woman. Why can't I just leave him? Didn't I already go through this kind of unsatisfying sexual relationship with Kyle?

Breathe Helen, pull it together! I can do this! I love Mark and he is a good man. I'm not in my twenties anymore and I have learned many lessons from past relationships. I am the queen of communication now; I can teach Mark how to love me the way I like to be loved.

I remember my mother's wise words, "Men

are simple. They just need sex, food, and to be told that they are appreciated." I can do that. Now, how do I teach Mark how to satisfy me in a simplistic way that he can understand? Aha! I need to call Mom!

"Hi, Mom! How's everything going?"

"Hi, Helen, what's shakin' bacon'?" Mom always sounds like there's a party going on in her life.

I break down. "Mom, I'm having issues with Mark. He's what every woman I have ever known wants.... A rich man, who has his own house, very loyal. He wants to get married and have kids and the white picket fence."

"And?" Mom waits.

"And I feel very lucky that he loves me, takes care of me, and wants to spend the rest of his life with me, but... I'm very unhappy! We can't seem to connect sexually and I think he wants me to turn into a more domesticated kind of woman. You know me, Mom! I don't cook and I don't like to be obligated to clean up after any man!"

Mom chuckles, "Oh baby girl. See, you have a good man who loves you and wants to take care of you. You have to learn how to cook and clean and take care of him too. Maybe the sex won't get better but you might have to sacrifice that to hold onto something far more valuable."

My heart drops! What could be more valuable than having sexual passion with a partner?

"I understand that, Mom, I do, but I think that may be a bit more traditional thinking. See, I have more of a modern view to this."

"Oh you do? Well, how is that modern view working out for you then?"

"I mean, okay, see, here's the thing, Mom, I don't believe that I should have to give up my sexual desires because my partner can't fulfill them. Mark's a man and men are supposed to be more sexual than women. If anything, Mark should be the one all over me, not the other way around. And I'm a great catch..."

"You are!"

"Thanks, and I'm trying to exhaust every creative idea before I get the urge to cheat on Mark...but to be quite honest... I may cheat on him. But I don't want to do that! I'm just saying, you know me, Mom, I am too young right now to be sacrificing what I feel is one of my rightfully so— required desires to make me happy. I'm sorry but I don't see all cheating as bad or wrong. I'm a good person and yes, some of the cheating I've done in the past was wrong and I'm sorry for some of it — but actually not sorry for some of the cheating because it made for lots of really funny stories." I laugh in embarrassment.

"Mom, I just can't live a life with one man who expects me to change and him not do the same. Ugh!" I cry in utter frustration.

My mom is my hero in life and I cannot believe I just puked a mouthful of my disgusting truth to her. She is probably going to be upset, wondering how I could believe in such foolishness.

"Ey yi yi, Helen…"

Oh God, here it comes.

"… this is all my fault," Mom responds.

What? Wait, what? I'm confused. Did Mom just say this is all her fault?

"I brought you kids up to be very independent. All of you kids are the same, just like me, always on the go. When I was your age I was the same way. After I left your Dad, no man was going to tie me down. I took you kids traveling and taught you to rebel alongside with me. Until I met your step dad, I didn't know how to be stable. He and I haven't had sex for many years but he's a good man and that's all that matters. Baby girl, one day you are going to be old and sex is not going to be everything; having a best friend and companion is! Now if you are going to step out on Mark, then that is your business but don't let go of a good man who loves you and wants to take care of you for the rest of your life. Get what you need from someone else if you must, but return to your home, to your good man, always."

This conversation with Mom is one of my most favorite conversations. She spoke wisely, without judgment, and with support. I thank the heavens every day to have been blessed with a mother like mine. I don't know many people who can tell their parents anything. When I was younger, I swore I would be nothing like my mother; as I'm getting older I can see so much of my mother in myself and I feel honored to carry on her spirit within my own. Mom is right about a relationship being more than sexual fulfillment. I understand that now. Although I do believe I am right as well. Therefore, since both of us seem to be right, the perfect solution is to mesh the two rights together and call it a day.

"Problem? Solution!" as Veronica always says. Except this time it doesn't feel that easy.

I talk to my mom for a few more minutes, and then we hang up. I put the phone down, but it feels as if my chest is getting tighter and tighter. The air in my lungs can't seem to get out but I ignore the feeling until late that night when my own head chatter wakes me up.

Breathe. I've got to breathe. Am I having an anxiety attack? I've never had one before. Is this what it feels like, or am I trippin'? Get out of my head! Stop talking! Why can't I sleep anymore? Why am I breathing like this? Am I making this up or over-exaggerating? OMG! Why can't I stop the chatter in my head?

I crawl out of bed and my body feels like it's going to topple over. I feel so dizzy. Mark is sound asleep. Ugh! I can't fuckin' stand him. What is wrong with me? I need to splash some water on my face. This is so not cool if I die from an anxiety attack all because I am stuck in an unhappy relationship that I know very damn well I should have gotten out of a long time ago. I turn on the bathroom light and glance back to see if Mark was awakened. Nope. Looks like he's going to sleep through this whole event. The cold water on my face feels refreshing and confirms I am not dreaming.

I gaze at myself in the mirror in disbelief that this is happening. I'm Helen! I'm the girl who made it through a divorce ten years ago that almost took her life! I'm the girl who goes to the motivational seminars, who gathers the girls to rally on a Tuesday night, who has traveled to seven countries and dances in the moonlight with exotic strangers! How is this happening? Why can't I get out of this? Why am I still in this fucking relationship? What am I going to do with my life? This worry is going to kill me! Where did I go wrong? I'm lost in confusion.

All of these questions are only making my anxiety get worse. I've got to stop the chatter. Breathe, Helen. Shhh... breathe. One inhale and one exhale at a time. Don't think about anything... just focus on your breath. I love you. I love you. I'm here. Lay down, close your eyes, everything is going to be okay. Trust. Breathe.

"Morning," Mark throws his arm over me.

"Morning. I think I had an anxiety attack last night," I spit out.

"Oh yeah. Why?" So typical of Mark to ask the question, "why" about all of my feelings that I ever express to him.

"I don't know," I swallow. There seems to be no point in making an explanation in "why" I thought I may have had an anxiety attack.

He doesn't seem to care that deeply about it anyway as he plays on his phone while talking to me.

"Oh why don't you know?" Mark asks as he is catching up on his fantasy football scores on his phone. I glance over at him realizing he isn't the least bit concerned about my well-being and my annoyance meter is at an all—time high. "You know what, babe, I just didn't get enough sleep last night. I'm good. Are you hungry? Let's eat breakfast," I politely gesture.

Most men are clueless as to what women want. There are books upon books about how to talk to men and how to talk to women so that each of us is heard. I've read quite a few and have practiced many of the suggestions in the ten years after my divorce. One of the main tools I learned is how to be plain blunt and straightforward with what you want from a man. It's said that women are more about their feelings and men seem to be more logical. So I practice being straightforward with men all the time.

"I want you to eat me out more."

"I need you to be more compassionate about a certain subject."

"I need you to tell me I'm beautiful at least once a week."

"I need you to talk to me in a kinder tone."

"I will cheat on you if you cannot fulfill my needs after I've exhausted telling you what I need a million times."

In the same respect, I let my partner know that communication is vitally important and he in turn must let me know what it is that he needs.

When I first meet potential partners, they all agree that communication is key. We pop some champagne and toast to the fact that we are adults now, about to embark on an adult relationship, and we throw a forever-we-will-communicate celebration. Aww, those were some good nights! Unfortunately, it doesn't always work out that way. Once the pheromone smoke clears from the romance stage of the relationship, boredom strikes. What's next? Where's the next high? Why is my partner all of a sudden, a jerk and not as sweet as before? Oh crap! Is this the real relationship? Wait, you mean to tell me this knight in shining armor is really a selfish shellfish? Bummer. Time to have a talk with my true self, my inner guru.

Glass of wine? Yes, please. Time to sit down outside under the moon and stars. Let's talk, Self. You know damn well this is not my first rodeo. How could I have been so blind and have avoided the signs of this coming relation shit! But he loves me and he is a good man... he's an asshole! Tears well in my eyes. I can love this man to the end of days. I can see our future together, me in the kitchen baking, while I watch him outside chopping wood for the fireplace of our beautiful big cabin that we built together.

Suck it up, Helen, he's only an asshole when you push his buttons. I mean, let's be honest, I can be a bitch and my moods can sway from day to day. Is this good enough reason for his lack of desire for me? Ugh, I can't stand how he rejects me when I want to have sex in the middle of the night. Such a douche bag who does that? I love him. I guess I should forgive him and look past that too.

Sip...

This wine tastes better than some of the sex we've had. I laugh. I think I actually have more fun without him here. What is the point of this man in my life? Exhale. Okay so maybe he is a jerk but he's my jerk! I just got defensive for this man and I'm the only one listening. Ha!

Another sip. No person is perfect, yes, I know. But let's not hide the underlying culprit of this future break up. He wants a baby and you don't. Tears flow down my cheeks. I smile. It's not fair, Universe! I asked for a good man and you gave me a good man! I asked for a man who has a good job, who has his shit together, who has a great relationship with his mother, who works out, and wants to be in a true committed relationship. Why?! I cry out to Universe. I even asked for a man who didn't live in Phoenix. (Long distance relationship. Yep! You guessed it.) You delivered that man to the tee, Universe!

I sob and sip.

What are you trying to teach me? Am I supposed to have his baby? A baby I clearly do not want? There are thousands of women who pray for a man like Mark. Was this the plan, God? Are you waiting to see if I will give him a baby or let him go to someone who will give him what he truly wants?

I wipe my tears and take another sip. I breathe in all of the vast night sky. It's beautiful... I love Arizona in the fall. Absolutely amazing at seventy-five degrees in the late evening. I nod my head. It's all going to be okay, Helen. I take my last sip and one last glance into the moonlight before walking back into the house for the night.

I whisper aloud, "Thank you, Universe."

145

Chapter 15

Living One Vibrational Energy

"My soul moves with
compassion and my heart
deepens with emotion."

I LOVE GOING TO PLACES where I can sit and
people watch, take in the colors of their clothes,
the wrinkles they have around their eyes when
they smile, their body language when meeting
one another, and sometimes I even eavesdrop on
their conversations - wink! One of the most
frequent places is coming to this cafe in Central
Phoenix, Lucy's Kitchen. It's open on one side
with fresh air flowing through and smells like
greens and fresh lemons. It's one of my favorite
places to eat organic food, bring my laptop and
write, meet with friends, and also spend time
alone in a room full of strangers.

I wonder if the young woman with short
brown hair, standing in line to get a coffee, is

happy in her life. I wonder if the two older businessmen sitting at the table right across from me are talking about football while their eyes graze down the back of the tall thin blonde who walks right by them; if they are wishing for a woman like that in their lives, or if they are secretly having quickies with that blonde stranger in their minds at that very minute.

This is one of those days when I can just BE. There are no obligations to be anywhere or expectations to be someone for someone else; life is in existence no more in that moment than any other moment. Living in America has its perks; it's the land of convenience. I'm sure if I had been born in another time or another country my beliefs about everything in this book could be completely different. However, this is not the case. I was born here in America and I have a deep understanding of how fortunate I am.

In 2011, Veronica and I visited five countries in a very short period of time. We experienced beautiful cultures, partied in underground European clubs, and were awakened to what real poverty looks like. Before I left America, I had been a huge believer in helping the homeless in the inner-city programs. I volunteered for four years straight. I spent my own money on supplies, gift cards, and clothes. I was broke after every paycheck but always felt that it was right to give because I still had more than "the homeless" in these shelters. After I returned from Egypt and Africa my perspective changed about homelessness in America.

Veronica's perspective changed too. She felt that her heart had opened up more and she began to have the urge to give more. For me, my eyes had changed the way I viewed what homelessness was. I no longer wanted to volunteer my time or give away any money or clothes. Instead I wanted to give resources and suggestions to people standing on corners holding signs. Time is valuable, and America is abundant with opportunity. There are libraries and programs that offer for free what college kids are out there paying thousands of dollars for - Education - to get better jobs and make more money. Something inside of me changed and when it did, I felt more empowered and I no longer gave out of sympathy or pity but out of love for another human being.

Some people only view me as this hungry sex addict who likes to go around and break hearts because it fuels my codependent need. Who knows, they could be right in their own minds. Agreeing with people who are determined to be right is not going to change my beliefs overnight, therefore, why not just say, "Yup, you're right" and go on with the day. The truth is, I have a heart, a big heart, and a very strong and deep connected heart. That connection is not just to have sex and intimacy with beautiful beings in this world, but it's also to be connected to every living source inside of me and around me. Here's the thing, don't be upset or spend a lot of time disagreeing with anything in this book. In the end we all want to say we lived as alive and charismatically as possible without any regrets. Am I right or am I right? I'm fucking right, biatch!

I was once asked how I could cheat without feeling any guilt. That was a great question because it forced me to look at my behavior and ask myself the same question... as if I had a super power (or a super problem) and I was desperate to find its source. The challenge is, I don't know where the source exactly originated just yet, but I do remember the first time I cheated, and I felt normal and free as if there were no such thing as a past or a future, just bodies in that time and space. I also remember the first time I realized an unknown time of death gave me permission to let go of any kind of guilt and live this life in any way I choose.

When Bruce Lee famously said, "Be like water," it made complete sense down to the core of my being. To "be like water" means to me that I can flow with whatever the universe throws my way, and if I decide to conform to any identity, label, or ideology, then this is only a temporary conformity, and I can choose at any moment to move on and flow again because water is a liquid element in which one can transform into many desires in this lifetime.

Take a trip back in time

"PACK ONE BAG OF CLOTHES each because we are moving out by the end of this week!" Mom proclaimed to the five of us.

Mom held weekly family meetings for the five of us kids to gather around and talk about our lives with each other. That was her way of connecting with us and keeping us all pulled together while she worked two jobs and did her best to provide a positive lifestyle for us.

"Where are we going?" our 13-year-old eldest sister, Margaret, asked.

I was next in line — known as the infamous second oldest, coming in at the tender age of 12. What a funny term, "second oldest." How does that even make sense?

"Mom, there is no way all of my dolls are going to fit in one bag of clothes," my sister Olivia stated.

Some people considered Olivia as the middle child, but to my sister Grazelda, who was the fourth child, Olivia was the third oldest child. Grazelda liked to call herself, "the baby girl." She and my only brother (and youngest of the family), Roster, considered themselves the babies and it sickened me. We were all babies at one point, but till this day the two of them, Grazelda and Roster, pull their "I'm the baby of the family" cards on us quite often. It was hysterical that there was some kind of higher privilege given to them when they used that term. I happened to fall for it every time, caving in to their wants and needs when they pulled the baby card — sickening I tell ya!

"Well kids, I bought a large piece of land very close   to Arizona and we are going to build our house on that land. Your uncle is coming in a few days to pick us up in a blue bus and it's going to be a new fun adventure!" Mom explained. Mom had finally left Dad a few years back and after sleeping in shelters and in the car, she had finally turned her life around with two jobs and a nice savings. She was moving us out of California for good.

"What about school? I'm not going to Victor Valley Junior High with my friends?" Margaret gasped.

Margaret and I knew our pre—teenager lives were about to take a whole new direction than the ones we had planned for ourselves in Southern California. My three younger siblings seemed to be open to the idea of this new adventure. I wondered what Arizona was like. I envisioned horses, cowboys, and cowgirls dressed in boots at my new school. We were all born and raised in Southern California in the barrios. We considered ourselves, "street," or depending where someone is from, "hood." Every race and culture we have known growing up is either Black, Mexican, or mixed as Blaxicans.

The very translation of Arizona portrayed only two words that scared the shit out of me, "White People." The only white people I'd ever known in my life were cousins of cousins or friends of friends who were also "street." Arizona was a new kind of white people that we had only heard stories of in history books or seen on television.

ॐ

Pause for a Thought

ISN'T THIS INTERESTING: Culture shock for a 12-year-old young California girl who's fearful of another unknown race in a state that is literally three hours away?

AT THE END OF THE WEEK my uncle arrived in a large blue bus to pick up Mom and the five of us kids and drive us to our new forty-acre property. On this vast piece of desert my mom declared that we were going to build our Earthship home with our bare hands. For those of you who don't know what an Earthship house is, it's made out of tires, cans, wood, and adobe. There is a lot more to it, but the main foundation is packed tires of dirt. That first summer on "The Property" as we liked to call it, was the worst summer of my life! The Arizona temperature was unbearable, reaching over 100 degrees of dry heat every goddamn effing day.

Over the next four years the six of us endured endless hours of hammering with a sledge and packing dirt into numerous tires only to come home every summer with a note from the fire department that the heat burnt down all our hard labor. I can't tell you how devastating it was for my mother but she just said, "Okay, well, let's start over."

There was no air conditioning in the summers, no heaters in the winters, and showers were given out of a one-gallon jug of water on the steps of our big blue school bus/RV. My first curling iron had batteries in it and the first time I shaved my legs was in a bowl. Needless to say, when the Biggest Loser and Survivor aired on television (when we got older), the five of us kids laughed in

153

ridiculousness.

"If we can do it as kids, any adult can do it!" my brother shouted. The Property was our home away from our California home where our father, Fred lived. It was there on the Property that the six of us slept under stars every night, danced around flames while cooking our evening dinner, slept with wet sheets at night to cool our bodies in the summer, played hide and seek with rattle snakes and coyotes, and befriended numerous homeless people my mother brought back to feed and employ. Life on The Property was like another dimension away from the life I had in school.

"We brown skins have to stick together," I proclaimed to a classmate at my new school. I'm trying hard to fit in and make friends fast. I've never been around so many white people before and it's freaking me out.

"We're not brown," my classmate laughed, "… we're red." I felt pretty stupid. I knew I was half Native American, but back then I was raised by my dad to be a proud Mexican. (Only to find out I was Spanish and not Mexican years later). Arizona quickly became my teacher of many cultures and races. There was racism both from my end and from others toward me. People made fun of me because I was really dark and scraggly from the sun, and because I lived out in the middle of nowhere on a piece of land. Our family was considered true desert rats.

Every day became a nightmare at school. Before we moved to Arizona I was president of my class and a straight-A student, but my entire time in junior high and high school in Arizona was a joke. To avoid pain from being teased I grouped up with the only blacks and decided to do whatever it took to be a bad-ass alongside them. My best friend, Kadina, who had come from South Central Los Angeles, clicked with my way of thinking from the get-go. Together we caused a ton of ruckus in school and involved ourselves in many fights.

I soon learned that a few kids in school didn't want me hanging around blacks, saying, "We don't hang around that kind." Mom would kick my ass if I chose to get rid of my friendship with Kadina since most of my cousins are blaxicans, so I ignored the threats and their ultimatum.

This caused years of "watching my back" and many days I faked sick or pocketed a small knife in my shoe while at school. My sisters and brother adapted very well and I felt extremely left out. My sister Margaret and I were best sister friends our whole lives — until we moved to Arizona and then most days at school she acted as if she didn't know me. I was heartbroken by this. School was very hard — that is, until my last year of high school.

After Grazelda and I returned from a year of living with dad in Cali, something changed in me. I realized how much I had grown to accept and love my Arizona culture and all the beautiful races and faces in both California and Arizona. As I prepared for my last year of high school at the age of seventeen, ready to be teased once again, I noticed kids look at me differently. The ugly duckling had turned into a beautiful swan. I was now the popular girl on campus and this changed the game for me. Girls wanted to fight me for no reason; boys from the football team wanted to date me, and kids I didn't know wanted to be around me. What happened? All I did was leave the known, travel to the unknown, then return to the known, and in the process my perspectives and self—image changed. Like a science project with an astonishing result. I was amazed about this. An awareness of evolution had happened to me. It's still happening.

ॐ

JUMP BACK TO THE 2011 adventure with Veronica and me. "OMG, dude! We are in Paris!" Veronica and I jump around screaming in ultra-happiness. Au Paris! We dance around with iPods in our ears and carry massive backpacks. Our hosts are two young men who allow us to stay in their flat for five full days. They show us around Paris, taking us to monumental places and areas that only locals know about. It's the first time I have ever met French Dominicans and French Rastafarians too. Veronica and I are in love with French culture, the beautiful language, and of course the French men. We both swear to learn French and return one day.

"OMG, duuuude! We are in Barcelona!"

For some odd reason, Veronica and I have taken on a vegetarian diet during our travels. If you've ever been to Spain, this is not the best place to travel whilst on a non- meat-eating diet. Can somebody say, "hungry?" We are so hungry because we can't find anything to eat that isn't meat-based. Luckily our friend, Sonia, flies in to meet us during our journey and she speaks Spanish - perfect for getting into a lot of underground playgrounds.

Soon after Barcelona, comes Venice, and then Rome where we have to part ways with Sonia. Seeing the Coliseum is one of my most memorable experiences. Talk about awestruck. In Rome, Veronica and I happen to find ourselves lost on the streets for hours, fearing for our lives even with the Roman police. Not speaking a language in other countries can be the biggest weakness of any scenario.

After Rome, Veronica and I make our way down to Athens, Greece and on to our last stop together, Cairo, Egypt. In Cairo my eyes are exposed to overwhelming poverty; I never feel so helpless in my life in wanting to give to the masses. Children sleeping on the streets in the cold; begging for coin; or 3-year-olds selling tissues. It reminds me of Mexico, a place I swore to never party in again because I couldn't celebrate while kids begged outside the door. Just not my style. Women cover their faces and bodies, people stop everything and kneel down to pray to Allah, and life seems completely different to people in Cairo. Our hosts are married when we arrive and divorced by the time we leave - a strange experience indeed. Veronica and I hug at the airport where she goes to catch a flight back to Phoenix and I go on to Rwanda.

Rwanda is a place I have wanted to visit ever since I was in my teens. After seeing the genocide on the news, I wondered why such a horrific thing could happen and life was still okay for people in America. I didn't understand humanity then. Visiting Rwanda, learning about the genocide, and getting to be a part of a retreat that embraced the art of peace, is a life-altering experience. I sit in the front row, listening to an interview with perpetrators who took part in the killing. I am able to meet with survivors who were kids at the time and who witnessed their loved ones die.

My soul moves with compassion and my heart deepens with emotion. I witness true forgiveness; something I had only been taught in churches throughout my life. Rwanda shows me what the human face of forgiveness looks and feels like. There are fifty-five participants sitting in the large circle of Rwandans and others who are there for the retreat from all over the world as an older man steps up to confess his crimes to another man, Pascal, whose family he murdered in the 1994 Genocide. Pascal looks about in his late thirties. He had a family of twenty brothers and sisters and a pregnant wife of nine months. He watched his wife murdered and the baby cut out of her stomach and killed. He fled for his life and found refuge in a safe place hidden with another family.

Pascal (who once was Tutsi) looks over to the other man (who once was Hutu) and says, "I found forgiveness for you." My heart just about died. I desperately held my tears back. I was about to lose it. Other foreigners began crying while many Rwandans looked at each other in disbelief. Mixed emotions flooded the room and soon people began shouting questions to Pascal like, "How do you forgive a killer who killed your wife and baby in front of you?" and "How can you trust the killer so easily?"

Some grew angry and shouted, "You are persuaded by the very church that turned their back on us!"

Pascal nodded in understanding and gently spoke, "It is not the church that I follow but healing. The problem I have with the church is they teach and tell too many people to forgive others when they need to tell people to heal themselves first. I chose healing and forgiveness because I found so much fear everywhere I went that I had a heart attack, so I had to find a way to forgive. It was not easy, but I must try."

Some believed, and others didn't, but that day and the rest of the time spent bearing witness in Rwanda revealed to me a deep humanitarian love.

It's unmistakably remarkable. Words cannot even fathom forgiveness in all of its power. It is that divine!

I leave Rwanda with many friendships from all over the world and return to the States with a new love and joy for life. Everything that once meant so much — like work, cars, and clothes — no longer has as much flavor. Instead I feel this hunger to travel more, learn more, and socialize more with unfamiliar faces and venture into the unknown... even on the simplest level like going to a new restaurant, trying out a new nighttime spot, or speaking up and talking to strangers.

As I look back, Mom did the best service for the five of us. She took us out of the barrio and into an unknown world. My sisters and brother are the most social and outspoken people. We still have some slang and ego pride about our culture within us which comes out every now and then, but we love and embrace every kind of culture there is. I often get this question,

"What are you?" and I often answer with, "I'm human." Then it's often followed up with this question, "No, I mean, what is your ethnicity?" I know it's a nice question for someone who is truly interested, but there will be a time where everyone is mixed and this question will no longer be necessary. I'm a half-breed and my son is mixed with four breeds. The evolution of culture can flower into a masterpiece of divine art if we just call ourselves, "Love." That's what I am. That is what I am made of.

After many travels and many learned cultures this is what I like to think. Everyone is everyone just in different time zones. Racism is ignorance. I refuse to watch any racial news, pick sides of ethnicities when it comes to political views; my mind is not concerned with such things when I have such a beautiful opportunity to spend my day working out, hiking, reading a positive or romantic book, or dressing up and having a glass of wine with friends who may not see the light of day come tomorrow. The only people I believe who are separated and excluded are the people who separate and exclude themselves. I know it is not an easy thing to let go of an ego that wants to believe another race thinks itself superior to you. It's taken me many years to work past my own feeling of inferiority, and sometimes I still hear false beliefs inside my mind; it's then I push past those negative words and choose to love myself and others more deeply.

Let me just say this last bit to you: If my words of wisdom don't help loosen up any human blockage you have toward another race maybe this will... if you've only had Mexican food your entire life and never tried Italian or Chinese food wouldn't you yearn for something different? As such, if your body has not had the taste of a few different styles of men, even just watching porn and fantasizing, baby girl you haven't lived. I'm not suggesting necessarily having sex with every type of ethnicity out there. I am speaking about connection. This can be addressed to any kinds of relationships: Friends, family, lovers, even strangers.

Life is now. Attraction is now. Race and color are perspectives and perceptions that can be altered and transformed. You and I are artists and creators constantly meeting and greeting each other. Embrace the taste for genuine connection. Isn't it about time?

Chapter 16

I Climbed the
Woo-Woo Tree

*"My true ecstasy is to hunt,
seek, and find new things in
life."*

"HOW LONG HAVE YOU BEEN on this spiritual path?" The Psychic Angels Group facilitator asked me. Spirituality meet-ups are one of the many interest groups I enjoy throughout the year.

"For about ten years now I guess."

The true answer was I had been on this spiritual path since my formation in my mother's womb. It's only been the last ten years I've been more conscious of my spiritual concepts and activities. I've been a believer in witches, gypsies, animal spirits, magicians, shamans, psychics, super heroes, energy healers, gods/goddesses and invisible unseen forces since I was a wee lil booger. If you had come to me in grade school and told me you could float off the ground or move an object with your mind, I would have been all ears and bright wide eyes, "Acca —Yes I want to see!" If you had asked me at that same age if I believed in dinosaurs and told me you have the bones to prove it, I would have smiled and thought you were coo—coo like Cocoa Puffs. Strange that it took me a shit ton of years to come to terms that dinosaurs did in fact, roam the earth at one time. Once I accepted it, I was fascinated.

"HEY, GIRL, WHAT A WONDERFUL DAY!" Jill says to me.

What crawled in bed with her last night? This isn't like Jill; she's all chipper with a pep in her step. We hate our serving jobs and each day as we set up our sections we pass sips of soda mixed with liquor to each other. Why isn't she up for drinking on the job today?

"What's up with you Jill?" I smirk.

"Have you ever seen The Secret?" She glees.

The Secret is running rampant all over the world and all my friends are into it.! Chills travel up my twenty-seven-year young spine as I watch this amazing documentary come to life on my TV screen.

"I knew it!" I shout. "I fucking knew it! God is everywhere and in everything and there is a divine design going on all around and through us. I knew it!" I rejoice.

The year before Viv and I had read, Think and Grow Rich, by Napolean Hill. We had decided that our lives and our mindsets must change in order for us to find the happiness we truly desired. I call Viv's cell phone immediately after watching The Secret. We laugh at the synchronicity that both of us happened to learn of The Secret and watch it in the same week. We're ecstatic!

Two years after my divorce and watching The Secret, Viv and I pay for our tickets to attend larger events and seminars, featuring big speakers. I feel this anger inside of me from not knowing about all of this "mindset shift" shit earlier. Why didn't anyone teach me about Law of Attraction or Positive Thinking or fuckin' Money Beliefs when I was a kid? I have this huge desire to share this information with the homeless community for free.

In 2008, I make my big debut as a Conscious Awareness Speaker in a large shelter in downtown Phoenix. I have never spoken in front of a large crowd before and am scared to death to present material I am barely beginning to apply to my own life. I quickly learn how to put together manuals, contracts, worksheets, and Power Points to make my workshops more professional. The workshops become very popular and I am soon asked to speak in other shelters for parents and teens. I make it a rule to never practice or memorize anything I speak about because I want passion to flow out of me. It feels genuine and authentic to be myself, relate to my class, and tell the truth about who I was and how I am learning to become more conscious about my own beliefs at the same time.

"We are all in this together. I'm going to be doing all of these worksheets for the first time along with you guys. Let's make some moves together!" I shout out!

My crew includes me, my brother-in-law, and our boom box. Every now and then we have the luxury of getting a DJ to volunteer time and the class loves it. Music has always been a part of my own self-awareness and growth; apparently it moves everyone else in the same way. After each workshop I quickly change into my club clothes and meet with my friends for a toast to another successful class. I am proud for staying true to myself and to every person whose life I empower.

"I'm not perfect..." I say, "I go to the club, I have some drinks, but when it comes to making moves, only one person can make that choice for you."

It's an electrifying four years to teach life

skill classes and encourage others to become consciously aware of their own beliefs so that they themselves can jumpstart a new optimistic mindset towards their goals.

Life is hectic in my late twenties. I'm juggling two jobs, volunteering a few times a week at the shelters providing these workshops, clubbing, dating, traveling, and being a mom. Where the hell do I find the time and energy? I am invincible and want what many of us want, to do it all and have it all – right now!

I publish my first magazine after I return from my travels in Africa in 2011. It's a great achievement, taking focus, money, and energy that I am not prepared to give. A few months after I publish the magazine, I shut it down, all of it! I close the entrepreneur chapter, burn the files, cease all speaking engagements, and shut her down. It's a move I make with careful precision; I am exhausted and have lost the passion I once had for the hustle. Everything becomes about business, I'm not making enough revenue from it, and I can't find myself anywhere from any angle within it. It's time to re-evaluate once again.

Maybe get a higher paying job, stop the hustle and bustle for a bit, be lazy, go with the flow, and spend time getting to know myself and what I want a little more. That's when it happens... I get addicted to documentaries!

Then I dig deeper and get addicted to TED Talks. It doesn't stop there, oh no, it gets bonkers - YouTube and Google Search - How to be more confident, Motivational Videos, learn how to speak French, how to speak Spanish, Do Mermaids Exist? how to cook, how to put on makeup (scratch that, never mind, delete), Deepak Chopra audio books, Money Hypnosis...

I am officially an informational vacuum about to explode into a thousand pieces of HTML codes. Learning happiness is at the tips of my fingers, or so I believe, until I learn I actually have to put all of this into physical action. What better place than in my dating life! Whoop! there it is! Problem? Solution! Genius! High-fives all around.

"You guys, I think I want to try Reiki or acupuncture," I proclaim with such uncertainty.

It's one of those rare Monday mornings on Labor Day where the six of us, my girls and I, finally have a chance to get together for brunch and catch up in person. The restaurant is small and intimate with lots of windows to welcome the sunlight, perfect for our wild energies to blossom. There only one large round table towards the side of the restaurant and somehow the waitress knew that we needed some space of our own. Viv, Veronica, Sonia, Dotty, Lumi, and I all order waters with lemon - your typical 'all about health' group of girls.

"I've done both and I like it. You should do it!" Viv encourages.

"Where I come from, it's very popular and helps a lot of people," Lumi adds.

"I feel like becoming aware of my wants and habits has been such an incredible journey. It's like I'm so conscious of everything now. OMG, and church this last weekend was uh—mazing!" Veronica excitedly shares. We all nod in agreement.

The waitress soon arrives with our waters and two coffees for Sonia and Veronica.

"Does the foam on top of my coffee look like someone in the back just shot their cum over it?" Veronica asks. We all break out in hysterical laughter.

"No. Why would you think that?" I ask.

"Because it does!" Veronica exclaims.

"Drink it! Drink it! Drink it!" Viv and I shout hitting the table with our fists.

Veronica goes in for the sip with hesitation on her face and takes a gulp. The cum—like foam rainbows her upper lip and we all shout, "OOOOH!!" laughing aloud, some of us with tears while grabbing our stomachs.

"OMG that was hilarious, Veronica!"

"So anyways, as I was saying, in CHURCH yesterday..." Veronica playfully redirects, "... there was also this hot guy sitting in front of

169

me who smelled fucking phenomenal! Helen you would have started speaking in tongues!"

"Aw dang, I always miss church on the good days." I laugh, still wiping my tears from the cum in Veronica's coffee.

"Look at us, you girls, we are all growing up so fast! This is really nice, we need to do this more often," Veronica smiles.

We hug and say our goodbyes, knowing that each of us is only a text away should we need to reach out to each other. Conversations of self-love, growth, psychic abilities, tantric practices, conscious awareness, life goals, and spirituality are daily discussions with my girls. When one of us learns of something new on the woo-woo tree we are like happy hipsters who just hit the jackpot running to each other to share the news.

Most people would not even realize how hippy we are until they start talking to us and realize we are "one of those" kinds of people. I've seen and heard some outrageously radical things on this particular path. There have been times when I've raised an eyebrow or two as in "What the fuck is going on here?" in some woo-woo situations. I've always tried to remain open and if I happen to come across something or someone extremely far-out it's in those moments that I remind myself — this makes for a great story!

I love when I come across such high and

mighty people. You know the kind who look at all hipsters like they are all crazy loony tree-hugging thugsters! Those are my favorite people to show some love to. I've been in marketing and sales for a few years now and have really polished my adaptive skills. Needless to say, I'm pretty good at adapting and communicating with all sorts of people. Therefore, when I come across a blue—collar kind of person I do my best to get to know who he or she really is and what he or she wants out of life. Guarantee you that all they want is what every hipster wants too... love. Boom shaka!

I've been involved in some kind of spiritual practice since I can remember. Catholicism, Christianity, and Seventh—Day Adventist were my main practices that my mother first chose for us to dabble in. The two first books I was raised to read were the Bible and the dictionary. I grew obsessed to learn more about the origin of the books of the Bible. Who was God? Where did God come from? When I was younger I actually believed I was going to go to Bible College, become a priest, and turn people's lives around in prison. I guess the Divine had other plans for me.

I knew my hunger for knowledge was outweighing my thirst for religious text in ninth grade. I was in a class with a boy who had a book with a star on the cover who was into Satanic rituals. This was Rocky, someone I mentioned earlier in this story when discussing my childhood. He instantly grabbed my attention and I wanted to know what he believed and why he believed it. This was a defining moment in my life, because for the strangest reason I was drawn toward the unknown, needing to learn about him like a science project.

When he spoke about his beliefs, I never disagreed or tried to change his mind to follow Jesus or anything. I just listened and observed through a curious mind and a compassionate heart. Intuition has been one of my strongest super powers since I was a kid. I didn't know about it then, but I knew something bigger than me or anyone else lurked around and connected people stronger than religions, beliefs, or practices. It's as if I always knew that everything outside of us is not real and just a projection. The kid who believes in Satan is searching and will probably change his mind one day. All of these stories are stories passed down, translated, restructured, and who knows what else has happened to original manuscripts of ancient writings.

I don't spend time arguing with anyone wanting to convert me to his or her religion anymore. I just say, "Okay." It's effortless and everyone wins. Some people might call me a heretic for acting so fraudulent in this case but honestly it's worked for me my entire life and keeps the peace for all parties.

Not saying I haven't had my share of debates, which are extremely fun when it's non-harming to the egos. My true ecstasy is to hunt, seek, and find new things in life. I mean, come on people, you only have ONE life! I don't know why I'm here, but I do know that once I climbed the woo- woo tree, I could see over the mountain peaks and beyond; there are many untraveled lands and seas of people to meet.

Life is beautiful, people are beautiful, different beliefs are mystical, and change is inevitable. I know how scary it can be to step out of everything you know to be right or to think differently than what you believe. I'm not trying to convert people to be as interchangeably believing as I am. I'm merely suggesting that an open mind and an open heart can offer new connections and possibly a deeper understanding of others — if you allow yourself to open up to receiving whatever it is that you are supposed to receive in the experience.

P to the S: If you ever come across some really weird shit and you start to feel majorly awkward and uncomfortable in situations or rituals always remember you can push the big red button at any time that reads, **PEACE OUT.**

Chapter 17

When the Lights Go Out

*"Relationships are fuckin'
hard; let's not sugarcoat it."*

"**Fuckin' hoe! That's what she is!**" Sonia snaps. "I know he slept with her! They work together and go out for beers after. I'm going to his job to confront that bitch!"

"Yeah, I would be pretty pissed too, Sonia. Maybe you should just get her number out of his phone and call her. I wouldn't go to her job though," Dotty says.

"I mean, you don't know for sure if they are sleeping together, do you Sonia?" Veronica says in the possible mistress's defense.

"Vince didn't come home last night! They are fuckin' sleeping together. I'm so mad!" Sonia sobs. "Will you come with me, Helen?"

"Nah girl..." I laugh, "Look, Sonia, you know me, I don't have time to get involved in that kind of shit." I smirk and continue, "I'm too busy running my own games and trying not to get caught."

"Right!" –Veronica laughs, stepping up to high five me.

"Fuckin' bitch." Sonia laughs. "But seriously, Helen, how do you play the games you do? Doesn't it bother you? What if your man caught you? You don't care how he would feel?"

"Sonia, since you have known me, how many times have I been caught?" I ask.

"A few times." Everyone laughs.

"That's right. A few fuckin' times! And I'm still alive, I'm happy as shit, and there are still a ton of men and women out there who are available. People are a dime a dozen. Lovers come and go. Nobody is permanent. I do care about these men in my life. I love them. But I love me more so I'm going to do what feels right to me," I state.

"Yeah, but you have been hurt before. How would you like it if you found out Dillon was cheating on you?" (Dillon is one of my many boyfriends after my divorce.) Sonia's question is fair. She knows I am one hell of a jealous bitch.

"All right girls, let's get something clear here. First, I don't do men with girlfriends or wives. I got boundaries."

Everyone nods in agreement.

175

"You know I definitely get jealous, but I work through that jealousy and I have never gone ape nuts on another woman or gone to her work or tried messing up her life in any way. As for a man, it's simple. I can't get hurt if I have been the one playing the game first," I wink.

"That's what I'm saying, girl." Dotty reaches up and high fives me.

"Sonia, ask yourself this and be truthful with yourself. Are you going to stay with your man either way, if he is cheating or not?"

Sonia's eyes and head lower and she goes silent. I can tell Sonia loves hard and the answer to that question is not the answer she wishes she could tell herself. Sonia is bright and strong. She is a world traveler and a beautiful woman who many men would drop on one knee for. Over our ten- year relationship I've watched Sonia go through men like raindrops into a puddle. Now she has fallen in love with a younger man and put all of her eggs in one basket. I admire her romantic fantasy of a white picket fence and a happy long-lasting monogamous relationship. I truly want that for her. I wish I could find the perfect man and give him to her.

Year after year, all I've ever heard from Sonia is her desire to find a successful rich man who will take care of her, have babies with her, and give her a lavish lifestyle where she will never have to work again. And year after year, Sonia is unsatisfied with all of the wealthy men she has managed to fit into her busy schedule. This one is married, that one is too available, this guy is a player, that guy is too young, this one is too old, that one doesn't have enough money, this one has a crazy ex, and so on and so forth. If I were a beautiful angel with wings who overlooked Sonia's life, I would probably have picked up a bad habit of betting and would have been cast down from the heavens already for not answering Sonia's prayers the first few times.

There we are, four grown women in different situations in our life coming together to relate, support, and have a couple beers to mellow the conversation. All the while sitting there listening to Sonia's broken heart, and making quick suggestions for her to "pull it together" and be strong, I can feel my own heart aching. Underneath it all I am not completely happy either. I cheat, I lie, I live for the thrill of my next adventure like a professional actor who lives for the thrill of her next box office hit. The observer in me can't help but realize that this too shall pass. Sonia's broken heart and jealousy will drive her mad until she decides she's had enough. That could be today or years from now; either way, it's all moving forward.

I once heard that the whole point of life is

to live to survive. Could this be true with everything? Relationships are fuckin' hard; let's not sugar coat it. Above all other species we have the higher intelligence, yet we are like the fish in the sea splashing fins at each other to take a bite at some good bait thrown in the water by some random fishermen. That bait is not so good after the romance period and the fishermen tells you, "Caught cha, bitch! First I'm gonna skin ya, then I'm gonna take your bones out, then I'm gonna fry ya in front of my whole family!"

We go through life searching for happiness and when we don't have our hearts filled with happiness, we are on autopilot survival mode. Surviving work, friendships, weather, relationships, bills, children — hell, everything and anything that is around us that we aren't happy with. Life really is a game and love really is the prize.

A week has gone by and I meet up with Sonia to talk with her alone. I've known her for many years now and never have I seen her this unhealthy and this stuck before. I'm worried for her well-being.

"Hey, Sonia. How are you?" I ask as we sit down at a lunch table at the Jungle Bread Restaurant.

"I'm doing better. Me and Vince are breaking up. I'm moving out. He won't confess that he cheated on me but I know he has and it's..." Sonia stops for a minute to contain her emotions. "… it's just not good for us anymore to be together. Helen, I'm just so mad at myself. I gave him two years of my life. I just thought we were going to be married and have kids. I just thought he was the one, you know? I'm feeling so lost."

"I know, girl. I know you thought he was the one. Don't beat yourself up too hard. You don't want to know if he cheated, trust me, you really don't want to know. Look, I'm here for you. If you need anything, I'm here. I know how hard breakups are, Sonia; I'm not going to tell you just to 'get through it.' It's going to suck and be hard. I would just highly suggest you do your best to start saying 'yes' to a social life. That can help distract you from the break up. I'm only saying this because it takes time to heal and saying 'yes' and getting out can be healthy for you. Okay?"

"I don't know how you do it, Helen... how you could cheat," Sonia snaps and the conversation just got intense. Sonia's heart is broken and I have to be careful with my words. Right now, all cheaters and liars are her enemies.

"Sonia, I know I joke about cheating and lying all the time. I know right now you think all cheaters and liars are the worst scum on the Earth and you think I'm some girl who goes around breaking hearts for fun, but that is not   the case and you know that. You are just upset and want answers why things didn't go as planned. I get it! But things are going to turn around for you and one day you will look back and realize you've learned a lot from this experience. As unpleasant as it is, you are going to probably one day be able to help someone else from your strength to move past this moment. It's going to be awesome!"

"Yeah you're right, Helen. Do you think I should contact the girl he has been hanging out with before I leave?"

"No, dude! Sonia, you are way above that! You are not the kind of woman who attacks or goes after another woman for talking to your man. We are grown now! I know when we were in our twenties we used to hate on other women and get all jealous and shit, but we have grown from that. Don't you want to empower women one day? Look, I don't care if this other girl knows about you or not, rise above this, Sonia! Rise a-fucking-bove! You will be glad you did."

We chat for a while longer. We finally hug goodbye and go our separate ways. On my way home, I reflect on our conversation. Every person I have ever met has done some wrong to someone they know. Throughout my life I've heard many women and men complain about their significant others or partners and then turn around and do some dirty shit behind their backs too, but as soon as an affair or lie is exposed all hell breaks loose and the person who lied and cheated is thrown to the wolves to be torn apart. Let me explain what I mean by that: Sonia thinks Vince is cheating. Sonia seeks revenge on Vince and whomever he is cheating with. Anyone who cheats like Vince is as low a person as he is. Sonia puts Vince on blast and now everyone thinks Vince is a monster of a man.

Here's a different kind of truth: Vince is a man. Sonia is a woman. They both emotionally and physically became attached through the mind, the body, and the spirit. Expectations were high and not equally met. Resentment and anger made its way into the relationship and devoured the commitment they had for each other. Maybe he cheated and it felt right to him. Maybe he didn't cheat but Sonia's accusations are going to drive him to cheat. Either way, driving oneself crazy to find out answers for someone's wrong toward you is not worth your valuable time, is it? The Universe wants to move you onto another road in life onto another journey and you dare defy the signs? I'm just saying. Signs only get bigger and louder.

Let's discuss something we all deal with: Jealousy. Now she's a bitch! I like to think of Jealousy as the name of a very nasty and evil Goddess of the underworld. She's spicy, hot, and licks her lips at the show of a wretched girl fight. I once was the slave of Jealousy. She had me wrapped around her finger the night my ex-husband, Raymond, and I got in our first physical brawl. I was in my twenties. We were going through our ugly divorce and still lived together. We both happened to be at the same club that night and I saw him put his hands through another woman's hair for the first time and lost my mutha—fucking mind! Jealousy knew she had me and used me at my weakest moment. It was a painful moment to be thrown out of a club by security onto the streets like a criminal for trying to hurt another woman who had no idea who I was.

It was worse when Jealousy took over my mind and drove me to my house to grab a knife and wait for Raymond. Raymond knew I had lost my mind that night; he had to physically drag me out of my own home because he feared for his own life. (Thank God Keme was staying at Raymond's aunt's house that night). After that night and finding forgiveness for myself and Raymond, I vowed I would never allow Jealousy to take a hold of me like that ever again. I would walk away before physically hurting another woman or allowing any man to drive Jealousy back into my mind. I'm not saying Jealousy doesn't creep around, oh she does! Jealousy whispers to us all, but we don't have to heed her call. You don't have to be the girl who puts down other girls. You don't have to be the woman who hates on other woman. There is no good enough reason to blast other women who are here in the same lifetime as you simply trying to survive the best way they know how. *So what* she's a hoe. *So what* if she chooses to sleep around. *So what*, she stole your man. *So what* if that girl makes more money than you. *So what* if she makes it by doing something that offends you. *So fucking what*! Don't attack and don't talk shit. You are wasting your time and everyone's time around you. You don't walk in her shoes or know the reasoning behind her actions in life. If you don't plan to help better other women in this world then keep moving, honey!

Chapter 18

The Prize of Love and Lust

"I'm open to the idea of soul mates and twin flames, but unsure of the idea of only having one in my lifetime."

I'VE BEEN IN DEEP LOVE. The kind of love when you feel like you could lay down your life for that person. Raymond was the only man I had ever felt this way about. He was my heart and I was his. Our love was magical from the moment we met. We were high school sweethearts. We were young and crazy in love. I've got to hand it to teenage lovers; they go all out for one another. All stakes are on the table and both lovers risk everything to be together. Shout out to hormones and puberty!

The evening Raymond and I decided to divorce I cried with grief and convinced myself the man I fell in love with was literally dead.

This "new" guy was not Raymond but some guy who only looked like him. My Raymond had suddenly perished, and I was coming to the reality of it in my mind. I was 26 when I re-programmed myself to think this way about him. I didn't know much about the mind, but even so I had been practicing this kind of re-programming since I was a young girl, which seemed to work every time I needed to let go of something and get the courage to move forward. I never thought I would have to use this coping tool when it came to Raymond.

After we divorced, I searched for a man who could equal the powerful love I had felt for my husband. I've fallen in love many times, with quite a few men over the last ten years, and still have not found the safety and passion I had shared with Raymond. Many have come close, but something was still missing from these men. Did my real love die when I convinced myself of his death? Is all this malicious behavior because I am searching for someone to love me as Raymond once did? Do I need Jesus? I know many people are saying yes right now. (I'm just kidding.) I have Jesus already, thank you! Everyone wants to give me an answer or a suggestion to my search. Hell, I even want to give a multitude of answers to my ever-rotating same questions.

What if there is no answer and the Universe or God has set it up this way for me?

Was I predestined? I'm open to the idea of soulmates and twin flames, but unsure of the idea of only having one in my lifetime. I truly and wholeheartedly believe in love. Pure love. I believe it's possible to fall in love with many people in a lifetime and to even be in love with multiple people at one time. Some have said, "Well if he/she loved you they would have never cheated on you." I'm not 100% sure I agree with that statement.

For example, I'm a big communicator. I pride myself on being able to communicate my needs to my partner. I even go as far as confessing that I have cheated in previous relationships and that I will exhaust all efforts to fulfill our partnership until I feel the need to step out. My friend, Lana always pokes at me saying,

"What the hell Helen! You attract nothing but vaginas! I don't know how you do it. You even tell them you will cheat on them if they can't satisfy you. Then you break up with them before you do and they STILL beg you back only to keep letting you down. No wonder you cheat. You warned them too!" She always laughs. Maybe Lana's right; like an exotic pet, I will eventually strike because it's my true nature to be free and not to be held in captivity by anyone.

Everyone's experiences are different, and I think it's unfair to pre-judge what someone else's experiences mean to him or her without understanding them first on a deeper level. So when I say this (breathe), it's going to sound very strange and hypocritical unless you understand me. I came to a realization that love is everywhere, in everyone at some point or another. When love recognizes love, it's like angels are saying, "What's up?" to one another. When I stopped fighting with myself about guilt and shame, and instead embraced lust, sex, and desire, I surrendered to love. Once I started communicating the love and desires I needed from the men who walked into my realm of life, I empowered my voice.

This is strange and absurd to many people, yet it boggles my mind that I go to church or read enlightening books encouraging us to "Be in the moment," "Let go of the past," "Love one another," "Grab life and live alive now," and it doesn't pertain to all matters of life. Do these instructions come with limitations? Let's be honest, everyone has limitations in his or her mind. This is our personal safety belt in the joy ride of life. Safety first?

Even with all of these limitations and instructions, and any other words to make you say, "Huh, interesting," I still think about what every human desires more than anything in life...and that is love. Can I be faithful? Of course, I've been faithful to myself for years now. Oh, you mean can I be faithful to a partner? Most definitely. Remember in a previous chapter I said I believe in monogamous relationships? This is true for even some who swear to be committed to open relationships.

Secret: People just don't know how to confess to wanting two things in opposite directions at the same time. It's considered "wrong" or "impossible" in this society. Some call it "duality," "polygamy," or "polyamory" to have love for more than one partner. I would say a dual life is something I do enjoy now.

Sometimes I think my true love is Ross. He's been my on and off lover for years. We have become best friends and are too much alike. I can crawl into bed with him and snuggle up to his body after two months of not seeing him. His touch still ignites my skin like electricity pulsing through my veins, arousing every cell in my body. I melt at the stroke of his fingers through my hair. We tried many times to be in a relationship and each time Ross or I stepped out and cheated. This was like a cruel game of tag we played: "hurt me and I will turn around and hurt you." It broke my heart that Ross would not stay faithful to me even after I gave up the game to forgive him and "start over" almost every year. It boggled my mind because he was the one I would jump two feet in with, and yet Ross still couldn't remain faithful.

I went crazy looking through his computer, phones, emails, and receipts. I drove myself mad always searching for something that he was hiding. For every one girl I found him only "talking to" that year, I filled my own cup with thirteen sexual encounters that same year to hit back harder. The only problem is he never knew; it was like a Jekyll and Hyde persona I took on to save face from falling apart and showing my true heartbreak to him. Everyone always asked, "Why don't you and Ross try a polyamorous relationship? Then you could be together and also have men on the side."

The problem is I won't share my men. Call it what you want but that is my choice of boundary. Ross is a reflection of myself, revealing to me that not all cheating is okay. It is not okay for someone to cheat on me when I have committed to him my heart and my golden vagina. So why is it okay to cheat on another? Great question. That is a question I think everyone needs to answer on her own and share with whomever she chooses.

I'm not a fucking guru and can't tell anyone else how she should or shouldn't live her life. However, I do know this: Women are divine, emotional, and sensual beings who happen to be a little bit more complicated than our male counterparts. Complicated and crazy are the two words I hear most often from both men and women when describing most females. The irony behind these two words is astounding, being that a woman is the one in the relationship who sticks around longer, coddling an asshole who possibly treats her like shit, talks down to her, cheats, lets his eyes wander to lust after many other women both in public and on the internet — for years and years... and yet she is the one who is complicated and crazy? I'm not suggesting all men are bad or assholes. No in fact, I'm going to be as blunt as I can get right now. "If you were my asshole, oh you better believe I would cheat on that ass in a heartbeat and not feel sorry for it!"

OMG, did she just say that? That is not serving the world! I can't believe her! How can someone even think like that? Oh cry me a fucking river and get over your righteous ass. Here's the thing, I'm not a compulsive cheater. I don't just randomly sleep with men I don't know. I've only had ONE one—night stand my whole entire life and frankly I didn't like it. I have boundaries too: I don't sleep with married men, people I work with, young and inexperienced men, or men who have an interest in my friends, men who have girlfriends, and especially the number one boundary (not to mention moral conduct) is to never sleep or even lust after a friend's man. Like I said in the beginning of this book, "I'm pretty much a fuckin' saint!" Do you know how many women and men I have met who play comatose dirty? As an on and off again notorious cheater and liar, I have met many other cheaters and liars on my journey. Just like bankers, cheaters come in all different shapes, sizes, ethnicities, and backgrounds.

Let's take a closer LOOK:

WE'VE GOT THE "I was drunk" cheaters who lose control of judgments and emotions because of alcohol consumption. Most of the time these ones get a free pass. They especially get you when they start crying and asking for forgiveness. Honestly, come on now... they were drunk! Forgive them already! Rule of thumb: One time pass only.

Then we've got the "I fell in love" cheaters who have literally exposed their hearts to lust and a high dose of dopamine. I don't mind these cheaters because I've met many of them and usually they are remorseful but unstoppable and make for the most tear-dropping-breath- stopping stories. You just don't know how the story is going to end and it puts you at the end of your seat to find out.

Over in the gold corner we've got your "I'm a player" cheaters. These are the under developed kiddos who like to play with matches, get burned, and are unsure of what they are doing at first. Many of these cheaters are usually going through an egotistical phase just trying out the "players life," if I may. It's more of a fun phase for people who are experimenting with the lifestyle. Some of these players go on to be compulsive liars, which is dangerous and not cool at all. Others try it and realize it's not for them while a small minority get burned, feel guilty, or get married and stop playing around. And just like the top 2% wealthy in the money market, you've got the 2% out of the players club who evolve into their own type of beautifully fucked up, artistically acclaimed, dual cheating arche-type. This type is rare and make no mistake, they do get caught — no matter what they brag about. Secretly people live their lives through these type of cheaters — their stories, songs, dance, food, laughter, celebration, and other positive vibrations. That's because these cheaters are like angels whose wings got clipped from doing one bad thing — but they are still good fucking people.

Now, when I say "comatose dirty" I'm talking about the cheaters who fuck it up for the rest of us. These are the devils who pop up in everyone's mind when the word, "Cheater" is used. They are the bankers who steal money from the poor and wipe their asses with it. They don't give two shits! These cheaters lie and cheat to intentionally rage in the cage with their lovers. They are the ones who do it for the **soul purpose to hurt** someone no matter who gets hurt along the way. They are driven by pure dominant ego and spiteful intentions.

You know these women and men as the ones who slept with your husbands, wives, girlfriends, boyfriends, and best friends. They are notorious compulsive cheaters who say sorry and keep doing it over and over no matter how good, healthy, and happy their so-called committed relationship is. Most, not all, sex addicts have these kinds of cheating habits. Six words for you, "Nope, not my style! You're welcome."

I can honestly say, I'm not a compulsive liar or a compulsive cheater. I don't start off with intentions to hurt or boast. I seek love just as much as anyone else when I'm romantically attracted and drawn to someone. This brings me to the special kind of cheater who should not be called "cheater" but rather Lover of Lovers. These are the believers of love at heart, the soft—spoken, often mistaken as mischievous and secretive, and when we are rash we are wildly majestic and seekers of passion. Sometimes we overlap our lovers and sometimes we take time to ourselves before seeking a new one.

Either way, we don't settle even in moments when it looks like we are weak and okay with being a frame on the wall; we are the type who hunt during the lightning storms and prowl under the solar eclipse for our lovers. Most of our lovers are called by our pheromones and attached to our box of mysterious emotions that we dare to share little by little. Our sexual lovers are well chosen and diversely selected. We have many needs and not one lover can meet the bar until he or she has proven him or herself. Call us what you will but our stories have the secret sauce that keep the lovers a cumin' back for more. Wink!

Both the prize and price of love and lust have been an extraordinary experience. Straying off the straight and narrow, onto the unbeaten path into the dark and mystical forests, has introduced me to transcendent pleasures only those with wanderlust can appreciate. Being in love over and over has its price and can be summed up in one word... broken. Broken is not a fun price to pay. It's not something that I want to have for the rest of my life or something I want to look forward to in my next relationship. The price of lust can also be summed up in one word... risk.

Risk is a word everyone knows because it shows up in every single person's journey through life. Risk lies at the feet of vulnerability right before love is reached. Perhaps we all lust right before we have a chance to love one another. Perhaps lust has been placed in such a dark corner of our terminology that it's not given a fair chance to reveal the beauty of its enchanted meaning. Could it be so?

Chapter 19

Understanding from a Distance

*"I hated the way you talked to
Mom and I prayed every night
she would leave you."*

Dear Dad,

*I'm sorry your life ended so soon. Geez, you were too
young. I mean fifty, Dad. Dang you could have lived
longer. Since you are no longer here in physical form I
am hoping by reading this, the spirit of you that lives
within me will accept it on your behalf. I've wanted to
write you for a while now and get everything off my
mind that I have never said. Let me address the fact
that I did not go to your funeral because I didn't want
my last memory of seeing you to be in a casket, not to
mention you weren't in that body anymore anyway.
Don't be mad. I did eventually cry, two weeks after you
died, while my friend Lana and I were having
martinis on her balcony. She's a good friend, Dad; you
would have thought she was cool. So, I'm currently
writing a book and it's pretty outspoken about some of*

my current beliefs. A part of me fears being judged, but I figure if I'm going to be judged, then I might as well make it worth the preconceptions. You knew what a little player I am and I appreciated that you laughed every time I told you about my "new boyfriends." Some people wonder about the relationship I had with you. This letter is to tell you what I thought about our relationship too. Dad, I'm not saying this to attack you but the earliest memory I have of you is no bueno.

***

"Leave her alone, Fred, she's just a child!" Grandmother snapped as she gripped my seven- year-young body into her chest to protect me.

"No! If she wants to disobey the rules then she needs to be taught a lesson!" Dad shouted back.

"These kids have enough beatings every day from you. Go to sleep so you can sober up!" she cried.

***

I remember the tears flowing down Grandma's face as she fought for me that night when you came home drunk once again ready to beat the shit out of the five of us. I took a run for it and she embraced me; I clenched her for dear life.

There was a wooden chest from which you had us take turns picking out the "tool" that we were going to get a whooping with that day. The chest was filled with belts, cords, wooden spoons, chanklas (also known as flip flops), and hangers. Once the chest tools were no longer sufficient you switched it up to a huge wooden paddle that looked like a flat—headed baseball bat; you had us write our names on it every time we got a spanking. As the five of us kids grew older we became immune to all of the spanking and turned it into a game to see who got their name on the paddle more throughout the year.

I don't remember how old I was exactly when Grandma died but I do recollect the resentment I felt when I saw how you, my aunt, and uncles comforted our cousins but shunned the five of us as if we were a pile of "nobodys" in the hospital waiting room. Dad, I have to admit... you were a real asshole for most of my childhood life.

You were always drinking, spanking, or making Mom cry, and to tell you the truth, Dad, I didn't really like you when I was a kid. I pretended to be your "lil Snott" just so you would be nice to me and give me a dollar to go to the swap—meet with Grandma. I am fully aware that as a child I learned how to avoid pain by masking and pretending to be kinder than I really felt. I'm sure I loved you as a young child; I just didn't like your actions as a person. You probably didn't like yourself very much during that time in your life either.

I hated the way you talked to Mom and I prayed

every night she would leave you. The night Mom finally left you for good haunts my memories of past times. In the middle of the night, seeing Mom's face wake me up in a panic was scary. It was cold, dark, and creepy; we had to act fast. You probably thought I forgot about that night. She tried to take all five of us kids with her but two, Roster and Olivia, stayed. I was mad at them for not coming with us. I was also jealous because I know that they were able to shower the next day while me, Grazelda, Margaret, and Mom had to sleep inside the car at a park for a few days without a shower.

At the time showers didn't seem so important but I sure learned fast to appreciate getting clean. Honestly, it wasn't that bad; we eventually bathed in creeks and park showers. Mom had a lot of courage. We learned how to survive in a car, in a park, in shelters, and how not to be fearful of random strangers. Even though Mom had us moving around constantly from place to random place, I felt protected with her.

Don't worry, Dad, I'm not mad about that part of life anymore. We had quite the adventure that still lives within me today. Besides, it was so long ago and Mom ended up taking the five of us away to Arizona, so I sorta' felt bad for you after a while. My relationship with you became closer after I turned fifteen. That's when Mom and I started bumping heads a lot and she said Grazelda and I could move in with you. It was fun living with you in California my freshmen year. You were like a totally different daddio! Every morning was hot coffee and oldies on the drive to school. I can still hear it playing on the truck radio, "Crystal Blue Persuasion… oooh ooh." After school barbeques at the cousin's house, you showed me how committed you were to our external family. Every day was a good day, every week was a quinceanera, and every month there was a baby shower.

I had so much fun that year. I know you think I left abruptly when I told you I wanted to attend high school in Arizona, but the truth is Uncle Jerk is the one who messed it up for Grazelda and me; he's why we left. I understand Uncle Jerk is your brother, and you lived together, but I'm your daughter and you didn't stand up for me when I told you how he freaked out after catching me outside giving my neighbor, Eddie, a hug goodbye.

As soon as I walked in the house, Uncle Jerk flipped out, "I see what you are doing here you fuckin' hoe! You are just like your fuckin' hoe for a mother! You are going to leave your Dad just like your Mom did! You better not let your Dad or me catch you with another guy again!"

See, Dad, I wasn't mad that Uncle Jerk was calling me a hoe, I mean, Aunt Jan had called me a hoe and wench since I was a little girl. Being called a hoe didn't faze me. It's the fact that Uncle Jerk had the audacity to put down my mother to my face, which is why I left, Dad. I know it broke your heart. I'm not sorry though. I made the right decision for myself and felt strong for not putting up with Uncle Jerk's negative accusations.

There is something very cool I've always admired

about you and Mom and that is your ability to stay friends throughout all the years I've known you until your death. Even after Mom remarried she stayed true to being your friend. I liked you both as friends. You were funny and romantic at times.   It was nice to finally see the both of you smiling, flirting, and laughing when Mom had you visit for one of our life events or birthdays.

Dad, even though you drank all the time, and spanked us a lot for really no good reason, I want you to know that I forgive you. You did the best you could with whatever belief system and control you had in life. Sure it may seem that you abused us when we were young kids but I don't like to tell the story that way. I'm no victim, I'm no survivor either; I am just a girl who was born with this deck of cards and became consciously aware that I can decide how to create the life I want with the programming I have.

OMG, I have to mention this memory that just popped in my head. We were in someone's car, not sure who, when we picked you up from jail after you were released. You were in jail for not paying child support. Dad, we made it fine without the financial support. Mom never kept us from trying to have a relationship despite the lack of support and that is what is so cool about her. You got lucky with a strong and fantastic woman who doesn't dwell on your bullshit. Hahaha! You know I'm right too!

I do miss having a beer with you outside by the barbeque howling in the moonlight. Arizona has some of my most favorite beautiful nights, but there ain't

201

nothing like Cali's crazy city moonlit skies.

"Howl like this, Snott, Aaaa Ooooooh!" you'd say. I was your runner for "another beer" and always made sure I had enough air in my lungs to blow into the breathalyzer for us to get home from cousins every night. By the way, fucked up, Dad! Haha drinking and driving is so wrong on so many levels yet you had us believing you were invincible.

In my twenties it seemed like I could talk to you about anything and I was happy that you felt proud of me. You even knew I cheated every now and then on my lovers and you would say it was because I have your charm. I think you could be right - I do pick 'em up pretty fast. I noticed your traits in the men I chose in my early dating years: Hard-working, construction field, hanging out at the bars every night type of men.

Olivia once told me, "If you keep picking men like Dad, it's like sleeping with him. You don't want to do that do you?" When she told me that it really freaked me out! Haha, sorry Dad, you were cool but definitely not the type of man I want to be with the rest of my life. I'm sure you would want to see me with someone better anyway. After that talk with Olivia   I started picking more goal—oriented and healthy—minded men.

One last thing, Dad, you never knew this, but I found out when I was seventeen that I was adopted by you.

"So Helen, there's been something I've been waiting for the right time to tell you," Mom said. "Your Dad, well he ain't your real Dad. Your real Dad's name is Dominic and I had an affair on your Dad and got pregnant with you."

We were on a long road trip up North to see Weta, Mom's Mom. I didn't like that woman but I agreed to go to keep Mom company on the drive.

"Woah, that's weird."

I had all of these flashes of daytime TV shows that I had watched about people who found out they were adopted and wanted to meet their "real dad or real mom" for the first time in public. Such drama!

"He worked at a gas station and he saw you up until the age of two. His wife was pregnant with a little boy at the same time that I was pregnant with you so you have a brother out there and other siblings." She waited for my response.

"Hmm. No wonder I look a tad bit different than everyone else," I laughed.

"I will leave it up to you if you want to find him."

"Yeah, you know what, Mom, honestly I don't really care to find him. I've gone this long without knowing and I already have Dad and a stepdad; I really don't need any more Dads to add to that list."

We both laughed.

"Well I just wanted you to know. Whatever you do, don't tell your Dad I told you, he would be so hurt," Mom admitted.

"No way, I wouldn't tell Dad," I laughed. "I mean, it's like whatever to me. My life goes on."

Mom went on to tell me about the affair and that you (her husband) chose to adopt me because you loved her and didn't want to divorce. After me, you and Mom had three more kids and tried to make it work until it didn't.

I never told you that I knew because I didn't want to hurt you or make our relationship weird. I know how labels can implant different thoughts in one's mind. To be honest, the fact that you are not my blood, Dad, doesn't mean anything to me. I don't care to search out my blood Dad. There is no point to it. I don't have time for useless reunions. Margaret, Olivia, and Grazelda often suggested I find out who my real blood Dad is so I could find out if I have a history of any chronic illnesses. I would tell them my life is in my hands and whatever comes, I will deal with it then.

It is nice to talk to you. Damn, it sucks you're dead. I guess anyone can go at any time. My time will come one day too. I don't plan to reunite with you once I die ... unless it's what really happens after death. Other than that, I think this is it for me, my heaven and my hell. It may sound sad or negative, but I assure you Dad I am not afraid. I have no feeling about it, not at this moment anyway. If there is a light at the end of the tunnel or family that will greet me at my death bed, then so be it.

There are many people that say they don't regret anything in life, but to be completely honest, I do regret some things. I don't care if choosing to not regret anything leads to glorious moments in life, I still regret things. I regret not spending more time with you before your untimely death. I regret divorcing Raymond; I loved him, Dad, he was a good man and I know I could have given more instead of giving up; I could still have my beautiful family together. I also regret putting past jobs and employers above important moments I could have spent with family. You know, I've lived most of my life as a puppet, pretending and putting on a false front for people to accept me and to avoid pain. I often joke with Mom saying, "Affairs run in my blood," to make sense of many behaviors. If you could speak to me now, I know you would say to live on my own terms and be myself. Make no mistake; I'm in a constant state of creation and making moves as we speak. I'm still a masterpiece in process.

Dad, I am your daughter. I am a strategic player in the game, I'm actively social, I like to drink and get a good buzz going. I like to party and howl in the moonlight and it feels fucking amazing. I'm also the daughter of Mom. I speak the truth, I am strong, I like to eat clean foods, workout, love deeply, and fly with the invisible wind to magical places. You both have your ego—spirits embedded within me. I'm quite the city and nature gypsy hybrid now. You both have a job well done in raising me. I'm blissfully thankful to you both and only hope I brought one of the greatest sunrises to your life while you lived alive.

Love,

Your second child, Helen ... aka Snott

I wanted to share this letter for anyone who had questions about my upbringing and relationship I had with my dad.

SOME PEOPLE MIGHT THINK it's crude of me to have not shown up to my own father's funeral. To be honest, if I had to go back to that moment, I'd rather smoke a cigarette and rock out to Taylor Swift. I don't think it's disrespectful at all. My dad kicked my mother's ass for no good reason and then died over the choices he made in life and I'm supposed to feel guilty for not attending his funeral? Uh—Uh, ain't happening. My view of death is simple. We are born, we live a little, and then we die. It will happen to everyone and there is no escaping death. We can cry and feel the pain of a loved one leaving, but on this Earth, we are in constant movement and life does go on. Disclaimer: The above statement doesn't mean I won't attend other funerals or sob hysterically the next time someone close to me dies.

My first experience with a heartbreaking death came when my beloved grandmother died. I was around twelve years young. It was a strange feeling to know someone you love, someone who has held you, molded you, and spoken to you is gone forever. Grandmother had talked about Jesus and God since I was a baby; promising that there was a life hereafter to see anyone who had died once again. She made it a daily activity for me to read the Bible out loud in the dining room while she did the dishes and listened. I was nine and still remember thinking, why can't the afterlife be now? It just doesn't make sense to have an afterlife unless this life is just a game and the afterlife is just a prize.

As I got into my twenties and studied on my own, I learned about science. I find it humorous that religion has such a horrible regard for science. The two are ridiculously similar — but use different terminology. However, I won't go there because I'm not a professional religious or scientific debater. Anyway, my point is death happens and if I'm going to attend a funeral it's going to be for a gathering to reminisce about that person's beautiful life. With my dad, it just wasn't the way I wanted to let him go. I wanted to know that the last conversation I had with him was enough and that he's still alive within my memories, dreams, and blueprint. He wasn't inside the body that everyone cried over. He was in the blueprint of his children now and that is his afterlife.

RIP, Dad.

Chapter 20

Multiple Flames

"I fall in love with different men and sometimes the same men every year."

"NO, ALL I'M SAYING IS I don't think it's going to last with me and Mark. To be honest, he's kind of an asshole and jumps right into sex like I'm an outlet to his plug. It's repulsive at times!" I laugh.

"Eww, have you tried talking to him when he does that?" Viv asks.

"Viv, come on, meow!" I laugh, "He's a good man, has his shit together, but I'm his longest relationship and it's only been one year! This relationship is still a baby and   it's supposed to be better than this. It's like I have to break up with him and then maybe if we circle back around we would have a better chance," I pause. "I've communicated everything and then some to Mark but it's like he's really selfish and doesn't think about my sexual and sensual needs… EVER!"

"Yeah, Brian and me have to schedule our sex on the calendar now. It's like he's not that into me," Viv admits.

My mouth drops, "Nooo, you guys used to be like jackrabbits, what happened?"

"Between his kids, my kids, and our jobs, we are exhausted all the time. When I try and talk to him about it he thinks I am putting him down. He says that I talk to him like I'm more intelligent than him; that I make him feel like I'm talking to a little kid. It's not that though, it's just our perceptions are different. You know what I mean?"

"Yeah, girl, I totally know what you mean! These men are not at the level we are at, especially with conversation and enlightenment. It can sometimes make them feel like we think ourselves better than them." I snicker, "This is why I have Ross! He's smart, thinks outside the box, and he gets it when I talk on levels beyond the realm of current reality. Honestly, I can be myself with Ross and most importantly we laugh all the time when we hang out."

"That's how I feel when I hang out with Arthur!" We both laugh.

"I mean, me and Ross don't have sex anymore, but we still cuddle every now and then. It's like I seriously need two or three, maybe four men to meet all my many needs!"

We both continue laughing.

"No, it's true! Arthur is that guy who I can tell everything to and there are no expectations from him. I told Brian it was better when we were dating. It's like everyone gets comfortable over time and everyone quits trying. I wish we could live in different houses and just date for the rest of our lives."

"You could!" I spit out. "Look at me, I fall in love with different men and sometimes the same men every year. It's fun!"

"That's awesome! I need to do that!" Viv laughs.

"Oh shit! I forgot to give you the update of my massage therapist, Alexander."

Alexander is a foreign kind of saucy that women dream about. He's a certified massage therapist — which means he's great with his hands and his electric energy. I met him through a work event, and everyone knows I have a strict policy about dating in the workplace. Alexander didn't give me any signs of attraction in the beginning; this is what I like to call, straight hit from the backside, metaphorically that is. Wink!

He insists I come to his massage studio because my back looked unaligned. My whole life I've never allowed a male massage therapist to touch me because I was too insecure about my body; the thought of a random male seeing every flaw on my body scared the shit out of me.

"Hi, come in," he says in his sultry low accent. Right away the sage and myrrh incense fills my nose. Mmm I instantly feel calm and relaxed. "Okay, are you ready for massage?" he asks in his deep Persian accent. "Just take off your clothes and lay on your stomach. Let me know when you are ready."

The music is a tribal meditation beat and as he caresses my back with his warm hands I become present. *Goddamn! What the hell is this?* This is a whole new experience that sends my mind directly into "I love My Self!" mode.

During the massage my mind reveals past times of being an Egyptian Goddess, being pampered by my man servant. I embrace being a true Goddess in this moment. Alexander's hands move slowly to my thigh area and in an instant my sacral chakra becomes a live atomic volcano. It's happening and there's no stopping it. I get wet! Oh no, I'm on his sheets in just my panties. Dammit, Helen!

"Relax," he says. The touch of his hands now rubbing my feet move me back into Goddess state of mind. Who knew the power of touch could launch one's entity into a multitude of trance-gasmic dimensions? I fall in love with myself. I desire myself. My soul and my skin become one. The experience is celestial... and then it becomes sensual.

Three visits later, Alexander locks me into

routine visits at his humble home for weekly massages.

"Would you like a glass of wine or a coffee before we begin?" he grins. There's something enthralling about him that I can't quite put my finger on.

"Yes, I'll take a glass of white if you have it."

As I lay on the table waiting for Alexander's brilliant profession to soothe my shoulders, I can sense something is different. He slowly massages my back in a circular motion. It's as if my professional massage has turned into a sensual escapade; his breathing is slower and deeper.

"Excuse me, one minute please," he says.

I lift my head to see if something has happened. Alexander returns to the room with a big grin on his face. "I'm sorry but I'm highly attracted to you and this has been my hardest massage ever. It is hard to control myself..." He looks down at his zipper, implying his hard on, "...but I will control myself. You don't need to worry. Trust me."

I am in a slight shock. "Oh." I gulp.

The sexual energy is floating all around us in slow motion. As I lay back down, Alexander respectfully places a cloth over my eyes to ease me back into relaxation. All I can think about is how sexy this moment makes me feel. I know he wants me! A woman recognizes when a man desires her from the look in his eyes, the crack in his smile, and the way he jumps to serve her in any way. An hour has passes and Alexander is still honoring my body with the touch of his hands; I am truly a queen in this moment. Another thirty minutes pass and I'm suddenly taken out of my trance to a sultry voice in my ear, "Am I going to be in your book?" he seductively whispers. His breath echoes through my body down to my toes; I'm in awe. "Um" I gasp shakily, "Do you want to be in my book?"

Alexander comes around the table over to my left, slowly lifts the towel from my eyes, and leans in with a gentle kiss to my lips. The moment freezes and I am in pure sensual heaven. He lifts his head back up, staring deeply into my eyes.

"Yes."

<hr />

"YEAH, SO I TOLD MY massage therapist that I am not trying to get involved with anyone because I have a boyfriend."

"What! No way! OMG, what did he say?" Viv squirms in her seat.

"He said he understands but that he wants to continue working on my back weekly. He also doesn't want me to pay anymore. It's free!!!" I rejoice.

"Helen that is funny! So he is going to just

213

give you free massages and you don't have to do anything?" Viv's eyebrow lifts in disbelief.

"Well I told him that I feel too guilty because I have a boyfriend and that's why I don't want to kiss or do anything with him. But girl, you know I don't like to kiss anyways! Plus, the real reason I stopped it beyond that point is that I don't want to lose a good massage therapist... plus he's now become a good friend. Honestly, I enjoy the sensual climax and need him to provide that high for me."

Viv agrees with my reasoning, nodding silently. She gets me.

"You know Viv, I have my men but when one comes out of the blue when you least expect it, wanting you and desiring you, it's like... Whoah! I did not see that coming! Um, excuse me, sir, don't you see my hands are full. Ya might fuck shit up for me!" We laugh hysterically.

Alexander opens up dimensions for me that I only daydreamed about. Every moment spent with him is a living-in-the-present moment for me. I embrace sensuality and allow myself to breathe through every hint of passion he feels for me. The power of touch from my massages change my life. It becomes my weekly time to love myself, my skin, and my soul. When you have a professional, who honors your body more than the man who swears to the moon that he loves you, something doesn't scream "satisfied" in that story. Then again, thousands, probably millions of women turn to professionals to get the love, seduction, and touch that they don't get at home. Once again, I believe it's okay to have many men with many talents to fulfill one woman's many needs. It just makes dollars more than sense to me. Wink!

Let's Go There

"KISSING" HAS ALWAYS BEEN a weird taboo to me. I was thirteen when I had my first kiss and it grossed me out. Someone's slimy tongue was mingling with my slimy tongue and then his face was all up in my face. I didn't like it! He was in my muth-fuckin' bubble, in my space! I had a hard time shutting my eyes during the process. I've always wanted to see what was going on during the kissing process. Are his eyes open too? Is his head turned sideways, straight up, or moving in circular motion? Does he have something on his face that I can't see? Here's my chance to find out, because he is closer than ever!

Kissing on the face lips is that one sexual part of the whole romantic experience that I really could do without, until I got in my thirties, that is. I once had a guy who had no

215

idea how to move his tongue in a sexual and romantic rhythm with mine. Ugh! Where the hell did he learn how to kiss, and how come no one ever told this twenty-something year old dude he's sloppy as shit? I had to blurt it out to him right away. Poor thing would have never known that he sucked face... literally! The worst is when you get someone who has a great smile, great teeth but his breath smells or he has unprocessed food in his gums. I'M TOTALLY GONNA VOMIT!! Men asked me all the time if I didn't kiss because I thought I was a bad kisser. Nah, homie! I can kiss like the phenomenon of the god particle, people wonder how the hell I do it! OH-kaaaay!

Over time I learn that kissing can be very intimate and sexy. It comes down to the sexual and sometimes sensual connection I have with someone. Like when a man has that hungry, "I want to devour that ass" in his eyes and his three- point-shot (great smelling breath, cologne, and saying all the right things at once) is a slam dunk, than YESSS — let the kissing dance begin!

Chapter 21

Every Day Missing You

"Take a deep breath. Exhale. Hold back the tears, forgive, and keep moving forward."

THE PHONE RINGS! "What's up, Lana?"

"Where are you? I thought we were going to meet up for happy hour after work today?"

"Oh was that today?" I laugh. "Girl, I'm in Cali visiting my son and... I'm also looking for jobs."

"Looking for jobs?! How long are you going to be there? Did you quit your job here? When are you coming back to Arizona? Where are you staying down there?" I know she is only asking me a thousand questions because she cares and gets worried when I make impulse moves.

"Raymond had to travel for work for a week and asked me to come down and care for Keme while he's away. I let my job know. While I'm here I'm going to try and find a job. I want to move here and be near my son. It's so hard being away from him."

"Yeah, I know it is for you, Helen. Did you tell Mark?"

"Girl, I didn't tell anybody." I laugh. While in California for that one week, I land four interviews and am hired by one small family-owned company. Keme and I are ecstatic! We stay up late that night talking about all the cool things we can do once I live closer. We are so happy!

A day before our week together ends, I get a call from the hiring manager saying they found a better candidate for the job. My heart feels shattered because I know it is going to be awful telling my son I will have to wait on the move. I fall apart and cry that night and Keme hugs me close repeatedly saying, "It's okay, Mom. It's okay."

I try a few times to move to Cali to be near Keme but fail at each attempt due to lack of time, money, and places to stay. I feel like a complete failure.

"You know I miss you every day, Keme. There is not a day that goes by I don't think of you. I'm still trying to figure a way down there." I say into the phone.

"Mom, it's okay. I want you to stay in Arizona. I actually like flying out there and getting away to see my friends there too."

"You know I tried, right?"

"Yes, Mom. I know you tried. It's okay. I have a lot going on here. I like going up there to visit you." He says so calmly and playfully.

I fly Keme back and forth a few times throughout the years to spend time with him. Each time we are together it's as if nothing has changed and we are close as ever. Although I live a pretty free and wild life, there is a mother's brain and soul within me that feels void without her child near. Even with all of the untamed adventures going on, once there is a sliver of silence, I can hear the anguish of her deep within me.

"Hey look at your school schedule, talk to your dad, and let's get your next flight out here to see me. I miss you!"

"Okay, Mom. I'll talk to my dad and get back to you soon about it. I love you."

"Thank you, son. I love you too. I'll talk to you later papas."

I hang up the phone. Take a deep breathe. Exhale. Hold back the tears, forgive, and keep moving forward.

Raymond and I try to remain civil and decide not to go with the court-ordered parent times. We had decided that we will work out the schedule from month to month based on what is best for all three of our schedules and with consideration to our distance.

Although it may be strange to some, at the

time, Raymond and I were trying to do the best we could after the divorce. Some things take time to learn and grow from. Parenting is definitely one of them.

Let's Go There

I PRETEND BEING AWAY from my son doesn't bother me to save face and show strength around other people especially other women. I pretend paying child support doesn't faze me, but it is the dagger in my back and the shackles on my feet. For years I've struggled to pay child support. Some months I would try to survive off of can foods, so I could make the payments. Everyone would like to believe it's because I want to do the right thing and financially support my son, but the truth is I pay to avoid jail time. Do you think parents actually would rather pay money than spend time with their children? Maybe some people want to believe that because they are too scorned or maybe they do have a good enough reason. I can't speak for every parent out there, but I can tell you that child support is both a money angel and a demon who taunts the soul unto destruction.

Chapter 22

Seek and You Shall Fun

"The pressure of the world weighs in on my shoulders"

"LET'S SEE, ADMIN, OFFICE, data entry, come on Craigslist give me something good," I whisper.

Job searching is a pain in the ass, especially if you are someone who doesn't like working for anyone else. Ever since I was a child I have been working and chasing the dollar; cleaning yards, washing windows, cleaning houses with Mom, and many more fun activities I got little pay for. I've worked restaurant, retail, sales, marketing, office, and the medical field. I'm exhausted! I'm 33 and still keep switching jobs.

The pressure of the world weighs in on my shoulders. Jobs seem to reflect my relationships with men as well. After the honeymoon stage of a job, when the reality sets in that I am under someone else's command, I want to bail! The similarities are astounding: I am overly ecstatic about both at first; I can't wait to learn more about them, I brag to everyone how awesome they are, and when I realize how unhappy I am, I fuck 'em both. The only difference is I usually put up longer with a man because I've invested my heart.

From time to time it gets lonely in my mind and my world seems so small and desperate. I can have both a good man and a good job and yet feel very unsatisfied. It feels as if "good" is not "good enough." I spend numerous hours asking Google questions like, "How to be a more confident woman," or "How to get out of a funk" and sometimes I even ask, "How to quit my job and start to live."

I scroll on Facebook and read numerous stories of people who quit their jobs and travel the world and blog about it. I am infatuated with people who post how they found their passion in life and are living their own dreams. It makes me happy to see friends and online "friends" enjoying their one precious life. Sometimes my mind wanders through cyberspace and peers into their random lives to see if they are like me, "High and Low" on multiple occasions.

When my thoughts are to myself and I am seeking change, my heart and soul long for the dream to run free throughout Earth's playground, but my logical mind controls my body and seeks to first find security. Find a new job that pays more, has benefits, and something that will keep me happy longer than a year. Am I this programmed to live the majority of my days on Earth in a box working for a system? Is the controversy between my soul and my body causing constant friction within my heart? I'm just like many people out there. I fuss and fight with myself quite a bit. However, that being said, I am my favorite person to make up with after a long hard struggle. I take myself out for wine, maybe some dancing, every now and then a movie, or I watch some YouTube videos on the hottest men of the month and I feel a hundred times better about life.

"Look, Helen, I'm not trying to be a jerk, but you don't have a savings, a retirement fund, a 401K, and you drive a piece of shit car. You need to try and get a job in a big company that can offer you a career you can retire in," Mark says.

"I understand what you are saying, Mark, but I just can't see myself working for someone else my whole entire life. I want to go to school to be a Yoga Instructor or a photographer or professional writer; do something so I can work and travel at the same time." I plead for his understanding.

"Come on, babe! You're 33 ... are you kidding me!? You can't keep switching jobs. You need to find one and stick with it. You need to save your money, pay off your debt, and then you will have money to travel when you retire. You are living in a fantasy land, babe! It's not real and you need to start getting it together because I'm not your sugar daddy!" Damn, well thanks for popping my eccentric sugar daddy fantasy I've had in my head since I was a kid, Mark.

Douche bag! Sigh.

Face it... I tell myself... Mark is right. His credit score is as perfect as the myth of the tooth fairy and his management of his finances is honorably respected. As for myself, my credit score is like a walking zombie, dead but alive with thousands of dollars in debt hanging over my head. I've read over twenty books, attended two classes and ten workshops on money management in the last eight years, and can't seem to remember much about them. I know Mark is trying to help but it definitely hurts to hear the truth about my financial flaws.

Don't get me wrong, I'm very aware of my money woes and the programming of money I've had growing up, but what Mark isn't aware of is how much I've improved my relationship with money in the last eight years. Any conversations of my desires to travel and see the world are argument starters in our relationship. Even though Mark pisses me off by talking to me like a teenager who doesn't have a clue about money, I appreciate everything he says. I practice a breathing technique while I listen and take deeper breaths when I hear something that triggers my defensive cells. I need to learn and not get so defensive.

Money... a peculiar word that rhymes with funny. Shut your eyes and listen to the way "Money" sounds spewing out of your mouth. Strange, isn't it? An illusion, a vehicle, an exchange of value, and something that is rather nice to have an abundance of. I've only dated one man in my life who had little money and the adventures we took were priceless.

In my twenties, I had a handful of jobs that paid me quite a large amount of money, and when I saved enough to travel, I dipped out and never returned. Now in my thirties I find myself questioning if I'm going to be the lady in her eighties working in a cubicle. I can't bear the thought of working for a corporation with bosses who are younger than me telling me when I can and cannot have a day off to live my one gift of life for years to come. Debt isn't real, money isn't real, but the value of everything is real and the attachments I have with different kinds of value are immeasurably strong.

IT'S NO ORDINARY DAY; there is something in the air and both Veronica and I know it. We look at each other, look back at the mountain, and then back at each other.

"Holy guac, dude! It's freakin' beautiful today!" Veronica says aloud as she opens her arms wide to embrace the spirit of the mountain.

"I know... right! I love Arizona in the winter. We are like seriously the luckiest state in the U.S. Three out of four seasons are uh—mazing!" I smile.

North Mountain is our sacred paved mountain. We both agree this mountain has a giant spirit that feeds us a vortex- like energy — every time we make our way to the top.

"So how are things with Mark and the job going, dude? Do you like it still?" she asks.

"You know, dude, I don't really like either anymore," I laugh.

For the record, Veronica and I are both equally "dudes and dudettas" without any prejudice or second thoughts about it. These repetitive names accent our conversations.

"Oh what happened? I thought you loved your job!"

My current job title is Marketing Director for a chiropractor. A job I jumped at because of the opportunity to expand the chiropractor's new health and wellness addition to the company, not to mention the financial sign- on bonus I was offered in the hiring process.

"I thought I loved it too! My boss docked my pay and I'm stressed out all the time. I am not happy, dude." I frown.

"I'm sorry, chicaletta," Veronica half-smiles.

As we continue to walk up the mountain a beautiful man without a shirt walks past us and we both turn instantaneously.

"Woah, dude." My mouth drops open.

"Yeah," Veronica gasps. The sun perfectly highlights his gorgeous tan muscular arms and tight sculpted six pack.

"What's he doing?" I ask Veronica.

"I think he is about to run up the mountain because he turned around."

"Do you think he knows we are staring at him?"

"No, dude, we look like we are walking backwards up the mountain. There is no way he thinks we are staring at his hot, sexy 'I wanna fuck him' body!" We both laugh.

"OMG!" I shout.

"What, dude!" Veronica laughs as her gaze is still on the shirtless hot guy running past us.

"I forgot to tell you... I did a nude photo shoot."

"Whaaat! Shut the hell up! Seriously? I wanna' see! Were you nervous? When? With who?"

"My photographer, Joanne. I felt totally comfortable, dude. She's super awesome. And..."

"And what?" Veronica is about to jump out of her skin waiting for me to finish my sentence. She knows me too well. All of my stories are epic.

"And... I slept with her and her husband," I casually say. Veronica's eyes widen as she breathes in the biggest inhale and exhales,

"Whaaaat?!" She is shocked shitless and laughs."Okay, I did not expect that but then again, why am I not surprised?" She laughs again.

"Well, the nude photo shoot was purely professional. A while later, Joanne asked me if I was interested in having a threesome. I figured, why not?" I laugh.

"So how was it?"

"You know what, dude, honestly, it was pretty damn hot! I wouldn't mind doing it again. I'm an adult who consented to it, I felt secure in my body, and explored new territory. I felt very safe and mature about it."

"Wow. Did you cum?"

I knew that question was coming. Hahaha."I came close; it was just so surreal." I laugh, "... but tomorrow I will make sure I do for sure!"

"What! Again?"

"Yup! She asked me over again. Why the hell not, dude!" We both laugh and high five each other.

"Helen, we have a pretty rad life don't we? And it's fucking beautiful out!" she shouts out loud.

We continue our trek, but my mind stays on our conversation. My mother is going to kill me if she finds out about Joanne. Yup, it's true. I've had sex with women too. And not just with Joanne. Right now, your mind is probably asking, "Is she bisexual? Or secretly a lesbian?"

Neither.

I explored with women in my twenties and early thirties. Many people do that; I'm not a unique case with this. However, I do think a woman's body is majestic and if the right moment presents itself again to be intimate with a woman, I'm in. I know some may think, "For crying out loud! Does this woman have any boundaries at all?"

Yes and no.

See, I'm in love with life and all the beauty in it. Labels are labels and will always be labels but people are rare jewels of the Earth. I want to gaze, taste, and touch the riches of this world; which to me can be a beautiful grown woman or handsome grown man. This happens to be both the masculinity and femininity of delightful consenting adults whom I get to know, trust, and share mutual attraction.

I've never questioned my sexuality outside of making inappropriate jokes about it with friends. Yeah, I'm kind of vulgar and hardcore disgusting when it comes to jokes with my closest friends, or if I've had too much to drink. Other than that, I've been true to myself when it comes to my desire and attraction to both men and women. I've never said to myself, "I'm straight, heterosexual, bi, or pansexual." I've only acted out of complete confidence that I am experiencing a burning desire to feel another man or woman's body and the intention takes flight from there. Where it lands can even be a surprise to me.

Chapter 23

Break-ups Sucka Defense

"It seems no matter how amazing and 'right' you may play your cards in the beginning it still does not guarantee the relationship will make it to the end."

UGH! MY STOMACH HURTS, not like a stomach ache type hurt but a "my soul got sorrow punched in the gut" type of hurt. Breakups suck! Doesn't matter how strong I lead myself to believe I am, when a breakup happens it never feels 100 percent good. My breakup with Mark is strange but apparently not unusual. We both have many complaints about each other but if you search the root of all problems, there is usually an underlying kink. Ours is something I wouldn't have ever expected: a baby.

Mark wants to have a full—blown family

whereas I don't desire to have any more kids. Just like any other relationships, I tried to convince myself that maybe we could still work. Nope! Eh-eh! This is one of those reasons that can't be overlooked. When we first met, of course, we talked about what we both wanted, and at the time it seemed everything was aligned. He wanted kids, a wife, and a best friend. I was open to kids and wanted to get married too. I wanted to travel the world. Mark was open to traveling the world. We fell in love with each other's strengths, which were our differences and BAM — two people on opposite roads going in opposite directions — got attached. What the hell were we thinking? We weren't. We were floating on high dosages of serotonin for sure! Almost two years later, when we least expect it, the thinkable happens. "Mark, let's not prevent the inevitable. You know what I'm talking about." I shakily say.

I can hear him sniffling on the other end of the phone. "I know. You're right," he whispers.

My hearts races; I can no longer hold back my tears. "We tried. We really did."

"You are the greatest woman, Helen. I just thought you would come around," Mark cries.
"Mark, I'm sorry but I don't want any more kids at all. You deserve to be with someone who will give you a baby." I wipe my tears and my nose with the same sleeve. I'm lost in pain

232

now. "You once said that it was selfish of me to not have your baby, but actually it's more selfish of me to continue this relationship knowing I won't ever give you one when someone else is waiting to give you exactly what you want." I pull myself together and feel strong. I'm actually doing something right! "Mark, this is it, you know. No more finding reasons to work it out. You have taught me alot and I am forever grateful for you."

"You have taught me a lot too. I'm sorry for ever being an asshole and not touching you or giving you what you needed," Mark responds. "I love you, Helen and I'm here if you ever need anything."

"Bye my beloved Mark." I cry and sob all night over our breakup and my heart silently mourns for quite some time after.

It's said that time heals everything, and there is definitely some truth to that. There are parts of me that wonder if I have made a horrible mistake by letting go of such a great man. He is everything I asked the Universe for... had I not thought this all the way through? Maybe I could have his child? Will I find another man as great as Mark? I wonder if we will circle back around again.

My fears come to surface when I feel vulnerable. Thank God I have a super gnarly sense of awareness. As quick   as these questions fill my head there is this divine voice within me that stands firm with my decision, as if I am protecting myself from running back. "I will be okay. We both will be okay. Day by day, Helen, day by day." There is a part of me that is hurting but a larger part of me is assuring me that this is what is meant to be for a higher purpose   for everyone. My, how I have grown! Once upon a time there were two individuals who celebrated coming into an adult relationship. Now there are two individuals having a mutual civil adult breakup.

"WHAT ARE YOU GOING TO DO NOW, Helen?" Veronica asks.

I smile, "I'm going to live!" I nod my head in agreement with myself. "You know, dude, I don't feel the need to be in a relationship anytime soon. I am learning to do things by myself and it feels good for once. I'm changing and I'm okay with that. I mean, it hurts — but I'm going to allow myself to feel the pain when it's there and just keep going, you know."

Veronica jumps across the divider in the car and gives me a big hug. "Dude, I love you!"

My girls, I can count on all of them to be my wing women and my shoulder to cry on. I feel blessed beyond measure. Sonia eventually left her man a few weeks before my breakup with Mark and the two of us laugh about our great adventures to come. Veronica and I get super stoked at the fact that we can hang out more with my relationship out of the way now. Lana's cynical but kickass—ass is all on board with my breakup recovery party. It's comforting to know that supportive friends are there to catch you when you slip, fall, or jump.

Even with all of the loving support and extra events that replace time once spent with a partner, there are still the un-busy moments when everything comes to a stillness and you are left with your thoughts. Sadness and grief can take over when realizing someone you've invested time, money, and heart in will no longer be there.

There is no doubt in my mind that I will be okay, but the pain of letting go of someone I fell so hard for and   put a lot of faith in just bites at my soul. Only time can heal the brokenness and failure I feel. Relationship after relationship, where am I going wrong?

Maybe, where am I going right?

Breakups are very painful. Relationships are super great in the beginning and after the honeymoon stage... relationships are work. Sometimes a lot more work than they need to be. Having attachments to other people has always fascinated me. There are times when I tried to be the observer in my own relationships as if I were the science experiment. I've tried it all from dating and telling the man all the reasons why he would NOT want to date me, to exposing all of my issues first to someone who is interested. It seems no matter how amazing and "right" you may play your cards in the beginning it still does not guarantee the relationship will make it to the end.

I'm definitely no expert on breakups because they hurt like hell and I still cry and wine a shit ton when I go through them, but here is a list below on the things I do to help myself get through breakups without breaking:

- ☆ Smoke some green and speak to the night sky stars
- ☆ Go dance with friends, A LOT
- ☆ Eat tons of gluten-free popcorn and watch Dave Chapelle and Amy Schumer stand ups
- ☆ Drink wine or dirty martinis while playing reruns of Sex in the City
- ☆ Create profiles and flirt on online dating until you fall asleep
- ☆ Spend time in Barnes & Noble a few days out of the week
- ☆ Write your own book, blog, or vlog about your experience
- ☆ Cry and then go look in a mirror and make fun of your crying face so you can laugh

☆ Cry and forgive yourself and practice letting go each day by breathing and moving forward

☆ Refuse to get depressed. Get pissed, throw your covers off, and get the fuck up and open the blinds!

☆ Hula hoop outside while watching the sunset

☆ Surround yourself with positive bad ass bitches who lift you high as fuck

☆ Go buy a new smokin' hot sexy dress, put it on, and go have a margarita

☆ Put your gym shit on and start a new relationship with getting ripped

☆ Turn up my music and shake your ass all over the place

☆ Spend time thinking about what pranks you can play on your friends now that your single

☆ Extra time to figure out how you can become a successful entrepreneur and get out of the jobs you hate going to

☆ Go through your closet and throw out everything that just sits there. You're no damn hoarder!

☆ Spend time with people who deserve your attention and time more than your ex ever did

☆ Go back to school or pick up a new educational something to dive into

- ☆ Attend Meetup groups and social gatherings that are fun and make new friends from all over
- ☆ Join free single groups or start your own
- ☆ Do yoga to get more flexible for your next man—just sayin'
- ☆ Travel. Just pack your bags and get the fuck out to some new adventure before you change your mind
- ☆ Keep writing down all the reasons why your ex is now an ex just in case happy thoughts and memories keep entering your mind
- ☆ Remind yourself every day that each day it will get easier just like all the breakups in the past
- ☆ Volunteer somewhere. It feels good to help another when you are hurting
- ☆ Hang out with a trusted fuck buddy if you really don't give a fuck
- ☆ Hang out with your best guy friends and refrain from sex but let them play with your hair
- ☆ Create a new YOU and sharpen the things you love about yourself
- ☆ Attend some kind of retreat that will lift your soul up
- ☆ Plan a girl's trip — Go on that trip — Get wild!
- ☆ Date yourself for a while. You probably will learn things about

yourself you didn't even know before.
How cool is that!

☆ Move. Forward. Somewhere New.

I OFTEN WOULD FORESEE my breakups before
they would actually happen. Sometimes I
wondered by foreseeing the breakup if it was
my fault for calling it into existence when it
would happen. I always hated the idea of "red
flags" because everyone has them. I have major
red flags and even with years of working on my
own red flags, I still have some left that I'm
working on and may be working on for the rest
of my life. It's finally hit me that I need to spill
the beans about my red flags and see if they
mesh well with anyone else's red flags. It's the
best way to do it because some people,
speaking of myself too, enjoy some of the red
flags in our lives. Example: A red flag for some
of the partners I've had is the fact that I
change jobs a lot. "Oh snaps! Run! She changes
jobs and could be a threat to my eternal
happiness. She's one of those!" I get it. Just
like when I hear, "Yes, I have cheated more
than once before in the past." Boom! He told
the truth and he's fucked for it. "RED FLAG.
There can't be two cheaters in the relationship.
Uh—uh, sorry buddy, you're not the man for
me. I know way too much about a cheater's
game and nice to meet ya but ya gotta go!"
Now if the red flags were something along the

lines of:

Me: "I've had a shit ton of jobs and am currently unsure about the one I'm in now also."

Him: "I mean, I'm not happy but it's job security."

Me: Possibly a red flag? "Seems we have the same problem. Or is it a problem? I mean, are you doing what you always wanted to do or are you unsure of what you want to do? Do you dream about doing something else while you work? 'Cause maybe we have the same issues. Maybe you and I were meant to travel and do something bigger?"

This open dialogue of two red flags now have the potential of becoming two red hearts. Something about relationships that I am guilty of is jumping in too fast. Perhaps I didn't spend enough time getting to know men on a deeper level or else breakups wouldn't happen as often. Or maybe, just maybe, karma does exist. It exists in the pain deep in my gut and in my throat when I can't breathe after my heart feels like it's been shattered by yet another breakup.

Who knows? All I know is break ups feel the worst even though they can be for the best.

Chapter 24

Conversations with Myself

"Random streams of consciousness"

FOUND IT!

No... I swear I've been through this before. I kinda remember but not sure... I can't believe I don't remember. What the fuck! Sigh... I'm exhausted... Okay, calm down, I can do this. Inhale, LIGHT BULB!! Oh, that's where I put it. I knew I would find you laundry key!

TRUST AND BREATHE

I miss him, I'm doing it! No, maybe I shouldn't. I just want to make sure he's fine... Texting... Thumbs going to town... Erase, Sigh...
Not a good idea dude. Shake my head, no... It's okay, everything is going to be okay. I nod my head yes. Deep breathing... Exhale. OMG, my life is about to spin out of control. I'm about to freak out! Screaming within. Breathe through this. I'm going to take care of you. I nod my head yes.... Agree, Okay. Now stop thinking about this and focus on the meeting before your boss notices.

CHECKIN' OUT DUDES

Goddamn he is fine. I wonder how long I can stare at him. What if he looks and catches me staring at him? Quickly turn away as if I'm staring at the tree in the park.

Who cares if he sees me looking at him. Not my fault if he's hot. Slowly move my eyes back to the hot guy. What am I so scared of anyways? He should be happy I'm checking him out. I want to hump his muscles... That's so weird. I laugh...

PUPPY

I want a puppy!

Hmmm... but then I have to pick up poop... But puppies are so cute. I could be happy with a puppy... No I can't have a puppy. Who's gonna watch the puppy if I wanna just go away? Maybe next year... That's what I said last year! Sigh. Thoughts of cuddling a puppy. Thoughts of moving every four months. I can't get a puppy right now.

Bummed.

REASONING

I'm lonely. I'm not lonely, I just want to be cuddled by someone new.

Craigslist?
No been there done that. Old news. Plenty of Fish? Match.com? Online dating? Hmm. I'm too lazy to look right now.

Netflix?
Oh Yes!!!! I'm going to masturbate first. Nah... I'll do that later. Too lazy for that too. I laugh.

RANDOM HUMBLENESS

Argh! Here we go again. Same old shit.
Come on, find something you're grateful for. Don't start the day like this. My job is just ridiculous! I know... We'll figure it out. I'm tired... Sigh.

I don't know what I want to do. Driving. I see people waiting at a bus stop. I notice a woman with two small children. Flashbacks of Mom and the five of us struggling. God damnit Helen! I have it good. I have it fucking good! I'm moved. I'm going into work and making the best of it.

TO GO OR STAY

I wanna go on that trip with Veronica. Fuck I can't go! I put my foot down... But I really wanna go... I'm going!!!

Dude, you can't go. I have to save money right now. I can afford it! I can find the money!! I've got to go. I've got to seize the moment! Visions of fun times on our future trip flood my mind. Okay, okay, I can do this! Thoughts of responsibilities replace my fun times.

What about the job? What about the bills? What if the car breaks down? I sink down. I don't think this is a good decision right now. Okay. Boo...! But who knows, I may change my mind at the last minute. Glimmers of hope return.

INTIMATE MIND GAMES

I wanna fuck, I'm so horny. I wish he would suck on my boobs more. Why isn't he sucking on my boobs? Is there something wrong with my boobs? Mmm shut your eyes and think of someone else. Yup, it's working, I'm getting wetter. I hope he appreciates this. OMG could he be taking any longer?! There we go daddy...

I wonder if it would turn him off if I called him daddy? Still getting pounded. I bet there

are a lot of people who say weird shit in bed.
I laugh in my head. Yeah and I'm one of
them. Focus, Helen, try and get off.

PISSED OFF AT FRIEND

I can't believe she stopped talking to me!
I want to punch her in the fuckin' face!!
What did I do? Was I a bad person to her?
I just don't understand. I'm so hurt.
Screaming within. I want to blast her on
Facebook! No. I can't put her on blast. That's
just not right. Fuck right! She fuckin' used
me! I was there when no one else was. I'm
more hurt than anything. I've got to let her
be her. Let her go. Just bless her. Crying.
Okay. Attachments to anyone... Ugh! I do
miss her. Sad...

DRIVING IN TRAFFIC — EP. 1

Is this guy seriously on my ass? I wish I
could throw eggs at his car and then a bag of
flour.
OMG, go around! I'm frustrated. Just move
the mirrors and then you won't see them
behind you... Great idea. Mirrors moved.
Music turned up. Honk! That's right buddy,
you have a good day too! I roll my eyes and
laugh.

EVOLVING

When's the last time I had sex? You know, I don't really want to have sex right now anyways. OMG! I can't believe I just said that! Surprised me. Hahaha Oh it's happening. I mean, it's not a bad thing. Hmm I bet I would have the best sex ever if I waited for a long time... I wonder how long I can go without having sex? I start to count months. Yeah—No. Uh—uh. I got to have sex! I'm not taking these hormonal balance vitamins for nothing. I laugh.

Actually, I really don't want to have sex with just anyone anymore. Okay maybe I do. I laugh again. Something is definitely changing and it's evolving me, I'm aware of it.

I want some chocolate! I think I'm about to start my period. Ah! Everything makes sense now...

CAR DANCING

Oh! This is the jam! Oh snaps! Get it girl! Dang this song is taking me waaay back. Head bobbing, body swirls. I wonder what I look like to other people in their cars playing no music. Calming down. Feeling insecure.

Aw fuck it! This is the shit! I can't care what anyone else thinks when a song like this is on. Turning up music. Getting crazy and fist bumping in the car.

DRIVING IN TRAFFIC — EP. 2

I'm going to pass you. Come on car! 45mph... 50mph... 55mph. Whoosh!!! Wow, that was amazing. I feel pretty bad ass right now. I wonder why it feels so damn good passing other cars? Ugh! Red light. Noooo! Here he comes...

Right next to me. Don't look. Can he see through my tint? Green light! Come on car...Go! Go! Go!

Maybe it's the song. I need a more gangster song. Then the car will go faster!

BATHROOM BREAKS AT WORK

It's so quiet in here. Someone make some noise. Why some noise? Why is shitting so weird in a public bathroom?

I wonder if the person next to me feels just as weird. Yes! They are done! When they flush I'm going to push! Damnit, not enough time. Flush was too quick. I'll wait till they leave.

Omg! Are they seriously going to wait in the women's restroom and do their hair? Why! How do they not know the rule. Do Not Hang Out in the bathroom ladies. Gross!! 30 seconds or less. Wash, rinse, dry, Go! Get the fuck out! Be gone!

Omg! She is still in here. Ugh. Cough, make noise or something. This is too weird.

I swear to god, someone needs to write rules of the bathroom. Why would anyone want to hang out in the bathroom anyways! Damn that shit felt good. Must get on Facebook and post positive quote.

WRITING THE BOOK

Maybe I shouldn't write this book. I should totally write this book! What if I can never get a date after this? Plotting my book escape. You're gonna feel so liberated. Trust me, keep going. I get stuck a lot. OMG I have writer's block. It's better than getting cock blocked. I laugh. I can do this! I'm doing this! Wooh! Cheers to the air with my glass of wine!

GOOD-BAD MOM BATTLE

Ring! Keme never answers his phone anymore. Teenagers! I miss him so much. Don't cry. Don't you dare you cry... I'm the worst parent ever! I've lost the best years with my son and it's all my fault. No! Stop it! Don't do this. Let's not go down this rabbit hole again. Breathe. Forgive... Wiping tears. Try to call again later.

GETTING SCOLDED AT WORK

Breathe. Just nod your head. This isn't your first write up. My boss is just doing her job. Respect...

This is so awkward. She's an adult. I'm an adult. How weird is this? I wonder if they feel just as awkward? They look stressed, I wonder if they are happy here or faking it like I am. Here comes the sheet of paper. Breathe. Sign and then get the fuck out. You got this!

Damn rat race, one day I will leave you. I swear to it!

Chapter 25

And Then There Was One

"Am I not the one who wanted a change in my work and personal life?"

SILENCE.

Staring into the beautiful blue sky, I nod and take a deep breath. "I think this is it," I whisper to myself. I'm at my peaceful place on top of North Mountain, lying on top of my favorite rock watching the one bird flying around in the open sky.

For the first time since I was fourteen I am not fucking anyone. I have no side boo or a piece of flirty birdy booty. I just quit my job, moved out of my beautiful palace of a house, and broke up with Mark, a man I thought for sure I was going to spend the rest of my life with.

My always-there-for-me lover, Ross, has moved on to a new woman of his own. I'm happy for him too. I've created great friendships and memories with my girlfriends and guy friends; we have lived a wild and delicious life for the past ten years.

What next? I ask the Universe inside myself. I smile. "What next?" I whisper again quietly.

***

IT'S THE BEGINNING OF A NEW YEAR and I jump at the chance to go to a Yoga Teacher Training School for three months.

"What the hell was I thinking?" I exclaim to Lana.

"Well who knows, maybe it will be good for you," she laughs.

"OMG! Lana! Ahhh!" I grab my face in disbelief. I don't know shit about yoga. I had only taken one-week class two years prior and thought, Hmm I could totally do this. From that moment I pondered the idea of becoming a yoga teacher, feeling magnetized by the community. I searched hundreds of schools and watched endless videos of yoga teachers and how they traveled all over the world; was this to be me someday? I fantasized about traveling and teaching yoga by doing the crazy pretzel body poses and turning my body into a sculpted sexy yoga machine.

"Okay, so I have to confess, I put on the prerequisite that I have been doing yoga for a year. A year Lana! What the heez-ell wasz-ell thinking?!" We both laugh.

"You're such a nut! Haha — Why are you worried? You are active and workout every day, Helen."

"That's what I thought, too, but then I attended this workshop this last weekend and they had a yoga class on the Saturday I was there. Girrrrl, I almost cried! I couldn't get my body to stay in a pose for long. My hands and feet kept going numb. Breathing through my nose felt like the air was burning my nostrils and I felt so fucking goofy, it was hard!" I laugh.

"Maybe I should get my money back," I announce.

"No, Helen!" Lana snaps. "Calm down." She laughs. "You are just freakin' out because you don't do yoga and your body is not used to that kind of workout. Give it some time and you will become a pro! Trust me, I think this is going to be great for you!"

I appreciate Lana's encouragement. She's right I wouldn't have invested the money if I didn't see myself having a solid chance at this.

The Yoga Teacher Training came at a perfect time in my life. I wanted to take a break from meaningless and lustful sex to focus on a deeper relationship with myself.

Something is evolving in me and I can feel it within my core. Spending more and more time alone in silence and alone with my thoughts has me analyzing my existing life patterns. Nobody stays the same, everyone grows; the question is in which direction are you headed?

My latest relationship with Mark had shown me a new kind of path that I wanted to travel. I never really cared for a trusting or loyal relationship before I met him. I watched myself grow more than ever before, through our relationship. The idea of trust and loyalty had brought such peace in my life when I first met Mark. It's almost as if this was my lesson that the Universe knew I needed. Clever Universe! Make me think I would get everything I asked for — and then take it away. Perhaps a little sprinkle of karma was thrown in the relationship too. I never believed in karma, and thought whatever happens is just meant to happen for who knows what fucking reason. There is no denying the design is flawless and there is no changing the dynamics of the laws of this great universe.

The next day, I sit on the mountain, once more, this beautiful morning I realize I desperately need a change of scenery. I am hungry for an adventure, for an awakening, for something profoundly different. Yoga teacher? I'm not even sure I like the sound of that or the politics of the business side of something so sacred, but whatever; what do I have to lose at this point?

It's been the longest dry spell I have ever had without any dick. This is strange, even for me! I wonder if I am going to meet anyone in the future or even worse, if I'm ever going to have sex again. Maybe this is the moment Mom talked about, when sex was no longer everything in life. Falling in love with Mark and then making an adult and responsible decision to let go of the relationship was another defining moment for me. It restructured my heart and showed me my true love for self and for someone I truly cared about. This time I had front row seat to my own motion picture as I was wide awake and aware as it happened.

You know there are millions of stories of someone who finds her true north or happiness through some radical event in her life. I can't really profess to one radical moment that changed me, or helped me find God, or happiness, because it took many small moments in my life to lead me up to a moment of maturity and an understanding of deep compassion for myself. I felt God, Universe, Source, I AM, whatever name you wish to use, in everything from a very young age throughout my whole entire existence. I fought with God, laughed with God, cried with God, begged God for everything, and even felt the touch of God physically and totally at various times.

I've lived a life that many only dream about in such a short period, one I am still dreaming about, one I want more of. "What next?" I wonder.

I look down at the city from above, breathing in the fresh air all around me. There is a young little child, a teenage girl, a twenty-something rebel living within my 34-year-old woman's body asking, "Where are we going now?" I exhale taking one last glimpse on top of the mountain before heading off. "I don't know where I'm going, somewhere green?" I whisper aloud.   I do know for this small moment as time stands still, I could live on the mountain for the remainder of my life and the life hereafter overlooking the city, watching the sun rise, watching the sunset, and just being and nothing more.

⁂

"SO HOW'S THE YOGA CLASS going for you?" Olivia asks over the phone.

"OMG, Olivia, its fuckin' hard! Like, honestly it totally challenges me and I literally have to stay present and focused every moment I'm in class. I definitely cannot be drinking while taking this course," I laugh.

"Oh that's good! Well, you know what, I'm really excited that you are coming up here in a few months to stay. It's going to be great having you here."

"Olivia, I can't wait to go up to Oregon and stay a bit   too. You know, I have been in Arizona for eleven years and honestly, it's time for me to have a change of scenery. This will be my first snow bird, or should I say, 'fire bird,' year and I'm super stoked!" I joyously say.

"Okay so how long are you planning to stay up here, Helen?"

"Um, all right," I say, clearing my throat. "So Olivia here are my thoughts and after I'm done telling you, if you don't agree then I can give you a date for how long. I kinda was hoping to come and stay, check out Oregon for a few weeks and if it all goes well, stay for the whole summer. And between me and you, if being up there is good for me, I may find my own place and make Oregon home for a bit longer." I pause for my sister's thoughts.

"OMG, yeah dude! That sounds perfect. You can stay for as long as you want. I mean, not as long as you want — but definitely for the whole summer," she laughs.

"Cool. I mean I just need a change in my life. I haven't had sex in a long time, I haven't gone on any dates, I'm only working part—time at a strip club, and I'm just trying to make it through school without any major distractions

256

or attachments."

"Okay, wait... sooo Olivia, do you want to know a little secret?"

"Um, yessss!" she quickly responds.

"Okay, well I kinda searched out single men on the popular dating site POF just to see what kind of men are waiting for me in Oregon." We both laugh.

"Oh and I didn't stop there, I decided to compare the type of men in Oregon and the type of men here in Scottsdale."

"Helen, no you didn't!" Olivia is hysterical. "And?"

"Aaand, the guys here in Scottsdale are all about image like every third guy is super—hot and the guys in Oregon are all lumber-sexual, like Paul Bunyan-type dudes. Buuut I will say the profiles of the Oregon men seem like they are much more authentic." I laugh.

"Wow, Helen." Olivia is in a state of disbelief.

"Whaaat? I had a lot of time on my hands last night and couldn't sleep."

"So this is what you do in your spare time? Shouldn't you be studying?" Olivia asks so motherly.

"Olivia, I've been blessed with major ADHD and not only did I study but I also worked out, went to my pole dance class, meditated, watched some Netflix, played on Facebook, worked out again, took a shower, and then tried to go to sleep. That's when the question hit me, what lucky man in Oregon am I going to give my half a year virginity to?" I jokingly but seriously ask.

***

THE DECISION TO MOVE to Oregon for the summer is an idea I had played with for almost two years. Each year I came close to making the move, I purposely would find a new boo to latch onto, thus making it an easy choice to stay and repeat the same cycle. I decided this time around I had all the necessary tools and discipline to defeat my habits. As I sat on the balcony of Veronica's apartment, guiding my fingers over every picture in my vision book a.k.a my road map, I knew the time for change had finally arrived. My vision book is a book I designed with photos I had printed off Google Images that portrayed what I wanted my life to look like. Example: I had a photo of traveling to Peru and Fiji because traveling to these countries is what I desired to do sometime in my lifetime. It's basically the same thing as a vision board except I had it made into a book so I can travel with it and look at it at anytime wherever I was.

AS TIME GOES ON, my experience in yoga teacher training reveals much more to me about myself than I ever could have imagined. The answer to my question of "What next?" comes alive every time I'm in my shavasana pose — also known as the death pose at the end of every practice. (Fitting for someone like myself, in constant search of a new beginning.) I admit my first couple of weeks were completely grueling.

Learning about the eight limbs of yoga, which included the Yama and Niyamas was as if Change itself was saying to me, "You want change, BAM, here I am girl!"

Basically, the Yamas and Niyamas are two of the eight limbs of yoga that every yogi must be mindful of throughout her daily life. Yamas are guidelines for how a yogi must ethically behave in relation to others. Niyamas are what a yogi has to be ethically mindful of regarding himself or herself.

I mean, I don't even know if I should be writing about any yoga stuff in my book, but the point is when I learned about the yamas and niyamas I was like, "Oh fuck! Does this mean no more lustful desires or watching porn?!" I am kinda freaking out here!

Quickly, the Yamas and Niyamas below:

YAMAS (SOCIAL CONDUCT)

- ∽ Ahimsa (Non-harming)
- ∽ Satya (Truth)
- ∽ Asteya (Non-stealing)
- ∽ Brahmacharya (Continence)
- ∽ Aparigraha (Non-coveting)

NIYAMAS (SELF CONDUCT)

- ∽ Saucha (Cleanliness)
- ∽ Santosha (Contentment)
- ∽ Tapas (Austerity)
- ∽ Svadhyaya (Study of Oneself)
- ∽ Ishvara Pradindhara (Surrender to God)

THIS IS IT. The place I've wanted to visit for many years but was too scared to explore because I knew it would require massive transformation. This is my chance to jump into a new body and mind. It's going to take some hard work and much practice but it's a place I've never ventured before. Can I give up my beliefs about sex, cheating, lies and my unconventional contributions to my deepest desires?

As I sit on the mat in my training class, staring at the words jumping off the page of my yoga study book, the teacher's voice becomes faint and drowns in the background of my own thoughts. I am happy with who I am. I love people, I enjoy sexual pleasures, and I practice many philosophies and meditations every day of my life. Do I really want to be a yogi and live my life practicing these ethical ways that are defined outside my realm of thinking? What is it I am afraid of letting go, my secret self-less but self-absorbed habits? Or maybe the question is — what am I afraid of learning to become a more enlightened human being?

Ahh... yoga... why did you choose me?! Okay Universe, you sly big huggy bear you, once again you give me everything my heart desires. Am I not the one who wanted a change in my work and personal life? Am I not a seeker on a quest for deeper connection with myself and others? I believe I am the one who sent the intention out to the Universe to send me on my next great adventure. This is it... what are you going to do, Helen? I take one big inhale and make the momentous decision that will forever shift my future — I'm doing this!

Chapter 26

U-Turn Yoga

*"Let's take a bunch of
Yoga selfies."*

WOOOH! THREE MORE WEEKS before the final
exam! I finally finish watching all of the
episodes of Dexter on Netflix and can focus on
studying for the final exam. Dexter was my
balance to all of the yoga philosophy I
immersed myself into daily. Sometimes during
class I would wonder what is going to happen
tonight on Dexter? Is he finally going to get
caught? I feel such a connection to Dexter's
balance to a duality life and wonder how many
people out there feel the same.

There's a struggle to get myself to class
after the first two weeks. Some days I don't
want to get out of bed and   I wish I had never
signed up for school. I often compare myself to

the other students who are much more flexible. I can't even touch my toes or do a safe low lunge. I have no body awareness and every pose I do is totally grueling. The first half of Yoga Teacher Training (YTT) is quite frustrating but I hold myself to it. I now understand why yoga is intimidating for many people. I think back to all of the videos and research I did to find out what YTT is all about; somehow, I had the notion I would come to school to learn how to put people in yoga poses, learn a little bit of anatomy, and come to understand what the term "yoga" meant. That's all I thought I would learn. Silly rabbit! Can I just say right now for the record, YTT is no joke! It's a history and philosophy program at the core. In my awesome opinion, I would even say it is one of the healthiest, holistic, and totally challenging therapies you can embrace.

Ring!

"Hey Dudeletta! Whatcha doing tonight? I need some help on my yoga homework. It's on the chakras and I know you know a lot about that."

"Acca Yes! Come over after class. Can you pick up a bottle of wine and a gallon of water for me? Thanks!"

I can always hear Veronica's smile over the phone. BFF night here we come! After class I scurry to get my mat rolled up and flee to my car like a girl on rollerblades. I stop quickly at Trader Joe's and rush over to Veronica's apartment.

"Veronica, Trader Hoes only had half gallons, so I picked you up one." I laugh.

"Really! I could have sworn they had full gallons. Oh well, it's all good. Thanks, dudecicle!" Veronica happily shrugs. "So how is yooooga going?" She waits with open arms to receive my glorious feedback.

I take a deep inhale, simultaneously pour myself and Veronica a big glass of juicy red wine and say, "Soooooooooo," and laugh.

"Soooooo?" She looks confused.

"Okay, so school is nothing the way I thought it was going to be. Honestly, it's hard and every day I'm fighting with myself to go to class. It's almost over and I'm questioning if I just wasted all of my money on this program. Dude, I tore my right chest fiber muscles! I mean, what the fuck! I've done CrossFit, extreme sports, running, biking, weights, and have been totally fine. I do yoga for a few weeks and suddenly I'm injured! I thought yoga was supposed to heal the body, not injure it," I vent in frustration.

"What! You injured yourself? Oh dude, I'm sorry to hear that. Do you think that the injury has set you back to maybe feeling this way about school?" Veronica asks.

Damnit. She's good! "You know what..." I

stop to breathe and center myself, "...I do think that is why I seem to be looking at all the negative right now. Honestly, again — hahaha, yoga has been hard for me because it's a mental practice unlike any physical activity I have ever done before. It challenges me to step out of myself and everything I believe is true for myself into a sacred realm of life. It's scary, weird, and uncomfortable. It's like a combination of religion, spirituality, science, and mathematics all rolled into one. All of the things I am so resistant to but undeniably can benefit from," I confess.

"Well, it sounds like this is exactly what you wanted in life, Hels. Keep going and soon it will get easier and easier. Hels, you are going to be a great teacher one day. I can totally see it! Stick with it! Cheers!" Veronica lifts up her glass.

"Cheers!" We laugh.

"So on another note, didn't you say you had a hot teacher when you first started?" Veronica snickers.

"Hahaha. Yeah so my 'hot' teacher — she's gorgeous! And my other teacher, Harris, is super handsome but looks exactly like my son. Super weird, dude! Super weird!"

"Nooo way! Hahaha, that is hilarious! Are you like always wanting to say, 'Harris, go to your room?' she pokes. "Ha ha. Funny, Veronica." I manage to comeback with a straight face without busting up laughing. "It's actually kind of cool because it's like seeing the future of what Keme is going to grow to look like and become. If I were to die before I see his age around thirty then I've already seen it. BOOM! Time travel baby, time travel!" We cheers again.

"Well... PS, my coffee maker behind you has a hidden camera in it," Veronica suddenly says with a straight face.

"Whatever, dude!"

"For reals! It's been recording us the whole time."

"Pshh ...You can't pull a fast one on me, but you know who we can pull a fast one on? Facebook friends!"

"OMG! Let's do it!" Veronica jumps around in excitement.

By now, we are two glasses in, and open our second bottle of wine. Somehow, we both believe we are coming up with fascinating ideas and making more sense than ever before.

"Let's take a bunch of yoga selfies!" she shouts.

"Woooh! Yessss, by the pool!" I shout back. "In the pool!" Veronica agrees, "With the dogs and on the couch, with the dogs on the couch!" She laughs harder.

"Yessss and on the balcony, by the fridge, in the fridge, on the car. Woooh!" Laughing and in disbelief that we have come up with such creative ideas.

"OMG, this is getting out of control!

Cheers!" Veronica professes.

I lift my wine glass up to meet Veronica's and thus the BFF night flourishes into music, hugs, many cheersings, laughter, and tears of joy for our many adventures and present journeys. I can always count on Veronica to give me the space I need to vent about anything in life. There is no judgment, but fun and laughter during our venting parties. There is also a lot of support and random ideas that have us laughing 'till early in the mornings, and memories that are priceless. I'm blessed to have a best friend as free- spirited as Veronica.

The test day arrives. I pass with ninety percent on my written exam and pass my final yoga flow sequence test. My mother drives up from Kingman, Arizona to come see me get presented my certification. I can't imagine anyone else I'd rather have with me at the certificate celebration more than Mom. My whole life I wanted her to see I could be great at something, for her to see she raised me for success, and this is a perfect moment for us to share.

Commitment is not one of my strongest traits but this time around, I made it from beginning to the end. I cannot believe it myself! There is a sadness and pride in this day. Sadness to say goodbye to new friends I've made and the routine of learning something new daily, and pride for obtaining what I had set out to achieve. I have flashbacks of all the times I was so very close to quitting.

I am a certified yoga teacher now. It feels so weird and foreign yet somewhat fitting. Whether I wish to pursue further or not, yoga has undoubtedly altered my inner truths by expanding my mind into the body and mind connection. I want to learn more about the "yogi's way." Maybe this practice can bring me peace and a new sense of purpose if I allow it a place in my everyday life.

Mom reserves a room at the Wyndham for a girl's night to celebrate together. We smoke a little bit of *medical mary* together, have a glass of Kahlua, and snack on seaweed chips. We laugh our stoned asses off and play on the video app, Snapchat, for a few hours until we fall asleep. I remember hearing once that when people are about to die they regret not spending more time with their parents. In this moment with Mom, I don't want to be one of those people who lived with that kind of regret. I am happy she is spending my celebration with me as if we are both teenagers.

The day after feels like I'm a new baby bird trying to get the courage to fly for the first time. I need an extra push and listen to a few

Joe Rogan YouTube Videos and a few Susan Jeffers quotes from her book, Feel the Fear and Do It Anyway. I post my very first Yoga in the Park flyer — and although only one person shows up to the event, the fact that I show up is enough for me to see the success in myself. That's what I need to believe, that I will show up for the leadership role I believe myself worthy of. "One breath at a time yogi, one breath at a time".

Chapter 27

I Am Movement

"Despite this realism, I trust my inner guru to lead me in the right direction."

LEAVING BEHIND EVERYTHING and everyone you know is much more challenging than I imagined. Although, I expect emotions of fear and sadness when I move to Oregon, I don't expect to wake up every morning feeling completely lost with a knot in my throat. Before making the commitment to move to Oregon to live with my sister, Olivia, and her family, there were many conversations with myself to prepare for these emotions in my new environment. I anticipate feelings of regret, fear, sorrow, and total homesickness.

Despite this realism, I trust my inner guru to lead me in the right direction. Everything points to Olivia's house. I am sure my sister's home is meant to be my next step right after getting my yoga teacher certification. I daydream about mountains of glorious tall green trees, small—town city folks getting along perfectly, festivals and fairs, and beautifully sunny but miraculously cool weather throughout the summer. Somehow, I am moving to Oregon to save everyone with yoga, create happiness overnight, and attract a hot, outdoorsy-kind-of-man to whisk me away on a camping trip where we can meditate together. Boy, is my head in the clouds of My Uranus!

Veronica so graciously makes the road trip to my sister's house with me. I realize Veronica is the last time I will see and feel the energy of my Arizona home. I am a total downer on our last few days together and Veronica can't wait to get back home. I don't blame her! I want to leave with her when I drop her off at the Medford, Oregon Airport. I drive back to my sister's house with tears of sadness and whispers of surety that this is supposed to be.

Olivia's house is a massive two-story, five-bedroom house on a half-acre lot. It's absolutely breathtaking up in the mountains and the running trails are full of nature's winning green and colorful blossoms. Olivia has quite a large blended family. The house is always full of teenagers, my niece and nephews and their friends. All of the rooms are taken, so the living room becomes my sleeping quarters, when unoccupied.

Four days into my stay I realize how estranged I feel from my sister and her family and how estranged they must feel from me. Olivia and I never got along in the past. She is one year younger than me, shorter, and much more demanding. She and my brother have gorgeous hazel eyes and this always made me a bit jealous. My first week with my sister makes me realize how my preconceptions of her were from childhood, phone conversations, and hearsay from my other siblings. Spending just one week in the life of Olivia forces me to step back and observe. She is absolutely brilliant! A mother, a loving wife, a strong woman, a CEO of their family's three businesses, and even a volunteer at a hospital. She blows me away! Who is this woman? I am captivated by her ruthlessness, intelligence, and perseverance.

We share many stories of the years we missed together and stories from our childhood. How different we both grew from the same shared experiences too. I immediately put together a summer goal plan to share with Olivia. If anyone is going to keep me accountable to get my financial life together, it is her. My credit is on the road to repair, getting a new car is around the corner, and she even offers the best constructive criticism for this book. Just when I think I am not a family person or someone who will ever be that close to my sister, I'm learning to embrace the family dynamic. Family is coming alive again for me in my life and it's like I have a second chance to take the opportunity to dive in and take part of it as much as possible.

She and her husband offered me a two-day-a-week bartending position at their bar for the summer. I took it! Working at the bar made me feel like I had taken two steps back but it is what I needed to keep the money rolling in and pursue my yoga goals. All of my daydreams about Oregon had started to vanish.

My life in Arizona was very different from the life I stepped into in Oregon. There, I had a single woman's lavish life, free to go, free to do, free to bring home anyone. I had the sexy dresses and heels, the wine nights with the girls, and the fashionable tasteful Scottsdale men and their money. I could see out on the horizon over the city on top of my desert mountains and find quietness in my own home.

Life at Olivia's was completely opposite. The green— filled mountains blocked the view of the open world. Although beautiful and full of oxygen, I felt as if the trees were caving in on me while driving through the curvy roads when I first arrived. *"This is going to take some getting used to."*

Olivia's house is full of teenagers coming in and out of the house, something I am definitely not used to. Every night Olivia and her husband shared conversations, family time, prayer, arguments and debates, and adoration for each other. It was both new and scary for me to see the family dynamic on a day-to-day basis. The town folk were nice but far from perfect. They were just like every other town or city, just people making a living the best way they knew how.

From my perspective, it was a country-type but also a mix of bluegrass with a dash of city folk in the small Oregon town. One thing that was surely different was many people chewed tobacco. Even a woman I met chewed tobacco. It was the most disgusting thing ever! Working at the bar and having to hand out spit cups was a mental exercise not to gag right in front of the customer. I'm sure there were people who did it in Arizona but I lived there for many years and only saw a handful of people who did it. It seemed so foreign to me to see so many people chewing, it was a bit of culture shock.

My new journey in Oregon seemed to be raining heartbreak instead of hope. I found myself sad and feeling very alone. I questioned every good reason why I made the decision to move here in the first place.

I'm not family material! I'm not a small town kinda' girl! Why did I put myself in this situation and how do I get myself out of it? What exactly was I thinking I was going to get here that I couldn't get in Arizona? What is to become of me?

Everyday seems like a battle of my mind(s). I thought about my life in Phoenix and how I felt like I was going in circles. Am I the problem and have I only brought myself in Oregon to create another circle?

As I sat on my sister's outdoor balcony staring off into the forest, I fantasized about my spirit running through the trees with the wind caressing through my long black hair feeling free as a bird. I remembered the sadness I felt from my broken relationships and my suddenly dissolved friendship with Sonia, one of my closest friends in Arizona. I could hear my inner goddess confer words of wisdom to me, "It's here where you are supposed to be to heal from the brokenness right now."

Letting my friendship with Sonia go was heartbreaking. I loved my friend more than she would know but an unfortunate decision on her end to cut off our friendship was what she felt was best for her to do for herself. For that, I must understand that nothing lasts forever and we all have our own path to follow. As much as I want to be angry for someone cutting me out of their life when I felt I was a faithful friend, I must control my emotions and bless them in their chosen endeavors. I do wish her the best, I truly do. Anyone who wishes to shut people out of their lives has that freedom to do so. I've finally come to understand all relationships run their course and all you can do is let it go when the time comes to say goodbye and hope the deepest friendships come back around.

I wonder, is this the part where I grow up to be the woman I have foreseen myself to be: Strong, confident, a leader, truly independent and emotionally reliable on myself.

The truth is I can go back to Arizona at any moment. I am free to leave whenever I wish to. No one is holding a gun to my head forcing me to be here in Oregon. No one is forcing me to work at my sister's bar or feel lonely without friends. No one is forcing me to not masturbate or find a man or woman to have casual sex with. My day- to-day decisions and choices are mine and mine alone. I've realized my commitment to myself to follow through with where I have visualized myself to be, has grown greater than my personal habitual desires. This is EXACTLY what I wanted when making the decision to move to Oregon for the summer. I can do this! I am doing this!

THE REDWOOD FOREST... where the giants found their wood to build their homes. I am but a tiny speck of human walking through the mysterious huge trees. I sit still in   the forest sending out thoughts of my life as if I'm having a telepathic conversation with the giants around me. "I'm here." I'm alone with myself. It's time to be still, Helen, and face yourself. I've come a very long way from who I was over a decade ago. My youth still lives within me but my elder wisdom is desiring to break through. It is time!   I am not sure where life will lead me after my summer time in Oregon. I'm not even certain I want to move back to Phoenix, Arizona. I do know that coming to Oregon has allowed me to face the woman in the mirror and to carry her when she is weak. My ego has done exactly what it has been given the task to do — which is put on the costume of whatever my heart truly desires.

I am recently asked by my new twenty-two year old friend Stan, "Helen, you seem like you get everything you set your mind out to do. Like you don't give a shit and just go for it! How do you do it, like what's your method to your madness? Like what do you do to stay so energized and happy? I mean, do you eat good and workout and shit?"

I appreciate the beauty of his intentions and his thirst for connection and curiosity. We share much in common and I'm thankful for any new friends that enrich the flavors of my life.

"Well, let's see, I have a vision board, turned vision book, that I consider my roadmap when I feel lost or confused. Then I have people in my life who encourage me with all my crazy and spontaneous ideas. I also believe it's okay to boast about your life, your goals, your steps getting to your goals, and random achievements.

Some people don't agree with this, calling it selfish, but it gives the chance for people to praise you. It feels good to be praised. Also, I let things go quickly and practice a lot of forgiveness. Meaning, I don't spend hours worrying about what people think about me and dwelling on it. It's too much energy that could be used for better things like goals, dreams, sensual pleasures and other truly healthy desirable passions.

I'm also conscious of what I eat and how it affects my body in performance. Oh this is a big one, every day I wake up I listen to meditations, motivational videos, or positive songs to get me going on a good one! Hahaha, I also am a wine enthusiast and love being social. Meeting new people is just a very fun and entertaining activity! But most importantly, I am open to hearing what people have to say because people need to be heard. Even if I don't believe what others believe, I

278

won't spend hours disputing their beliefs because everyone changes. Someone today could be totally different five years from now based on the experience she goes through. Therefore, it all comes down to what makes me a happy person, and that, my friend, is love. Just giving love. Genuine, fun, silent, loud, courageous, simple, transcendent... love. Oh, and being authentic. Like if you can't be all love and positive, be raw and badass." I laugh...

I'm not one hundred percent sure of what my life may look like but I can say that I am now open to having a family again. I'm also open to the possibility of having another child. There is this small hope in me that believes it's now possible to have the family and the glorious adventures together. I'm working toward releasing the fear that family holds one back from traveling and fun. I also foresee myself being a magnificent and outstanding yoga instructor, writer, and who knows, maybe a badass women's speaker. Whether family or more single adventures await me, I'm ready and excited about the surprise path only because I'm finally strong in my authentic kick-ass self. BOOM! "Pour me another glass bartender!" LMVT!

I also believe I have made my world a better place by being true to myself and walking this path with an open heart to give and receive many different experiences. My beliefs may not be the beliefs of many, but I've chosen to keep some of those beliefs that were bestowed on me and discard some that don't serve me in the ways in which I desire.

I've also adopted new beliefs and continue to seek and stay curious about everything there is to experience in this one beautiful gift of life. My practice in Yoga is daily transformation in my life, and my freedom while pole dancing is blossoming exactly as I imagined... hot! I continue to passionately write as it is my mind's sole liberation. I am way happier than shitty, and more faithful than hopeful.

Life is my teacher and the Universe is my conscious voice. As for sex and cheating — to each their own, and to own their each. Wink!

Finally, for the record, the best relationship I have ever had, is with myself. I made Love, I receive love, and I give love. My words of suggestion for all who read this are to live alive, breathe, and go the distance! You'll be glad you did.

Chapter 28

Bailar Conmigo

"Dance with me!"

"**UGH! HE HASN'T TEXTED** me back for almost twenty—four hours!" I express.

"Maybe he has a lot of work and he can't get back to you," Veronica replies over the phone.

"The men here kinda suck right now! I can't sleep with them because the town's too damn small and chances are I will definitely run into them in the only Walmart and be asked why I suddenly stopped talking to them. Urrr! What the fuck am I doing in this tiny town, Veronica!" I laugh.

"I know! Pack it up and come back already! Plenty of hot men out here just waiting for you, Helen!"

"Okay, I know what I have to do. I'm going to focus on me, get what I came up here to do done, and then I'm going to hoe the shit out of this town right before I leave. Hahaha!" We both laugh.

Even though I am living out of the matrix and finally focusing on my ultimate spiritual new-found high in Oregon, there's no getting away from my amazingly talented wild self. I love my alter ego and the wild child inside my soul. I finally find joy in meditation, health, and the glorious trees all around me, but inside my body still lives a true divine character of radical rhythm, and a girl who just wants to have fun!

I'm someone who cannot be held down for too long, not even by my own self. No! The woman with wings inside my heart is meant to fly as free as a bird, run as wild with the wolves, and dance with bare feet on top of satin bed sheets. So I do!

His name is Farmer. He is a 6'3", gorgeous white male with an athletic build. We originally connected online when I was on POF for a very short time. We didn't meet for almost two months and I forgot I gave him my phone number. He randomly wants to meet all of a sudden. I'm already seeing a very hot and sexy body builder, whom I will call OC.

The chemistry I have with OC is pretty saucy and I don't really care to meet anyone new. However, my alter ego reminds me that we can't place all of our eggs in one basket.

Therefore, I decide to see what Farmer has to say. Long story short, I'm at it again! I have Farmer, OC, and two other hotties back home in Arizona who constantly ask for my precious time to talk. It's starting to get overwhelming.

At this point in my life, I'm open to dating but not breaking a sweat over mating season. The days when I feel overwhelmed and question if I'm repeating the same pattern with these new doggie dogs, I step back and return to myself. Dancing is always a favorite ritual. This time I feel fit as fuck and fine as wine.

Spanish music brings me back to my childhood days with my dad and grandmother. The family gatherings, the howlings to the moon, the food, laughter, and joy of celebration for no reason besides spending life together. Anytime I dance in my room, I feel the moving spirit of celebration. I dance on the bed, in the bathroom, and jump all over the place. I sway back and forth, flinging my hair, waving my arms in slow and fast motion. Sweat dripping from my face, my abs, and my arms; I am hot!

Incoming text: **WHAT ARE YOU DOING?**

Return text: **DANCING IN MY ROOM. WHAT ARE YOU DOING?**

Incoming text: **THAT SOUNDS FUN. WHAT ARE YOU DOING AFTER?**

Return text: **HOPEFULLY YOU. ;)-** (Winking,

283

tongue out emoji)

Incoming text: **OKAY SOUNDS GOOD**.

Seriously? Sounds good? This muther fucker! Who teaches these Oregon men how to flirt?! Omg, boring! I'm sure this is Farmer's way of flirting but it's so blah! Sometimes I feel bad for the men who don't understand women, nor take the time to realize how vital it is to learn the woman species. It really should be required to learn in grade school about male and female emotions, hormones, and how their brains differ. There probably would be an increase in happier relationships throughout the world.

I decide to drop Farmer and all of the other forest men I'm talking to for the summer. I don't want to spend the whole season trying to feed off male attention. Spending time in nature already provides me the peace and attention I need to be happy. Dancing and drinking wine in my room with Christmas lights on is the perfect club life for me.

"Olivia!" I shout.

"What's up, H?" my sister runs downstairs to my room.

"Queres bailar you little coconut?" I laugh holding out my hand. Olivia grabs my hand and we dance rounds and rounds to our Latin roots.

"Eyyyy-eyyy-eyyyy," Olivia howls. We are like teenagers all over again, dancing and

284

laughing with no cares in the world. My niece, Violet, races downstairs to see what all the commotion was about. "What are you guys doing down here?"

"We are dancing!" Olivia shouts as I swirl her around. "Eww you guys are dancing with each other. Mom you're being weird," Violet giggles.

"It's weird that you aren't dancing, Violet!" I laugh. "Dancing runs in our veins, mija! Dance with us!"

For a minute my memory brings me back to the times when Raymond and I circled and cheered on Keme when he was a baby. Keme danced and danced as if the world consisted only of music. He danced in super markets without a care in the world about who was watching. My son had the spirit of dance within his soul and still does to this day. I miss him very much in this moment. Tears almost consume me until I see Violet's smirk as she watches us. I grab Violet's hand and twirl her around. "Dance with us, mija!"

She awkwardly joins in with motions of happiness I have never seen before, and together the three of us celebrate life together.

ॐ

Pause for a Thought

AS THE YOUNGER generation grows so does the older generation. It's important to keep music and art alive within the home. Kids need to see the art of motion released out into the open. Music, which is art, means everything to me. Kids need to see their parents dance and move to the beat of their own drum. Parents need to dance with their kids and bring more life into the homes. There is something magical and unifying about sound. Even when you are alone, music and dance unify the soul and the body. It's incredible!

Please, please don't ever forget to release the magic, the unity, the music into your homes, into the cars, and into the hearts of every possible moment. Don't be the one who wakes up the next day regretting having not taken that last dance with a loved one or even with yourself.

Chapter 29

Trust Know One

"Trust is the angels smiling when I'm crying because they see the other side of the world I haven't come around to yet."

TRUST, THE WORD GLIDES down my moist tongue like an invisible super heroic light coming to restore the chaotic mess I've created of a world. "Trust..." I whisper with closed eyes. I'm in my morning meditation outside among the tall Redwood Forest in Northern California's natural theatrical setting. "Damn, God, you did hella good!" I smile in awe. The Redwood Forest must have been a place where ancient giants lived, or perhaps it's a garden for the larger source that the naked eye cannot see. Plants greener than green, waterfalls miraculously spewing out of random areas; the air brisk and full of oxygen. I'm but an ant in the Earth's backyard boogie.

Who am I? Where am I going? What makes me happy? Questions I'm finally ready to make peace with by forming no answers but only smiles. I've come to a place in life where everything seems to be better in silence. Tranquility has found me and stillness has taken a place in my heart. It's getting dark and I have to make it back to Olivia's house before dinner.

Evening has set in and at Olivia's house, big family dinners every night are still a holding tradition.

"Does anyone want to go for a walk after we're all done eating?" Olivia asks at the dinner table while everyone boasts about the great food.

"I'll go with you," I reply.

The trail is peaceful, right outside Olivia's driveway. Her house and yard look as if they are a newer version of Little House on the Prairie - a show I watched growing up.

"Olivia, I want to thank you for allowing me to come to your home and stay for the summer. I know you want me to stay longer but it is soon time for me to leave."

"I know, Helen; I hope you consider staying. I've been so happy having you here, sister."

"Me too, Oliva! I've grown so much since I first arrived. You guys have taught me a great deal of things, like how to respect family again and how I really need to get my financial life together. You showing me that a housewife can also be a boss woman has allowed me to see how closed- minded and judgmental I had been toward you because you weren't as free to just go as I am. This place taught me how to let go and dream differently. Like I want a big home on a big piece of land like you now. I love it here more than any place I have ever been in my entire life. Honestly, I feel like this was the best move I've made in ten years. For once I can feel the maturity and wisdom growing inside. It's almost as if there is a new me birthing from within." We both laugh.

"I don't want to leave but I must go on and live my life."

"I understand, Helen. I want you to stay, too, but yeah, you've got to do what you've got to do. At least come back and visit."

"Of course, Olivia. I plan to visit and will even think about making Oregon a second home. This may come as a shock to you but I am ready to settle down now. I'm going to be thirty—five and all of my friends are moving on in their lives. I want to be able to come home to someone or something. No one would believe me if I said this, but I want to build a home again. A real home. Maybe even a family again."

The look of shock runs across my sister's

face. "Oh wow, okay, I could see you doing that." Olivia surprisingly agrees. "Lately I have been pondering the idea of another baby," I blurt out.

Her face lights up. "Really?! Omg, Helen, for reals? Yeah, you should totally do it!" She enthusiastically bounces back.

Olivia is the first person I share my open future thoughts with. I can trust her with my feelings and wild thoughts of wanting to settle down. We walk longer that summer night, talking about the possibilities of motherhood and marriage. Things I swore to never speak of again since my divorce in my early twenties. There we are, two women being true to our natures like young girls planning our dream weddings to our Prince Charmings, giggling in excitement about my future fairytale.

We each have our place and path in life, but everyone views his or her path differently. Keeping quiet for once about my new thoughts about this new life feels good. I'm no longer at the mercy of outside influence because I no longer feel the need for anyone else's opinions. By leaving my beloved Arizona, traveling to new scenery, and reconnecting with my sister, I discover a new part of myself that I have been longing to meet. The person who has grown and revealed herself is stronger, wiser, and has a whole new agenda about the future. For as long as I can remember, I've wanted to travel and live a wild, free life. This new me wants restoration, security, responsibility, a home, a dog, a family, and a fuckin' garden. What the fuck is going on!

So what happened to me?! I did everything right! I let everything, and everyone go and flew the coop onto a new adventure. I'm the girl who joins the other adventurous free birds out there — determined to live their lives abundantly out loud and alive. I didn't want any more babies, no more husbands, no settling down. Uh-uh-oh-no. Not for me! No domestication, no cooking for a man, no waiting at home in a box. Hell no, count me out! I'm the traveler, the wild and free bird, Miss Independent, true player for realz... that's me and I fuckin' love it! Aaaaahhh! So what happened?

I will tell you what happened. Over the summer Olivia and I found out my grandma (Mom's mom) was dying. Neither one of us cares for her. She's a wretched old woman who treated my mother like a piece of shit her whole life. In my view of things the child abuse my grandmother allowed to happen to my mother is unforgivable. However, my mother yearned to have a real relationship with my grandma no matter how awful she was to her.

My grandma developed dementia and ended up in the hospital due to elderly abuse by someone who hasn't fessed up. My mother ran to her rescue, bringing my grandmother into her home to be her caretaker for the remainder of grandmother's life. Olivia and I decide we should go and see my Mom because it's very difficult watching her own mother die at home.

The day Olivia and I walk into the room where my mother has my grandmother resting is the day that time stands still and reality walks into my life. My Grandma is laying there like a vegetable and my mother waves us in.

"You've got to talk to her like a baby because she is like an infant now," my mother whispers.

"Pancha, these are your grandkids; they've come to see you." She caresses my grandmother's hair back and holds her hand.

My heart is instantly overwhelmed with compassion, an emotion I have not felt in a while. It's as if I was too busy to recognize the larger design in life other than my everyday goals. Here's a woman who lived a very hard life of her own, gave birth to many children - including my mother - who had to deal with some horrible relationships herself. Without this woman's breath of life, I would not be standing here. For the first time I bow my head in honor of being born from her seed. I hold back the tears and feel awe struck from the unconditional love my Mom is bestowing unto her infant-like mother. I stay in that room with Olivia and my Mom, just taking in everything life and love have to teach me in that moment.

Two weeks later my Grandma passes away. Life reminds me we all meet death at some point. Death reminds me it's nothing to fear but cause to celebrate and appreciate the ones you love. One day I will be saying goodbye to my own mother and my son will be saying goodbye to me. This is the circle of life and there is no stopping it. It's bigger than me and the reality hits me like a big bag of concrete.

As the summer starts to wrap up in Oregon, I begin to realize my greatest teachers are nature and family. I also meet the person I long to spend the rest of my life with — Happy Helen. Happiness is an everyday effortless attitude and feeling in Oregon with no stress of where to be, what traffic is going to be like, if I'm going to be late to work, if I'm too tired to meet up with friends, and so on. I start to enjoy staying home, hanging out in the yard, making dinners with Olivia, hanging out doing family activities, and every once in a while, dressing up and going out.

I spend time outside with Olivia's whole family playing ball or watching meteor showers at night, things I had never done before with my own family, and it brings so much joy and fulfillment to my life. Spending time in nature allows me the silence and stillness I need to reflect upon deep, quagmire subjects — such as the meaning of death and life. I spend many hours a day thinking about all my past relationships with men and how I viewed them as "failed relationships."

I spend time thinking about how I view myself, how others view me, what my fears are, what I'm chasing, what's chasing me, and what the possibilities would be if I could have a family again.

It is clear something has shifted when the finest of fine men walks into the pub where I'm bartending. He's tall, with a muscular build, beautiful white teeth, gorgeous smile, and super fun to talk with. He is totally into me and undoubtedly makes me nervous while I pour drinks. When my shift is over I decide to hang out with him for a bit and stay for a drink. We definitely have chemistry and I hope he's single. Hours later, he confesses to being in a "complicated" situation with a woman. I take a deep breath in and suggest he figure out his complicated situation before trying to get to know someone new.

"Well at least let me walk you out to your car," the super fine—ass guy offers. I hesitate, but damn he is fine.

"Um... okay." The super fine ass guy walks me to my car and says,"I just want to kiss you so bad, would you let me?"

I gasp. The sexual energy is ready to blow

like Mount St. Helen from within me. I have not had sex or masturbated in so long; this is my chance. I should live in this moment! I could totally have him, fuck like crazy and release him. Boom Bam, thank you man! What comes out of my voice box next throws my ego for a roundabout loop.

"Oh honey, six months ago I would have taken you home two hours ago. You're in a complicated situation with your lady. I don't know what it is and I don't care, not my style. If you love the woman, work it out because the grass is not always greener on the other side. I'm sure if she were in your same situation right now you wouldn't like it."

He nodded in agreement with me. "Yeah. I guess I wouldn't. Damn, you are an amazing woman!"

"Yup! I know," I sarcastically whisper. "Sooo, it was nice meeting you and I hope you figure your shit out." I laugh.

We hug and say goodbye, and all the other bullshit people hate to utter when they do the right thing... but really want to fuck the shit out of an attractive random stranger. LMVT!

On my drive home that evening I cry, wondering who the fuck I am and if I've gone mad. I just don't understand my reason for not taking that fine—ass man and making him mine for the evening. He wanted me, I wanted him and yet I turned it all down, for what?

Saying goodbye without getting any pleasure of any kind, not even a phone number is not my philosophy in life. I mean, he's in a complicated situation.

Usually that means I'm not breaking any rules   if there's no real commitment with the other woman. Am I getting old? Is this me being wise? Has it been so long without sex that I'm intimidated by sexy men? Did I do the right thing or the thing that's considered right by society? Am I turning into someone I've dreaded turning into my whole life — an honest woman?!

What's wrong with being an honest woman? That question boggles my mind for two weeks straight as if it were a mathematical equation I have to figure out no matter the cost of lost sleep. "Honesty" doesn't sound like a dirty word and it's almost spelled like honey. Seems safe and tangible. Maybe, just maybe I can find some balance by integrating honesty into my life.

Honestly, let's face it, there's no hiding what is tried and true. Truth just is. When truth wants to be louder than everyone and everything else, it makes itself known. I've had an estranged relationship with trust. There was and still is this naïve but powerful soul within me who guides me to safe and mystical paths in my journey where Trust is always met. Although, it may seem lying came easily for me at different times through the years, I am confident I did the right thing in some of those deceitful moments.

Trust for me now, is a relationship with myself. It's what I think, say, and do with my inner world and my visible world. Trust is working out my body, or challenging my judgments and beliefs when I feel uneasy about a choice I've made. It's smiling at work and believing we are all in this world together and we all have our bullshit and hidden agendas...so stop judging and start laughing. Trust is speaking up to the man who wants to create a relationship with me, and telling him how I feel in a manner we both can understand. Sometimes this works by using sports or money as the metaphor. Just sayin'! Trust is in many forms for me now, such as saying no to that gluten-free ice cream because I have to go to sleep and stop eating for the day, or laughing at myself because I am totally freaking out sending flirty texts to an ex who is still single. Trust is clicking "Send" on an email for a job I'm not one hundred percent sure I'll get, but yet I believe I will. It's climbing those mountains that suck ass on the way to the top, but believing I will feel *hella good* once I'm all the way up — which is most likely the case every time! Trust is the angels smiling when I'm crying because they see the other side of the world I haven't come around to yet. Trust is toning up the heart when the heart is weak. It's the light I wake up to every morning when I open my eyes first thing, and like a life coach, Trust says, "Congrats! You made it!" It's the sound of music, the color of math, and the seed of intuition. The cousin of Forgiveness and Love's bestie, Trust is solid like a rock and liquid like water. There is no safer place I'd rather be, than with Trust when shit hits the fan.

It's in Oregon where Trust, Love, and Forgiveness have an intervention with me. I'm sure everyone has had an experience with these three multiple times in life. They come dancing through the woods toward me like angelic, lit—up thuggy, ruggy gangsters with smiles on their faces.

IT'S ONE OF THOSE eighty-six-degree sunny days in Grants Pass and I'm sitting outside on Olivia's balcony overlooking the beautiful forest. Her house is in the mountains and coming from the city — it feels like I'm camping every day. I'm relishing the present moment, gleaming without a worry in the world, listening to MC Yogi on my phone, when the three approach me.

"Beautiful day isn't it!" Trust casually dances up beside me. Oh shit, what's Trust doing here?

"Yeah. It sure is!" I smile.

"Hey, Helen." Forgiveness creeps up, tapping my shoulder.

"It's time." Forgiveness reaches out for my hand. Fuck! I know why they're here.

"Yeah. It is." I tear up.

"It's okay to let it all go girl. We got you!" Wonderful Love swoops in and shouts while raising the roof dancing around me. I knew they were going to show up at some point in my adult life, but three at the same time, there's no getting around them.

I take a deep breath and exhale, "I'm letting it go! I'm letting it fucking go!" I stand up and open my arms, taking in another big breath of fresh air.

"Helen, you have been here for thirty-five years, girl, come on now! You ain't gotta lie no mo', you ain't gotta hide no mo', and you ain't gotta face it alone no mo'! You are at a new place in your life. You are free from all that shit now. You had your fun playing games. It's time for a new body, mind, and celebration!" Trust proclaims.

Damnit, I hate when Trust says all the right and honest stuff at all the right moments. I am open and ready to grow at this point; I am all ears and heart.

"You're right, Trust. I mean, when are you not?" I laugh. "I want to step into the new me. I feel ready. It just feels hard at times to be honest — especially when it comes to relationships with men. This is my normal. This is my wiring and I don't think I'm going to be able to be honest all the time," I admit.

"Oh no you don't, Helen! Do you know who I am? You can't lie to me and think I can't see right through your bullshit. I'm fucking Trust! Try again." Trust slams down like a serious mobster not to be reckoned with.

"I'm sorry. I should know better than to tell you white lies. Look, I'm fuckin' scared all right! I'm scared if I'm honest to the committed men in my life I will hurt them and lose them. I can barely tell myself the truth. I'm afraid of rejection. I'm afraid of having a partner in life because all he's going to do is leave me, if not on his own, then through death. I'm afraid of getting close to kids because I left mine and it kills me every fucking day! I'm afraid to tell people I have to get checked for cancer every three months, that I have an autoimmune disease, and I'm scared I'm going to die young!

I'm afraid to live wildly free and brave because I don't want to leave people I love behind, or be ridiculed because I'm living outrageously. I'm scared that no one will love me because my emotions can go haywire every now and then; sometimes, I don't know who I will wake up and be tomorrow. I'm scared of any of my friends or family dying before me because it sucks getting old when the body gets weak and tired.

I'm scared that being honest means I can't play around behind anyone's back and I kinda enjoy it! It makes me happy to love myself enough not to deny myself the pleasures of this world. Okay! Are you happy, Trust? I like fucking around because life to me is a game, and in this game some make it and some don't. Once I die I won't have a conscious, a spirit or an afterlife to give a damn! There. I'm a selfish bitch and sometimes I fucking dig the high!"

I rant with tears in my eyes. "I'm scared that once I trust again, I will be cheated on just like every other time," I sob. Trust looks over at Forgiveness and then to Love and the three of them nod at each other. Trust smiles and says,

"Now you are ready."

"Come here, girl." Forgiveness pulls me close to hug me in.

"Healing is going to be your life's journey. It's okay to be scared. It's when you aren't that I worry."

"You will be tested," Love explains. "You will go through more ups and downs, and you will tell lies again but from here on out you will have more trust and forgiveness for yourself than you ever had before. You might not see it now, but you will shine love, breathe trust, and wear forgiveness, and you will have the love you truly seek by *being* the love you truly seek." Love smiles while wiping the tears from my eyes.

"Our little baby girl is growing up! Come on now, this is a time for celebration! Turn the music up!" Love shouts. It's a glorious moment with the three.

"You guys are real assholes," I laugh as I wipe away my tears.

A week later I am tested by a love interest I have been seeing on and off during my Oregon summer.

"Did you just lie to my face?" OC confronts me. He's hot but I did not want to fully commit so I only went as far as foreplay with him. I am also seeing Farmer periodically and OC sees a text come through while we are at the diner having a bite to eat.

There it is. Moment of truth. I take a deep breath. "Yes. Yes I did lie. Honestly, I lied to protect you because I knew the truth was going to hurt you."

"You don't have to lie. I'm very intuitive and I hate when my intuition is nagging at me to try and find out the truth." He stands his ground.

Why does this make him sooo much hotter all of a sudden? I am instantly horny. I just wish I had fucked him. Now, it's too late. I'm busted in a small lie and having to confess the truth.

"I apologize. You deserve someone who respects you and doesn't lie to your face. I'm not that person right now. Again, I apologize." Oh God that was hard as shit but there it is after my intervention with Trust, Love, and Forgiveness. Damnit!

They got me! Ugh! It's like a smack in the face — Wham! Wake up, Helen! You don't have to lie anymore! Be you. Be strong where you stand and who you are! No need to lie, to cheat, to hide anymore. Step into bravery, girl!

I mean, who am I to be the only one with the power of intuition? This fine-as-wine, sexy-as-hell older man called me out! I stand there like a puppy with her tail between her legs until I realize there's a place called The Store that serves something called Wine. Amen! Hallelujah!

That night, I feel like I learned some valuable lessons. One, no need to cheat when I'm not having sex or committed to anyone. I can stand in my truth and hang out with who I want as a single woman. Two, when I'm ready to commit, I will be the best damn partner because I will be strong in who I am. I'm in my thirties for fucks sake, no more hiding, lying, or denying myself intimacy and sexual happiness. All I have to do is say what I want and be honest to the men who come into my life. If they are still there after the truth is spoken, then sweet deal and if not, then bless and release them. And if I'm going to be totally honest with that statement, I will not only bless and release them, but most likely text until the flame dwindles out. Hey! I'm just being honest! You ladies know what I'm talking about. LMVT!

From that moment on, I decide the relationship I need to be in is with myself for a while longer. This doesn't mean no dating or spending time with some hot masculine energy. It means I put myself first in a healthy, vibrant, kick-ass way. I wake up every morning with gratitude, play a motivational video, and work out. I shower and put on clothing that makes me feel like a rockstar. I adorn myself with sexy panties, perfume, and saucy accessories. I start to love myself without any compliments from anyone else. The only attention I want or need is my own. Fuck yeah! Month after month, I know something has changed. Trust feels good! Trust feels right! Trust feels whole! I trust myself to be sufficient now.

Although love is the force behind

everything and the most powerful thing ever, the point of Love, Trust, and Forgiveness is to obtain the sacred and majestic inner Peace. Hmm… very interesting.

Letter to the Great I Am, (Summer 2015, 35 years)

GOD, I'M OVERFLOWING with gratitude today. The past few days I have been in a funk. I really got harsh with myself. I kept thinking I wasn't worth this life. My brain kept fighting like two warriors on the battlefield. One warrior as my self—worth and the other as a demon destroyer. I hid under my blankets for three days straight and had to literally roll myself out of bed after the noon time. Ugh! I kept thinking I wasn't good enough and felt very confused about my life. I was angry at myself for "not knowing" and came down hard on the idea that I am 35 and don't have a place of my own, no retirement savings and a child I barely see.

I felt like giving up, God. But, I did not give up. I actually thought about praying one day and thought…'Nah, no point. God isn't even real.'

I was invited to a Back to the Future party by some friends and even thought about not attending because I was in such a funk. I conjured up different white lies in my head to make myself look good *to get out of going to the party. You know how I can't stand when people cancel on me so I couldn't bring myself to back out of the event. I eventually pulled myself together and went to the party.*

I'm glad I did. The party was such a blast! I talked, I laughed, I drank, I ate, and I danced! Toward the end of the night there was a girl who was hula hooping entrancingly. I lay down and gazed at her like I gaze at the stars, with such wonder. In the corner of the living room space where this took place were two other hippy gypsy women, singing. Another fourth girl was twirling and dancing along the hula girl. All four of the women sang harmoniously to the song on iTunes. I listened and observed the moment and it's as if time chose to stand still for those glorious five minutes. I felt as if it was a forever moment in time. Something magical and unexpected happened; I saw you, God. I felt you all around. It brought tears to my eyes and I was effortlessly moved.

I wasn't on any medicinal or any type of drugs at all. I only had been sipping on one vodka apple concoction and I literally surrendered the moment when I became aware that it was happening. I heard your voice in the sound of each woman, I watched you dance, and I saw you smile. We are you and you are Us. There is no separation. I had been subconsciously waiting for a sign of hope that I was worth this life. I had started to give up. I started to wonder if I was indeed alone. You came to me at the least expected moment. I saw you again this morning when I went to a mechanic who lived on a farm land. I let a random dog jump into my car as I drove on the mechanic's property. I didn't want to run the dog over and   I didn't hesitate to let the pup jump in. I've never done that before.

While the mechanic took a look at my car, I noticed a ton of horses in the pastures afar. I walked over to them and spoke to them.

I felt their energy and two of them stared back at me. I was moved to tears feeling their true beauty and connection to the Mother Earth and to you, God. I believe you are me and I am you and the horses could see it and I could see you in them. I saw you in the grassy fall fields, in the trees full of birds, and in the gray blue sky this morning. I even saw you in the loompa loompa looking mechanic.

After the mechanic's, I went to a store called Magic Man and purchased a twenty-five-dollar hula hoop. My first hula hoop! I had no hesitation to buy it, nor the Ganesh earrings I saw as I walked through. I also bought my first black light poster and a weed smoke pipe. I've wanted a black light poster since I was a teenager. I never got one before because I listened to my harsh judger inside my head that told me I was either too young, too old, or it was others. I got the pipe because I enjoy smoking the herb when I meditate, and I haven't done it in a long time. I figured, why not! Now is the time!

God, you never leave me, you are me! I've just been so busy and clouded by everything in the outside world that I never slow down to see you. I've felt you in yoga and I've felt you in meditation, but I SAW you at the party. I SAW you this morning. Thank you for appearing to me. I'm more than okay to just see glimpses of you. You are like a mysterious creature who reveals yourself throughout my life at mysterious times. I'm happy about that.

You knew I wanted to pray that morning and saw my hopeless heart. You revealed yourself never the less. It was a divine experience to see the spirit move in me, outside of me, all around. I remembered pure love and the force behind all that feels good and is good. I felt awakened. I feel cleansed. I feel new. There is no attachment to another. Just love for others. I feel very strongly that you gave me a sign and that is a sign of love. I had forgotten about love in the midst of pursuit of everything else. Even inspiration and motivation sometimes cloud my vision of love which is the very essence of God, for God is love and love is the Great I Am. I get it now. At my core, I Am Love. Thank you!! I am overflowing with gratitude.

With humbleness, Helen.

Chapter 30

Little Desert Hole

"My health issues force me into a healthier lifestyle and that's the ultimate truth."

I PACK UP, GIVE OLIVIA A HUG, knowing this is the last time I will see my sister and her family for a while. I believe I am the happiest in Oregon; still, I decide to leave. My journey from Oregon to Arizona is full of mixed feelings. I feel wonderful and free on the road as I drive through the Oregon mountains on the 5 freeway. I want to pull over and camp out in my car for days, but every hour counts to make it to Arizona in a good time.

Every part of me longs to turn back but it's as if I'm on autopilot. I drive a straight twenty hours without rest, reaching my sister Grazelda's house   in Bullhead City, AZ at six o'clock in the morning. I decide to meet with my mother and stepfather for dinner to talk with them about my decision to go back to Mark. Everyone knows exactly what I already knew myself, it's not the wisest decision — yet I do it anyways. Everyone wants to know the reason I could leave the place I found myself the happiest for someone I had logically left.

To my surprise, my brother, Roster shows up with Mom and Step Dad. Roster and I have always been the "wild ones" of the family. He had been staying with them to get his own life together. Something I had done a few times myself before.

"Helen, it's going to be a hard life with him, you understand, that right?" Mom asks.

My step father agrees with her. This is first time in thirty-five years I'm getting the parent talk and it's actually pretty nice.

"Listen here, Helen…" My step father says in his Georgian accent. "Mark is just like me. Your mom is right, it's going to be a constant struggle. Let me ask you this, do you accept Mark for the way he is… just as he is?"

I hesitate a bit, "Yes, I do." Roster can't help but sneeze a fake, "bullshit" at the table. Mom snaps at him like he's a little kid.

"Okay, now does Mark accept you for you? Does he understand that you are wild, just like your mother, you ain't ever gonna change. Does he understand that?"

Again, I hesitate, "Yes. I mean, I've

310

explained it to Mark over and over that if I come back to him and we do this again that there must be compromise."

I can sense my parents concern and sadness. They are just as doubtful as I am uncertain for myself. Although they like Mark and agree he's a great man, they know he's the kind of person to hold me back from my true self to be free, alive, and wild.

That night after dinner, Roster and I meet up with our sister Grazelda in Laughlin, Nevada convincing her that we have come up with a brilliant and rebellious idea to get compass tattoos.

"You know you don't wanna be with Marksickle, why you lyin' to yourself Helen?" Roster pokes fun at me.

"Whatever bro you don't know shit!"

"I know that you left him like a thousand times." He laughs. "Just come and live with me at mom's and the old man's house- then we can get in a lot of trouble together."

"I know Helen, move over here with us." Grazelda chimes in. Another memorable night with my siblings and too many beers later, we woke without any tattoos to the smell of Grazdelda's famous big eggs and turkey bacon breakfast. It was always a bummer to say my goodbyes to my family, pack up and carry on.

AFTER A MONTH IN ARIZONA with Mark, memories of why I had left him the first-time flood back. I remember everything; how I felt like my spirit was dying back then. How could I have been such a fool not once but two times over? I grow insanely angry with myself. It's as if a thick dark cloud of muck from the bottom pits of the devil's laughter seizes my mind. All I can entertain are suicidal thoughts and questions as to how I allow myself to live with such a stupid heart and mind.

I found happiness and I let it all go to return to the same damn soup bowl that nine months earlier I had celebrated leaving. My head hangs low and I can't even bare the sight of my own eyes in the mirror. I was so sure this was my next move I was supposed to make to get to where I was truly meant to be. Although I was happy in Oregon, something deeper was calling me back to Arizona. I thought it was a life with Mark again. Could I have been wrong?

"No, you don't get to give up again," I whisper. "You know what you're doing. Trust."

I look up at my reflection and assure myself this is all for a larger purpose. I do love Mark. We did say we were going to try harder. I believed his words and I believe mine. All my life I had run when shit got tough. I return to Mark because he's a very good man and I love his values. His values are the complete opposite of mine, and I had not had enough time to process what needed to be learned from our relationship. I want to prove both to Mark and to myself that I can "work through things" and not run on a whim when things don't go my way.

The decision to come back to Arizona is a long deep thought process. Returning to the city could help me improve my yoga teacher experience and give me the opportunity to save money to get out of debt. Mark came to see me while I was in Oregon and he shone like the man I had first fallen in love with when we met. I dated a total of eight different men in Oregon and out of all of them, Mark dominates with his masculine traits and values, things that appeal to me as I become more mature. This is why I made the decision to return to Arizona. Even though it saddened me to leave, I knew deep down this was worth a road to take again.

I tell myself to pull it together and find a way out of this dark depression I've fallen into since returning to Mark. Thanksgiving Day arrives, and I want more than anything to be back in Oregon with my sister, Olivia. Mark has to work out of state and urges me to go to his parents for the holiday. Many of my friends invite me to their homes for dinner. Even Grazelda and Mom invite me over for some Tofurkey. All I can think about is my son not being with me and my soul still behind in the forest. I don't want to be around anyone sulking or pretending to be thankful. I want to be alone with myself.

Aha! That is what I will do. The sun's about to set and I suddenly feel life renew within me. I grab my hula hoop and jump in my car. I drive a few blocks away to a secluded open desert space. I blast the radio and hula hoop as I watch the sun slowly set in the West. I stop to sit down on the hood of my car. I suddenly am overwhelmed with gratitude. Mark is a good man and he has invited me into his home, his heart, and his bed. I am thankful the man loves a wild woman such as myself. I have a car that is falling apart but it brought me all the way back from Oregon safely with no problems. Holy shit! I'm so blessed for that alone. My son has an incredible dad who takes care of him better than I could with my crazy ups and downs. I'm thankful Raymond has been such an amazing daddio. I gave more "Thanks" on this Thanksgiving than I could ever remember giving before.

From that night forward, I change my depressing attitude and swear to myself that somehow, I know exactly what I'm doing even though it seems shitty at times. It isn't easy at first, although something deep down tells me that my return to Phoenix is temporary. I'm not sure if Mark and I are going to work and move out of Phoenix, or if it means I will leave again on my own. I do feel strongly that I will one day return to Oregon to the mysterious, happy energy I felt being there every day.

I begin teaching yoga at a martial arts studio and quickly realize the answer to one of my questions as to why I am back in Phoenix. It's easier for me to get yoga jobs and there are more clients than a small town in the woods. I want to become a sought—after yoga instructor and I see this return as a chance to sharpen my skills. I enjoy teaching restorative yoga and intertwining mystical science with anatomy spirituality. It's my thang and that is how I perceive yoga, therefore, I only teach what I'm most passionate about. I soon pick up a bartending position and another corporate cubicle job in Central Phoenix. My hour-long drives to and from work are my time for education with audiobooks and podcasts. Working out and healthy organic foods are my fuel for this on—going juggling act. I've always been health conscious, but I dive more into it since I'm thirty—five and gravity is after my goods on my body.

The thought of turning forty in five years suddenly hits me like a bag of weed. Holy shit! Everything is going to shit. I notice my libido starting to decrease and my metabolism slowing down. Crow's feet around my eyes, boobs just get saggier, and spider veins are making their debut. What the fuck is going on?! There's no time to waste. I've been active all my life and maybe I need to speed up the restorative yoga to power yoga.

No one ever taught me to embrace "getting older" and those sure aren't the books I like to read. Mom would always mention she was "old now" and it always made me feel bad for her. Why do I feel bad for her? Isn't this a part of life? Did she have any regrets from her youth? Am I "old now" too?

Am I going to try and have a baby and be too old to connect with her once she becomes a teenager? Will I be "too old?" Sigh.

Fear. Fear. Fear. Where is all this coming from? Get a grip, Helen! Everything you need to know is on the internet. Afraid? Find out how to overcome. Old? Find out how to slow down the aging. Kids? Blogs, Vlogs, and Facebook links. Libido problems? Porn. Problems solved.

However, the internet alone isn't sufficient for answers. I want answers to show themselves in my body and in my everyday lifestyle. I want to help people by helping myself. I study everything there is about nutrition I hadn't known. I'm obsessed about the body and its connection to food. I run into a teeny-weeny problem along the way of my research to a healthier lifestyle. Sugar. Need I say more?

Sugar and I have had a lifelong relationship. When I was born, I swear there were candy-coated sugar cubes in my mother's breast milk. I pretty much had cavities installed in my teeth before they launched when I was a toddler. How do I stop eating sugar when I'm a walking sugarcane? I finally get a grip on my addiction to sugar and calm down after watching a ton of nasty-ass documentaries. When people ask me how I became "so healthy" I reply with, "Watch a documentary on it and you won't want to touch the damn thing for a while. That is your chance to change the habit!" It's like a super small window to change everything before you pretty much backslide back to your normal bad unhealthy habits.

My relationship with food has always been a challenge. Meat grossed me out ever since I was young, cutting up the pig and cow intestines with my grandmother. Even thinking back on it grosses me out. Because of that fact alone, I'm scarred from ever touching one of my family's favorite dishes — menudo. On the flip side, I can't wait to be invited to any barbeques that have some bomb carne asada and ceviche. There are so many debates about food it can be overwhelming. I am no food expert in my life right now but I can tell you what foods make me feel the most energetic and which ones bloat me up like a lethargic balloon.

I went from feeling like shit for years every morning without even having any alcohol the night before to everyone constantly asking me how I have so much energy and happiness all day long. The year before I met Mark, when I was 32, I finally decided to chillax on the alcohol, parties, and social realm in exchange for raw foods and juicing. I've been a gym goer and avid hiker for years, but still had no abs or buff arms to prove my consistency. Since the age of 17, I've had an autoimmune disease that has been a total asshole and thorn in my life. I was fine and sexy until I developed the disease and once it did, depression hit very hard. It's now been two years since I have had any symptoms and it's unbelievable how the power of a shift in diet can influence the body.

I also had CIN III, which is basically a step away from cervical cancer grade 1. Technically it's a grade 0. From eight years back I can remember bleeding during sex and always thinking, "This is a lot of blood, did I start my period?" The blood only came when I had sex and then it was gone. My first-year meeting Mark he urged me to get checked. That is when I found out it was CIN III caused by HPV. Oh, that made sense. I remember getting diagnosed with HPV ages ago. They advised me to have a colposcopy which was a small surgery to cut out the CIN III. I agreed. A few months later the doctor called me in for a consultation about the check up I'd had after my colposcopy, and she urged me to have another more in-depth removal of any remaining traces of the CIN. I disagreed. I was raised with a different mentality and had to at least try and heal the leftover traces on my own. This meant, changing diet, exercising consistently, and stressing way less. After two pap smears, I had proven that changing my diet and lifestyle had worked. I knew it would work but secretly wasn't a hundred percent sure.

The change in my lifestyle worries me that I can't dance the night away or ever have crazy nights to talk about with my friends. The change scares me but the idea of breakouts during my relationship with Mark scares me more. I don't want to avoid him, or lose jobs, or hide myself any more. My health issues force me into a healthier lifestyle and that's the ultimate truth. Mom used to teach us about food when we were kids but we rarely paid attention. She had us switch from cows milk to rice milk in our teens. Can't tell you how hard that was until she told us how cow's mucus would get into our milk and that's why we had green boogers. Gross! "Okay, Milk, I love the fuck out of you but it's over."

Coming back to Phoenix presents itself with many exciting opportunities that I had taken for granted or never had taken advantage of before. Now I long to do everything I can that's possible in a city — a wide range of classes from pole dance to learning French, raw cooking to tantric sex, and money courses to "bitch betta have my money" seminars; the city is the place for all level of achievers. My love for Phoenix and the Arizona desert makes its way back to me and this time I'm going to ride the desert train. "Oh it is so on!" Atlas! The raw photo in my vision book from eight years ago is now making its debut. I'm learning all about food, nutrition, and fitness on a larger scale. Even Mark's talk about hunting has piqued my health interest. I want to learn it all, everything from raw foods and essential oils to raw meats and paleo.

Once I get out of my head and start to put everything on paper like a road map, I see the steps I need to take to live a more fulfilling life. I redo my resume and blast it out on Indeed.com and Careerbuilder.com feeling certain that I will land a great new day job. I do land a job and a good one too, in the medical field. Things are looking up!

Finally! I find my oasis in this little desert hole that will bring me back to life.

Chapter 31

Tennessee Tea Bagging

"The best manifestations are the ones you don't see heading your way until you wake up and realize you are living the manifestation."

I GET PLAYED! Boy, do I ever get played! I get played like the hand plays the joker; I get tossed to the side. I get played like the kid who finds out Santa Claus and the Easter Bunny don't exist, you're kidding right? I mean, I get played so bad not even Jesus could warn me of this coming, (it only lasted five seconds) but still, I get blindsided by a freakin full-blown Bible thumper. Not only was he raised by God himself, this man also graduated from a Christian high school, college and taught daily music classes in his church. To top it all off, he was a 33-year young virgin. Ugh! Damnit, Lucifer, you must have sewn that sheep's clothing yourself, because that shit was straight imitation Versace! I cannot tell the difference between the real and the fake. Damn!

"No, let me tell you girls how fucked up this is..." I vent to my female coworkers. "I swear, we looked into each other's eyes and I told him, 'I can't tell you how good it feels to be with someone who feels the same way at the same time. Do you know what I mean?' He smiled back, kissed me and said, 'I know what you mean.' What the fuck! I was so vulnerable. I cannot believe I let my guard down for one minute and this." I laugh in disbelief.

Six weeks ago, I was in my normal awesome routine in Phoenix, Arizona:

4:30 AM - Wake up

5:00 AM - Gym

7:00 AM - Head to work

8:00 AM to **5:00 PM** - Sit in a cubicle box at work, stand up every now and then to stretch, do lunges and squats, with a thirty-minute lunch break and then get back to work.

6:00 PM - Arrive at home, make dinner, eat dinner, watch some T.V.

10:00 PM - In bed, falling asleep.

Next Morning ... REPEAT.

Every morning I condition myself by beginning my day with uplifting my mind before I start my own head chatter. I listen to motivational videos, maybe some Joe Ro Experience or Dave Ramsey podcasts. I'm always flooding my mind with some good empowering shit. Doing this makes me feel totally ready and prepared to take on whatever is thrown my way. I fuckin' devour it!

The next morning, it's one of those normal corporate work days. I walk in, say my "Good Mornings" to everyone I lock eyes with and robotically show myself the way to my little assigned box. Can you hear the sarcasm? Not going to lie, I resent the box. I resent any box for that matter. Moving along, the bosses call a few select names to the meeting room and proceed to deliver the news of an offer that the majority of us can't resist. We have thirty minutes to make the decision to leave our families and lives in Phoenix behind to take on a six-week work assignment in Nashville, Tennessee the very following morning. I make two calls, one to my son and one to Mark to get their blessing on a swift decision, I decide to go to Nashville.

A group of my coworkers and I arrive in Nashville and learn we are to live together at the Sheraton Hotel, drive and ride together in five shared vehicles, and eat, breathe, and work together in a small training room set up like a high school classroom.

"I don't think we are in Kansas anymore Toto."
— Dorothy, Wizard of Oz.

323

There are only two men in our group from Arizona and the rest of us are respected female warriors. I only know one person, Yana, because we had hung out in Arizona during our breaks and lunches. I find that I get along with all of the other women too. This is important to note because when we arrive in Nashville and join the training with other Nashville locals, things are really hectic and out of control for the first two weeks. Within one week our well-respected supervisor and friend, who led us from Arizona, is falsely accused of racism and then suspended. It feels like a high-school war zone coming to work.

A friend of mine back in Arizona, who is originally from the Louisiana area, phones to remind me that we are not in Arizona anymore; we are in the South now.

Hashtag #Whatdoesthatmean

Our Arizona team works overtime on overtime. Grueling hours, no weekends off, and the people start dropping like flies. Even through all of this, I maintain a sense of positivity and surety that this is where I am supposed to be in this moment.

Let's get to the juicy juicy. Mikele is an instant cutie pie. He's dorky, super sweet, and his eyes and smile are bewitching. He's a Nashville local and works in a different room than my team but often visits because he's the official tech guy. Easy on the eyes, this one. I don't know how it happens, but I have an instant attraction to him. (Also, probably easy to fall for another man when the man at home never touches you and is addicted to porn – *this girl has got needs.*)

For the first three weeks, Yana and I make up code names for all the hotties we gaze upon in our new city minus the married. The ring is always code for "Stop. Move along." Mikele handles all of our technical issues with such grace. I think he's the hottest thing since sliced gluten-free bread. On our third week I find out that he feels the same attraction for me.

Our short romance is one of the sexiest and fun times I've ever had with a man before. He's almost everything I could ask for in a man. He's funny, smart, caring, spiritual, handsome, attentive, affectionate, and the conversations are mind blowing. We laugh, play, joke, and flirt. A lot. He tells me all the right things a man tells a girl when he is falling for her.

Word gets around fast that sparks are in the air. I did it. I broke my rule of no mixing work and romance. It's funny how you can go so long without breaking rules and all it takes is the right persuasion to reverse that. I had never broken the "no mixing work and romance" rule. Ever. Is it the fact that I'm in a new strange city that makes me ease up?

Mikele pursues me and soon we are texting flirty messages all day. He invites Yana and me to dinner with him. All the girls think for sure he's gay. I don't care. This merely triggers my predator and prey instinct. We are going to dinner and I'm going to find out. I play dumb of course as he flirts with me at the dinner table.

The next day, I confess to Yana that Mikele and I have a mutual thing for each other.

"He is sooo into me, Yana. Swear!" I proclaim.

A few weeks gone by, all the girls have warmed up to each other and we all become very close. Being that we left our families and friends behind, we are all we have to lean on in Nashville. Surprisingly, once we put our egos aside and open up to each other, we allow ourselves to be seen by each other and express ourselves more courageously. Many of these female coworkers of mine instantly become lifelong soul sisters. I confess to them my struggle of rejection and my challenge of finding happiness in my relationship with Mark.

"Wow! We had no idea Helen. You are just so happy every day at work. You're so beautiful and fun, how could any man reject you, especially your boyfriend?" They all question.

Of course, I'm ashamed and embarrassed to be in this predicament yet again with Mark but I assure my ladies I know what I'm doing.

"You see ladies, I'm a runner. I run when shit gets hard and I dated like eight men while I was in Oregon last year and Mark is a good

326

man. I said I was going to give it a year and that is exactly what I'm going to do. I am not dumb. I am saving money and in exchange I am helping him with renters. It's a win-win financial situation. There is an expiration date to this madness and trust me ladies, it's just around the corner. For now, I can stick to my commitment and make the best of it."

They are all amazed and a little concerned. I can tell they feel bad for me by the look in their eyes when they say, "Okay, Helen, well, as long as you know what you are doing." Mikele is a complete romance surprise during our work trip in Nashville. All my ladies are so happy and ecstatic for me. They mention seeing my face come to life in a new light. They're right. I see it in myself and feel it in my soul. I feel alive, sexy, and sky high — like the world is painted in fresh new color with lots of bright boisterous hues. Mikele has me shopping for sexy dresses and wearing stockings to bring about his naughty fantasies he has described to me on our dinner dates.

Time seems to go faster, accelerated by our crazy desire for one another. His hand against my cheek as he presses against me and leans in for a kiss drives me wild. He always leaves me wanting more. Six days into our romance on speed, I start to wonder why he never makes a sexual move on me. Kissing is more like heart magic whereas sex and foreplay is like dessert all day long. I want dessert all Nashville day long. That's my plan with Mikele, to enjoy his presence and intimacy until I head back to Phoenix.

"I don't know, you girls, something isn't right. He wanted to eat me out and he didn't do it good. So, I jokingly asked him if he had ever eaten out a girl before and he said he did. Then he said he wasn't sure if he did. I had to teach him how to eat out and make me orgasm." I am perplexed.

The girls instantly break out in laughter. "What! That is sooo weird, Helen," they shout.

"Maybe he's a virgin?" A few of them start to question.

"Noooo... there's no possible way... He's 33, you guys!" I stammer. "He's definitely not a virgin. First of all, he would have told me and second, there is just no possible way!" Again, I shut down the possibility of it. The girls laugh and poke at me for the rest of the day.

Later that day, Mikele and I plan a dinner date at a very nice restaurant. I text him to pick up some condoms. I can't wait any longer. The thought that he's a virgin leaves my mind and all I can think of is that I'm going to get some later on.

The dinner's absolutely romantic, everything I'd been desiring and fantasizing about for years with a man. There he is sitting across from me, rubbing my hand, staring into my eyes, telling me how beautiful and amazing I am. The words of the girls earlier suddenly pop into my mind and I blurt out, "Are you a virgin?!" I hold my breath and wait as I look into his stunned face.

He smiles, "Yes."

I begin laughing my ass off. He's totally joking. He laughs too.

"No, I'm not," he says. "Just kidding. I am. No, I'm not." He pauses for a drink.

I'm laughing so hard. This fool is totally fucking with me. He's not a virgin. "No serious. Are you?" I wait.

He smiles. He takes another sip of his drink slowly. "What if I am?" He pauses.

Again, I hysterically lose it laughing. "I mean, you're not, right? Because there is no way I could take anyone's virginity. Just not my thing." I laugh and sip my cocktail.

The food arrives diverting us to a whole new conversation. Later that night at the hotel our make-out session gets hot and heavy. I reveal my sexy black lace lingerie underneath my dinner dress and his mouth drops. He's instantly hard and he asks to take a pic. I'm so smitten by this man. After we make out a bit more, I suddenly stop and look in his eyes.

"I need you to tell me the truth, Mikele, this is a serious question okay?"

"I won't ever lie to you, Helen."

"Are you a virgin?"

"Yes. I am."

I sit back shocked and instantly reach over for my glass of wine and chug.

"Does this bother you?" he asks.

"Look, Mikele, it doesn't bother me. I just don't want you to do anything you'll regret later in life."

He reaches forward to grab my hand and looks in my eyes. "Helen, I won't do anything I don't want to do. I want to do this," he assures. We begin to kiss again, moving forward with the night.

After trying to get five condoms on he eventually goes soft. I give up and reassure him we don't have to keep trying. "It's okay, Mikele. Whatever is supposed to be, will be." We fall asleep cuddling.

Around one o'clock in the morning Mikele wakes me hard as hell. Groping, fingering, and kissing all over me. He's ready and so am I. Before I know it, he's on top of me, missionary position and as I wait for him to stick it in, or so I believe it isn't in yet, he comes. Apparently, he is already in, and I must be half asleep or too wet to tell. This is the weirdest thing to me. He comes! That fast! Holy shit, I thought this was only something you see on T.V. Well, I testify it does happen in real fucking life, people! He lasts less than a minute and I have officially taken this man's 33-year young virginity.

The next night we hang out the sex is better, and he lasts about five minutes instead of under a minute. We lay on the bed with smiles as we gaze at one another.

"I'm off this Sunday, we should totally do something this weekend!" I suggest.

"Oh, I thought I told you I was going out of town. I'm going to Texas for the weekend."

"No, you didn't tell me. That's cool. What are you going to do down in Texas?"

"I thought I did tell you. I'm not trying to scare you, or hide anything from you, but I am talking to another girl. That's why I kept saying this was bad timing."

"Wait! You told me you were talking to the girl but is she your girlfriend?!"

"No! She's not my girlfriend, but we had already planned this weekend before I met you." He pauses, "I have to go. I already told her I would go."

There's silence.

I smile, "Okay. Well, you have fun. I'll see you when you get back."

The weekend arrives and it seems to drag. I think about Mikele the whole time. He never once texts or calls me. It's strange. It's as if he never existed. I think about reaching out but maybe he's with the other girl and I don't want to side track him.

Soon Monday rolls around and Mikele's back from Texas at work. I feel something has changed with him. He seems so distant. He avoids our training room which is abnormal behavior for a tech guy in the company and for someone I had seen multiple times a day while at work.

I feel a rush of sadness. After a week Mikele tries reaching out to me through phone calls and texts. I have already put up a guard. We play the cat and mouse game for awhile and finally I decide to make peace with this man because face it, we work together and I'm not about to make the next three weeks of my time in Nashville an awkward place to be.

Later on in the evening Mikele confesses to feeling extreme guilt for spending time with his girl in Texas and thinking about me the whole time. He feels bad for leading me on and returning to Nashville as a committed man in a new relationship.

I'm a bit shocked that he left unattached and came back over one weekend with a girlfriend. He admits to kissing the girl but swears he didn't have sex. Yana and I use our Facebook stalking skills and find his new girlfriend online. She's pretty, in her early twenties, blonde hair, blue eyes, and a full-blown Christian too. I end up breaking my second biggest rule (sleeping with a man who has a girlfriend) and only a few weeks after our initial cat and mouse game. I feel nothing from breaking the rules.

Mikele can't help reaching out to me, and I can't help inviting him to my hotel for more pleasure. I mean, technically I feel he belongs to me because I took his virginity, and I'm the only one sleeping with him, and because I'm in Nashville- his girlfriend is not, which makes her irrelevant. Seems a valid point to me.

Two weeks before leaving for Phoenix, Mikele suddenly stops talking to me AGAIN! He withdraws with guilt again. I'm confused because it seems he wants me as much as I want him, although he struggles with his Christian convictions. I understand these convictions very well, as I share with him how I, too, had once been heavily involved in the Christian church and had felt the same conflict between my faith and pleasure. We talk about our struggles with the timing, and how I have a boyfriend back home, and he has a girlfriend now in Texas, and why it's tough for both of us to dump our lovers and shoot for the stars.

In my heart, I know I'm totally capable of making the jump if Mikele could too, but he can't. Instead Mikele comes down hard on me, blaming his desire on lust and temptation, and saying I'm a heathen compared to his young Christian girlfriend in Texas.

"It's just you two are so different. I know you can understand and are strong enough to handle this more than if I cut things off with her."

I grow furious. Before Nashville, I would have been silent and allowed time to heal things as a new yogi would... but I can't hold it in this time.

As Yana runs into the beauty store to purchase some goods after work, I pace back and forth outside thinking that his behavior is not okay. I have been honest. I have been patient. I have been understanding, but this is not fair. I call him ready to release my inner beast.

"Hello," he sheepishly answers.

"I'm soo mad at you right now!" I firmly say. I can hear his fear on the other end of the phone. "You think it's okay to play with my heart just because I'm from Arizona and I'm only here in Nashville for a few weeks. YOU are the one who pursued me, Mikele, not the other way around! I was fine with just sex. I was honest with you from the beginning, but you drew me in and then pushed me away over and over. What the fuck, man! You definitely need to grow up and become a bigger man about shit." I pause.

"You're right, Helen. I'm sorry to both of you," he sadly admits.

His apology only infuriates me more and I can't help but pull out a can of whoop-ass.

"You think because you're a Christian you can use me to backslide and then return to God? Like you are so holier than thou? You

334

think you can treat me like a heathen and then praise your chick in Texas as if she is a mutha-fuckin saint? Guess what, Mikele, she might be slutting around too with all of her Bible verses and you would never know because good girls do scandalous shit too, so don't compare me to her! I also was a Christian once; I know exactly what you're going through with your spiritual war, feeling guilty, but don't make me feel bad for what you feel bad for. I don't feel bad. I enjoyed every moment together. I enjoyed the lust and temptation!" I snarl, and continue to rant at him...

"I believe different than you do and I won't feel bad for it! I also won't allow you to treat me like some floozy just because you have a girlfriend now. You need to grow the hell up! If you feel guilty then stop talking to me...period! Don't play me back and forth because I will show you what playing looks like if you want to go there." I take a moment to catch my breath.

"You're right. You're absolutely right with everything you said. I'm sorry to both of you. I have to make a call to her right now and tell her. I'm sorry."

I suddenly feel bad for him, but also a release from the deep feelings I had developed for him. It's as if I wrote a letter, burnt it in a fire and am ready to let him go. Yana walks out in the middle of my bravery and when I hang up she gives me a high five saying she's proud of me. I feel proud of me too. Sadly, it's been a few years since I have stood my ground to a man. This feels amazingly good. Secretly I can't wait to do it again. Who's next? LOL

The next day at work, Mikele messages me saying he told his girlfriend everything and they are going to work through it. I laugh and smile.

Yana sees the message and looks at me. "What do you think, Helen?"

I smile and whisper, "They are perfect for each other, Yana."

Right before leaving Nashville and returning home to Phoenix, I thank Mikele for reminding me how I want a man to look into my eyes with that passion and desire. Our few weeks' romance was spectacular, and it brought a sensual life back into my spirit that I hadn't seen in a few years.

Let's Go There

I KNEW MIKELE was a hardcore Christian when I met him. I had even quickly laid it on the table that our spiritual beliefs were very different and that I would not judge him and asked for the same respect in return. After his fiasco with my heart, and blaming it on his spiritual backsliding, I was able to accept it the first time around. After the second time, it did put a sour taste in my mouth for Christians. It wasn't Mikele's behavior that flooded me with harsh judgment regarding Christians, it was the reminder of what I had endured on my own walk as a Christian. His blaming of backsliding or falling for lust or temptation irked the fuck out of me.

To me, it was a dirty excuse for adhering to his natural human behavior. To him, lust and temptation were bad, therefore, I was bad - yet he wanted me. It infuriated me that two people could come together on opposite sides of the country, fall for each other, and because of a belief that had been twisted and fabricated over thousands of years - so embedded into his blueprint - he dismissed me. How many times did I dismiss my true desires, my happiness, my joys and love for life experiences for the same Christian beliefs years ago? Ugh! I don't dislike Christians or their beliefs. I'm not saying that at all. I'm spewing my personal beliefs about Christianity, lust, and temptation between lovers. I am very intrigued by Christian theology and philosophy. I like it. It's fuckin' intense and interesting throughout history. Some of it, I totally believe in and some of it I call bullshit — just as Christians feel about secular, spirituality, pagans, or other labeled fufu fluff historical enlightened paths.

All I'm saying is if you are going to ask the

world to accept your choice of faith, then it is only courteous and polite to return the acceptance. This is my rant. It is over now. Forgive me or not, Christians, I don't care. I still love you and feel you are needed in this world. It is not for me to judge you or God. I am just hurting because I really had developed major feelings for Mikele. Maybe, just maybe, it's not Christians I should be sour toward but perhaps it's forgiveness, the main foundation of Christianity, that I need to apply and practice myself.

"I forgive you, Mikele."

———————⌒〜⌒———————

DURING THE ROMANTIC ESCAPADE with Mikele, my female coworkers bring me the most happiness away from home. I have an epiphany one night during meditation as I sit in lotus pose on the floor on a towel in my hotel room. I have a candle lit, rosemary incense going, the sounds of native flutes playing, and beautiful roses in my creative wine bottle vase sitting in front of me. I reflect how before the trip to Nash, I had been constantly Googling "Women's retreats" to attend. I was in dire need of uplifting women and had already hosted my first women's circle earlier in the summer, which eighteen amazing women had attended, including my mother. I was seeking a getaway of my own. As I meditate it hits me that this work assignment is in fact the retreat I've been seeking.

I call my female coworkers "my g-work girls" because to leave the fam and jump on a plane on such short notice, that takes some real gangsta shit. Not to mention, they have real names like: T—Money, J Daddy, Easy Street, Jiz Jazz, and they call me H-Town. These are only a few of them; in total there are twelve of us. We began our journey in Nashville as strangers, and by the third weekend we lean on each other for sister support. I had been spending a lot of my free social time in the yoga community and with my close friends in Phoenix before Nash. The type of retreat I have been seeking was something to help me tap into my inner power, sexuality, and self-love again. I often observe my g-work girls in Nashville and find myself laughing every moment I spend with them. We spend weeks together every single day with hardly a moment by myself unless it's to sleep or meditate or a few moments at the gym. There's no hiding who we truly are from one another. Everything's exposed: moodiness, dreams, jokes, attractions, tears... everything. Our characters are tested daily as we are the team from the West, and like a lone wolf pack, we have to keep watch at all times for any type of attack from other healthcare teams in the South. It's a work-assignment opportunity game we are to win.

All twelve of us range in age from early

twenties to late fifties and there's an equal range in ethnicities. The one common ground we share is we're women and we understand each other on many levels of life experiences. I had not seen this type of "retreat" coming in my future. I can tell you the best manifestations are the ones you don't see heading your way until you wake up and realize you are living the manifestation. We all learn many things from each other.

I become a health guru and everyone comes to me to learn about exercise, yoga, supplements, food, raw drinks, how to increase energy, or get rid of a cold, lose weight, or relieve stress. I motivate seven of my g-work girls to get to the gym with me and it feels great to see my wellness passion help others. I wonder if I'm in the wrong line of healthcare and if my true passion is in some kind of nutrition path. Ever since I can remember from a young age, I always dabbled in nutrition and have always been active. Before yoga, I had thought about going raw and getting a degree in nutrition. Why haven't I looked into this profession before?

The exchange for healthy advice is something I never imagined I needed. Such as "release your inner beast, Helen." My g-work girls have no filter.

There's no everyday positivity and yoga enlightenment kinda talk. They aren't negative or gossip girls either. These girls have sailor mouths, gangsta tudes, and keep the laughter constant all day long. "Vagina, dick, asshole, bitch, slut, and muther fucker" are words that fly around out loud no matter where we are - at work, in a restaurant, in the car, at church (just kidding. Not at church). Every day brings me back to my inner youth-self, when I was crazy wild, no filter, gangsta, and didn't give a fuck. I miss that part of myself very much.

Somehow, over the years I let it go to become more positive, enlightened, and loving. Hanging around my g-work girls feels as if I'm being refueled by a new but familiar type of empowerment energy. I can speak anything out loud and say anything out loud and not get a smudge face look. You know that look... like someone is trying to pass a hard mountain-size log out of his or her asshole.

I realize during my meditation that this is the retreat that's essential for my life in this moment. Deep down my soul wants to release the beast and run with the wolves once more. This moment and the epiphany make my heart smile.

"Crazy Universe, you trickster... you always know what's best. Ya got me again!" I softly laugh.

I return to Phoenix with new close girlfriends, awakened sensual sassiness, and the boldness I had been seeking to release the beast within. I'd do it all over again, even without the financial incentive, if I knew these were my only gifts I'd return home with, especially the gift of new friendships that are certain to last a lifetime.

Chapter 32

Me, Myself, and Time

"What I want is to FEEL alive."

RETURNING TO ARIZONA from Nashville, I still often think about Oregon as if it were a magical boyfriend I left behind and constantly daydream about. Nashville's lush green environment and tall trees reminded me so much of my happy place in Oregon. A large part of my spirit stayed back in the forest. Jumping back into the city life and caravanning with strangers through afternoon traffic annoys the shit out of me much more than it ever did before. Mark is ecstatic to have me back in his arms and to be honest it feels nice to be held. My time is consumed by day jobs and home life, and soon I'm back to the grind - except this time I feel as though I'm a droid sleep-walking through my life.

After Mark kisses me and prepares to leave for work, I smile and see him off just like I used to do before. Our relationship is feeling like a boring cycle once more. I wake up daily wondering if I dreamt up the forest and majestic mountains I once gazed upon a summer ago. I find myself day dreaming throughout of hiking and sitting on Olivia's porch meditating on my pure happiness. When my Arizona friends ask me about travel I vomit my love for Oregon until they can't stand to hear about it anymore.

Besides missing Oregon, I can tell things are different with me. I've been swinging in and out of manic depression and some mornings I have no idea who I will be when I wake up. It's been such a struggle that I try my best to hide when Mark is around. He's a great man and I can tell he loves me very much. I don't want to put my burden on him or make him worry. To be honest, the man really has no idea who I am most of the time. Sometimes I don't even know why he wants to be with me. We rarely see each other, nor touch one another, and barely say a word when we are in each other's company.

Before Nashville, when I had returned from Oregon to Arizona, I caught up with my bestie, Veronica, and finally found out why she had stopped talking to me for a few months while there.

"I thought you were using me like you use your men," she announces.

"What! No! Are you serious? Omg, Nooo! I would never do that to you, Veronica. You are my best friend, not any man of mine." I hug her.

We both cry, hug, and laugh the night we reconnect. It's us being us once more. However, as with all healing — it takes some time.

A few weeks pass by after Nashville. Coming back to Arizona and starting my routine over is challenging. I am already used to being apart from friends and spending time at home. I still feel distant from Veronica. Even though I travel quite a bit, we always found time to talk over the phone or social media. This time, we are more distant than ever and it still bothers me that she waited months to tell me what I had done that bothered her. I can't believe Veronica would think I would ever use her. I can't believe she felt she couldn't even talk to me about it the instant she felt that way. I wonder if I'm a problem to my friends due to my behavior and my beliefs. My friend, Sonia, and I had already broken the ties of our ten - year friendship earlier last year; is my best friend next to sever ties with me? I spend more time away from all of my girlfriends and more time at home by myself with the TV and food. I begin to give up on working out, going out, or doing anything fun.

Somehow, I put it in my head that all of this pursuit in life is bullshit and worth nothing if you can't be happy. The idea that friends are chopping ties with me and questioning my actions literally hurts. I just don't understand. I have been the one who would drop everything and come to them if they needed me. They could tell me the craziest secrets and I wouldn't judge them. There is no fucking way I would ever use my friends. I valued my friendship for years and now I just want to be alone and away from them. I don't want a man, I don't want friends, fuck... I don't even want a good time out. What I want is to FEEL alive again, FEEL my spirit dance with the wind and nature around me, FEEL love energy from all parts of the Earth and the midnight skies; that is what I want.

Speaking of Sonia, I miss her. I was devastated when Sonia had suddenly viewed me as a person who wasn't good for her circle anymore. The rejection really broke my heart. She was family, like a soul sister to me. Even worse was when I thought the conversation between Veronica and me had solved everything on my return back from Oregon, only to find out she felt it was unresolved nine months later.

We had written letters to each other while I was in Nashville and decided to hash out our issues with one another. Surprisingly the letters we wrote were exactly alike - almost as if I wrote her letter and she wrote mine. We are definitely soul sisters.

She explains to me in the letter that my cheating behavior is disliked, and she shouldn't have to accept it. She ends the letter with, "but you can tell me anything." I realize from that moment, I have to respect her wish because she's in a new place and I don't want to cause conflict to her morals. Speed up the weeks now back in Phoenix, Veronica and I are driving to a 5K run when I mistakenly forget about my boundaries and expose a story about Mikele.

"Oh. And did this Mikele come back to your hotel room?" she sarcastically asks.

"Nooo. He was a coworker." I laugh.

This moment hits me like a scary, haunted, eerie movie; I just lied for the first time ever to my truest best friend. She thought I treated her like "one of my men" on the ride up to Oregon — when I had no such idea in my mind or heart ever before. Here we are, and I am treating her like one of my men by lying so effortlessly. I feel unsafe to be myself and to tell the truth. It breaks my heart, but I shake it off. I want so desperately to tell her the truth and blurt out, "Okay I lied! I took his virginity and it was a high I had never had before!" but I can't do that to her, knowing she feels the way she does about my habits.

After I drop her back to her apartment, I

come to the conclusion that I can no longer talk about any other men besides my current boyfriend. I'm not sure how long this can go on or if she will respect the fact that I lied to protect her conflicting morals. I feel as if my own best friend's losing touch with who I am or who I am becoming - as if she only wants to see me in a positive light and no other way. I don't know how to perceive this because honestly, I don't want to believe this can be us after all that we've been through. I make a pact with myself that I'm going to be honest with her and never lie again.

Even though I lied to protect her wishes and morals, it doesn't feel fair to me or to our relationship. Friendship is one of my highest values in life and to hide who I am or what I do to my own friends is not okay.

I have a hard time with boundaries but my Christian bestie, Dotty, is open to my revealing all of who I am without judgment. It didn't make sense to me that Veronica and I were in this predicament. Finally, I take a breath and let it go. I have to make peace and let it go. She may not accept what I do and that's okay. We can still be friends, best friends, with respect and boundaries. I would do anything for Veronica and accept anything she does within reason. If Veronica cheats, lies, or hurts someone and comes to me I would do my best to understand. If she does it repeatedly, we would definitely have to dig deep. For that, I could understand any disapproval she would have toward me.

Veronica and I eventually get past one of our biggest battles. I believe it makes our friendship stronger. I also come clean about Mikele over a glass of wine not too long after and Veronica hugs me and showers me with tears. She understands why I lied and we vow once more to let it all go. This time we do and are totally us again. She really is the bestest effin friend ever.

After the whole ordeal, I question my habits once more. Do I want to change? Is cheating a part of my continued path? Am I a bad person? Am I going to lose friends over my habits? Are my friends afraid of bringing their men around me? Am I a psychopath? Should I just be polygamous and call it a day? Am I a nihilist? A moral nihilist? A hedonist? What is wrong with me? Am I truly alone in this? Am I a bad friend? Do I even deserve to have good friends? Am I hurting people by being true to myself? Maybe I need to change for them?

I head home and pull out my hidden stash of mary-ju-wanna. Not surprising, I'm alone for a week; no one is home and I can let loose. I turn on some Blackmill soft ambient dubstep. I sit outside in the backyard and stare up at the night's sky. Puff, puff, hold. "Fuck, I need to change." Ugh, why does it feel so good but feel so bad? Why don't I just leave Mark? What am I afraid of now? I've left before, what am I attached to? Why do I have to have this conversation with myself every fucking year! Puff, puff, hold. "Damn this shit is good." Exhale.

The world is so big; I'm like a tiny ant. A meteor can hit at any moment and wipe us all out. The air is brisk, feels like a wind bath, so relaxing. Coyotes are howling. What a dope sound they make. Coyotes speak their own language, birds speak their own language, nations speak their own language. Ah, but sex and love are a universal language. Lol Why can't I find a guy who wants to touch me all the fucking time, who isn't my now best friend and lover Ross?

Why do I need a guy anyway? Men have porn and I have lots of men. We are now equal. Hahaha!

I have a major issue with my men once I catch them watching porn. It's like once I find it on their phones or computers, that's it! They are fucked forever. I subconsciously build resentment. After that, cheating is like whatever to me. If they feel hurt or pain, I could care less about their feelings. It's one of the first things I tell my potential relationship partners when I first meet them—to beware that I will not tolerate the porn addicts cause it will trigger me the wrong way. Like the time I caught Kyle watching porn and ran straight to another man I had on   the side that very same day. Same with Mark in our first year together. I found the porn and drove his truck to Ross' house that same day walking in saying, "I need you to fuck me right now Ross!" The list goes on. Is that it? Is that my problem? Is it with men who watch porn? Lol. I'm high as fuuuuuck right now!

Why am I thinking about men or my problems? If I break down this body of layers there is nothing here. I'm a false image. An imagination of my brain. I'm probably not even brown. Holy shit! What if I'm grey and it just looks brown through my lens?! Whaaaat ifffff... my brain is the real alien? No one knows EVERYTHING about the brain! It's in my head and controls everything in my life...and yet I don't even know anything about it. It's a fucking alien in my head. Calm down. It's giving me anxiety.

I love being by myself. It's a peaceful feeling to sit here, get high, and look at the sky. I'm okay with whatever happens each day. I'm okay with friends choosing to still be friends or choosing to have their space even if it's forever. Honestly, I'm okay with everyone's opinion about me. I like me. I like the card I was dealt in life. This is a fun card! Okay so I had a rough childhood, who hasn't? I had a horrible divorce; okay, agree, that was painful as fuck. I never want to go through another divorce, like everrrrrr!

Okay so some people don't like what I do. They have that right. Who am I to be mad about it? Or to make others see my perspective and approve my message? I tear up thinking how I almost lost my bestie. I am so lucky to have her as my friend in this one precious life I was given. I love that betch to the moon and back! I'm soo lucky that all the people I love are still alive. I've got a gang of siblings and a gang of friends, and a gang of lovers. My life is totally abundant. I have created an abundant life! Light bulb! Woah! Life is good, man. If this is it and the least of my problems is others disagreeing with my way of life, then life is fucking good! I'm blessed!

"I need some water... and some chips. Maybe some pumpkin pie. Oooh and some popcorn. Yeah, popcorn for sure. I think I have the munchies." I laugh out loud.

Chapter 33

In This Game

"What I do know is that I have definitely evolved from who I was in my twenties to who I am in my thirties."

AS TIME GOES ON it's inevitable that people evolve. To try and go against the current flow of progress and evolution shows significant signs of wrinkles and ignorance in one's reflection. How do I know what I'm talking about? I don't. In fact, I could be speaking complete bullshit, but then again, maybe I've gotten wiser and it's pouring out on paper. What I do know is that I have definitely evolved from who I was in my twenties to who I am in my thirties.

For example, in my twenties when I was daring, most of my daring activities stemmed from two mindsets - my drunk mindset and my

"I'm young and invincible" mindset. The two mindsets combined were dangerously bold and adventurous. However, my heartbreaks were just as dangerous and unadventurous. My twenties taught me lessons and gave me tests I wouldn't want to ever retake. Now in my thirties, I'm daring in a different way. I'm daring to be greater, stronger, and kinder to myself and others more than I ever cared to be before, and I fucking dig it! This time, booze and invincibility are not the leading factors to my motivational mindset. No! Instead this time around, the two leading motivations are health and fitness and a determination to be happy.

In my twenties and even early thirties, while I was so busy trying to figure out my own life, I didn't even stop to think about the lives of those who had brought me into this world. As I get older, my mother and stepfather get older too. It's always hoped that parents die before their children and unfortunate when it's the other way around. No one wants to see anyone he or she loves go. It's the way of life, or the circle of life, or whatever, but how fucked up is that everyone dies. Ugh!

"Mom, how young are you? Like, what is your real age cause I don't even know?" I'm curious. I've never really stopped to ask my mom how old she is. For some reason it seems like a taboo subject to ask her real age rather than her always answer, "I'm 25 again."

"Oh, let's see, I'm fifty - something." Mom chuckles.

"No, Mom, for reals. How young are you? You can tell me your age. I want to know." I speak up.

"I'm fifty - seven."

I gulp. All these years with the only age she ever confessed was "older" or "25 again," and here the truth finally hits my ears. "Fifty—seven. Mom, you are so young! Do you know how many 70-year-olds would trade places with you in a heartbeat! You've got to live your life, Mom. You've got to set some goals for YOU, like you used to do." I hold back my tears.

"I know I do. I used to set goals, Helen. I just don't have money. I give it all to your step dad. I can't do anything right now." Mom confesses.

I'm not about to let her sulk. "No! Mom! This wild and free spirit that lives within me, within all of us kids, is your spirit! The spirit that you bestowed within us...your kids. You did this. All the creative, fearless, adventurous sides of us... this is you!" The passion is trying to light my mother's once wild spirit on fire.

"Yeah. I know, I know. Sometimes I feel like I'm dying inside, like I don't even know who I am anymore. Like I'm losing the person I once was."

There it is. My own mother, my teacher, my mentor and friend confessing to me what I feel every once in awhile, in my own life. It crunches my stomach to hear my own mother feeling the awful death of the grand and wild spirit within herself.

"Oh Mom, I know the feeling. Look, why don't you set a goal? A health goal. You know, like maybe being in the best shape, the best attitude, and best energy by sixty. Start now reclaiming the parts of yourself that you love and don't look back. This is the best time of your life, Mom!" I cheer.

"You know what, you're right. I'm going to do that," Mom agrees.

The eerie sense of Mom feeling as if she's dying inside remains for a few days. She is the woman who brought me into this world. Much of my free-spirited personality was passed from her and who I watched her "be" growing up. I couldn't stand the idea of my mother living out the rest of her life feeling helpless and stuck. She's better than that. She deserves to give herself everything her heart desires!

I think about all of the people who have inspired me: Zig Ziglar, Greg Laurie, Tupac, Bruce Lee, Tony Robbins, Deepak Chopra, Wayne Dyer, J Krishnamurti, Sark, Joe Rogan, Sid the Sloth, Aubrey Marcus, Neil deGrasse Tyson, Napolean Hill, Maxwell Maltz, Dave Ramsey, Jesus, Danielle LaPorte,

Yanis Marshall, Kung Foo Panda, Mike Rowe, and did I say, Joe Rogan? Yeah, he's pretty much my main man. Anyway, all of these inspirational people who've had a small or large impact on me made me realize that my mother has been my greatest inspiration throughout my whole life.

I've been a seeker my whole life. I've never stopped being curious, asking questions whether out loud or in my head. There are so many self-improvement experts who have read thousands of books and been to a gazillion workshops, and they want to turn around and give others advice - which is brilliant. But when I stop to think about my own life at this point—Mom has not been given the medal and praise she undoubtedly deserves.

Mom is one amazing woman. She was a rape baby and was hated by her own mother. She came from a family of abuse and incest. It was Mom who took us out of la barrio and into a new way of living. She had dreams of owning a beautiful large piece of land with a sixteen-bedroom house so she could have a place for us always and a place for others to find peace. Now that I recall all of this, I realize I have the same vision. This is what I am working toward a property to start a women's retreat. Veddy interesting... Didn't even realize this until I wrote it. Ha! Mom's spirit truly lives within me.

Everyone has some kind of mantra he or she lives life by. Mine just happens to be that I see this life as a game, or as some would say, "the game of life." Mom played her cards to the best of her ability with five little ducklings attached. My duckling is with his father and I have no one except my lovers. I may play my cards well, but something tells me that Karma - may it exist or not - played a card against me long before I started the game. What if this game I play with hearts has cost me my own heart long before I came about living? What if my life was predestined? My heart, my son, what if he was predestined to live with his father to protect him from my malicious behavior? What if the Great Spirit told me in a previous life, "Helen, in your next life you will have an abundance of lovers, adventures, friends, and palaces... but this will cost you something great. This is your opportunity to experience life. Do you accept?" What if my dumb ass was like, "Yes! Whatever it is. Yes!" I'm just sayin'…what if this was the case?

Now I play to win at this game of life with a thorn in my side. Constantly thinking about my son. Constantly praying for his wellbeing. I know I am destined to achieve but it cost me. It's heartbreaking to say the least, but I couldn't have raised my son the way his father has. A man raised a man and my son is turning into a fine young, smart man. I couldn't be more thankful to his father.

Struggle and breaking through obstacles are a part of life. In order to get to where I want to go, I've got to take risks. I foresee my legacy — not sure exactly how I will get there, but I've seen it in visions and dreams. Like I've mentioned before, I'm a signs person. As *Ace of Base* would say, "I've seen the signs and it's opened up my eyes, I've seen the signs."

When it comes to laying out my week, I like to have some kind of ritual or routine. I try to stay away from happy hours and avoid restaurant dinners these days because I want to save money and get physically shredded. I start with motivational videos and sometimes oldies each morning. I like to dress in tank tops almost every day. It's kind of out of control to be honest. I have a closet full of beautiful and awesome clothes, yet I will wear the same jeans and tanks day after day if I can get away with it. (I often do). Most days I get hyped up to be the best version of myself as I can be while I battle my array of multiple personalities and emotions like a badass warrior playing tennis. I whack these emotions to the side. I go to my corporate job and play around with my coworkers, cracking jokes all day and planning our escape from the cubicle life. I have a good workout routine before work, during work, and after work. It's definitely not ADD or ADHD, it's just me being me. I meditate with music late at night after I turn on my Christmas lights in my room that I keep on all year round. Some nights I turn on my music really loud and dance as if a hot next-door neighbor is secretly watching me through the window. I fling my hair everywhere and swirl my body in front of the mirror. I seriously think I'm the shit. Before I go to bed I let my mind drift into different dimensions of life memories and future adventures. I plot my "next move" toward a happier life for the next day before I drift into the realm of sleep dreams.

Once I'm in my sleep dream life, I lose control unless I find myself lucid dreaming. The next day I repeat my routine unless there is some kind of class or spontaneous adventure I want to take on. To me, it all seems like a game of chess or Tetris, especially in the city. The city is full of different people, places to go, and foods. It's like I can swim in an open and waterless sea of faces and stuff. People avoid people, often in elevators, bus stops, and checkout lines. We just stand there, play on our phones and avoid eye contact. Fucking weird, right?

You go to the forest and everyone's friends or acquaintances. It's as if everyone desires abundance but not with people. LOL... I totally get it, too many people every single day for years is a lot of emotional bullshit. That's why

I believe everyone needs to get away at least once a year to the forest or somewhere with more nature and less people. In this game, everyone needs a break to refuel, recharge, and jump back in full throttle.

Some people do not see this given life as a game, but more as a gift or a blessing. They believe in before life and afterlife. It's all a choice. That is the coolest part about it. Sometimes I, too, weave in and out of the teachings of the Bible. Sometimes I find myself talking to God and Jesus. I weave in and out of my mantras and beliefs and it bothers many people. I understand how it could be bothersome, but this is how I like to play my game and it works for me. Compassion and forgiveness are not something I weave in and out of, but these are actually the most consistent traits in my life. For some reason, my emotional blueprint is designed to be very compassionate and forgiving. I do my best to step back and evaluate when I give too much or allow too many people to step all over me because of my ability to forgive so quickly. Other times, I feel as though I am hoarding my compassion when I know it's the most amazing part of my love for another.

When I view this life as a game it allows me to feel more empowered. I acknowledge that my body is my vehicle with a ton of super, awesome powers, like my five senses, to help me navigate through the game. I see my "wins" as something that happens throughout the day, all day long.

When I am suddenly laid off or quit jobs I dislike, I don't freak out. I take it as a sign that I'm supposed to move forward to the next '*thing*.' I often wonder what the next '*thing*' is going to be. Like a kid getting a surprise gift from her parents on her birthday, I anticipate and wonder, "What did they get me?" Part of me is nervous the Universe didn't get me anything, but then I rest assured that based on my past, the Great Spirit has never not delivered. There was a time when I didn't view the world like this. I was negative and thought that bad things always and only happened to me. Sure enough, negativity showed up when I spoke it into existence. Once I learned about what all the "Greats" do and how they believe and speak, my ass changed real quick! (Okay, maybe quick in "Helen time," which could be over time and patience in real life.)

I realize to be handed the card of being a woman in this life may come with some pretty tough obstacles, but we've got the best allies in the entire world to make it through life with a shit ton of wins — each other. We've also got the ability to carry babies in our bellies. WTF! Babies in our bellies! How fucking alien is that! Incredible bitches! Sit back and take that in for a moment... it's just fuckin incredible!

Chapter 34

Owning My Self

"Truth: I don't want to settle but I am afraid I will be alone if I don't settle down now."

REMEMBER HOW EARLIER in this book I mentioned I don't like labels and I'm aware that I have manic depressive tendencies? Well halfway through my 35th year on this planet, I realized my emotions were spiraling out of control and no self-help book or peace-making meditations can silence the "I wanna kill myself" voices in my head. What is triggering all of this? Where is anger and pain coming from? Is it the fact that Mark is still part of my life as my main boyfriend and we are just not right with each other? Is it me? Is it hormones?

I'm teaching yoga, working out regularly, and having wine with my girlfriends again; life is feeling really great. Then one day... BAM! I wake up pissed, livid, angry, resentful, sad, depressed. I'm hating every part of me and all I can see are the problems in my life.

Truth: Mark and I are barely having sex, but he doesn't go soft any longer when we do have sex.

Truth: My confidence is not as high as it was when I was in Oregon for nine months.

Truth: I'm not a holy yogini. What would people think if they knew I was a sex-craving, gangsta rap playin, slang-talkin, Walking Dead-lovin' sweet piece of ass?

Truth: I'm weak and I always hold back my tears but can vividly see myself crying, screaming, and breaking chairs in my mind.

Truth: I get bored of jobs every three to six months. I like changing jobs... I fucking love it! There I said it!

Truth: I'm faithful to Mark for a few months and I like being faithful, but I don't like that I'm settling. I don't feel like my true self without passionate-hot chemistry with a partner.

Truth: I don't want to be labeled as bipolar god damnit! But I'm aware that I am manic and it's not because there is something wrong with me. It's because I'm a fucking woman, and I sometimes have a lot of estrogen and serotonin, and all that other fucking stuff that makes my emotions much more heightened

364

than men, and in some cases — more than some women.

Truth: I don't want to settle but I am afraid I will be alone if I don't settle down now.

Truth: I truly believe I'm an honest and good person despite what anyone thinks. It may sound psychotic to some but it's what I honestly believe myself to be.

Truth: I think I am losing my memory at a young age or... I am so ADD that I don't give myself time to rethink many short and long-term memories.

Truth: I love Christmas lights and Christmas trees up from November to April. Makes me happy.

Truth: Owning my Self - all of me not just the good parts but also the cray cray parts, feels Uh-mazing-like I can breathe! It's a Kodak moment, not gonna lie.

So here I am, confessing all of my "Truths" again. This time I am at the point in my life where I'm owning my own shit and I'm at peace with it... Yup! I'm crazy but hot, indecisive but smart, goofy but poised, gangsta but classy, stealthy but strategic, and extremely emotional but controlled.

My biggest fear, which I believe is probably ninety-eight percent of all people's fears, is what other people think. The two percent who don't care are either lying assholes, pioneers, or in my own words... Winners of the Game of

Life. If I can get to the point of not caring what other people think, and I mean, really not caring what other people think—holy shit. Life would be radically different for me. Every now and then I think, what would bold look like in my life?

I picture myself so happy it's insane. I feel free for a brief moment. I wonder if that's where I'm paving the way for myself, but am too afraid to face it because it's too unfathomable to be in the two percent. Can my true and higher self be subconsciously plotting the glory of my life's road without my knowing? IS THAT POSSIBLE? I mean, let's be honest here, we are living life forms, LIVING on a living life form known as Earth, which is spinning in space around dark matter in perfect mathematical equation.

Here's another truth I think of often: I am blessed. I am lucky as fuck! I mean, seriously, I got dealt a good hand in life. I was born in America. My mother is so rad! I had a relationship with my dad. My stepdad is the best stepdad anyone could ask for. I have a healthy, smart, and courageous son. My ex-husband is an incredibly good man and amazing father to our son. My siblings are amazing. I've got the most supportive and free-spirited friends. I'm healthy and beautiful. I have a car that runs, and I sleep in a bed I feel safe in. This alone brings me to tears. We don't choose our parents and we don't choose where we are born or where the game starts for us. It's fucked up for millions of people who get dealt the shittiest hands.

My heart weeps thinking about it and it's happening as I'm writing this and as you are reading this. Some babies are born with a shitty, fucking horrible hand and it is sooooo fucking unfair! (Knot in my throat - fuck, I can't stop the tears...here they come.)

Pause. Breathe. Continue...

This is the cold, hard truth of life and if my being an extremely emotional being is the worst part... then I'm still blessed and lucky as hell!!! Mic dropped!

Here's the hand I was dealt: I'm a woman. I've got a shit ton of emotions I'm still trying to figure out at thirty-five. There is a promising idea that I will be spending the rest of my life figuring out my Self. Maybe the whole "point of life" is that we are supposed to figure out our Selves. Because maybe, just *maybe*... if we figure out our Selves, we will know God or Source, Universe, or whatever it is you believe to be the Higher Creator of you.

Okay that totally sounded all guru cliché and it's probably because I've heard this before, but I swear it's as if I just figured it out on my own for the first time. It's also probably because now it actually makes "for real - for real" sense to me. No wonder all of the master gurus and spiritual teachers of ancient times said the same thing but in more enlightened terminology. Yeah, my mind is totally blown right now! Game over!

Pause. I'm getting a glass of wine. This is getting heavy.

Truth: I'm a product of an affair. I like to call myself *'an affair baby.'* After I was born, my mother took me to see my biological blood dad for two years of my life. Can you imagine how this may have developed my brain and my nervous system? Is this why my cheating habits seem normal to me? Does the desire to have multiple partners and keep secrets run in my blood? Who knows. Who really knows...

Chapter 35

The Three Heads of Her

"The goal is to have our dual selves become one and balanced. What if it's backward?"

I HAVE A LOT OF TIME to think on my drives to and from my corporate job, taking me one hour to get there and one hour to get home. The time alone gives me the gift of reflecting on my life five days a week. I got this job when I returned from Oregon through a temp -to- hire agency. This was only my second time going through a staffing agency. It got me thinking that based on my pattern with past employment, going through multiple employers a year, this may be the best solution for me.

I become bored with both men and jobs after the first few months; maybe temporary employment is the perfect job for me without getting fired or quitting on the spot. So here I am, back in a corporate building, forty hours a week, Monday through Friday, eight to five o'clock; your typical rat in the cubicle maze. I find myself going along with the herd to beep our badges through the security door before flocking to the fourth floor to report to our desks.

Omg, I laugh, this is so weird. This goes against everything I believe in. Hahaha! Focus, Helen. You are on a mission. Your job is not 'this job.' No! Your job is to get in, make all the money you can under this short-contracted time and pay off all of your debt! Wear the rat disguise and when you are ready, take it off and throw it on the mutha fuckin' ground. For now, do what you have to do to work your way to the larger goal.

I am at this job for a reason. A larger purpose. I have to keep reminding myself of this.

Monday through Friday I work the cubicle job and on the weekends I teach yoga in the daytime and bartend at night. I am busy as shit but yet I still feel very free. Old wise words echo in my mind about freedom being a state of mind. Absolutely agree. I wouldn't say I'm one hundred percent feeling free but I definitely don't feel over-burdened with all three of my jobs although there are days when I feel as though my life is not my own and I'm in someone else's shoes.

Today I have the most unusual thought,

the goal is to have our dual selves become one and balanced. What if it's backward? What if the point is to accept the dual as one? Thinking back when I cheated, and how it felt so normal, yet others asked how I felt no shame. I feel as if there are always two or three of me inside. I say two because of my so called "good" me and the other "badass" part of me. I say third because she is the "one" who is aware of all and everything inside and outside of me.

Here I am trying to fit my whole entire life, into everyone's mold of what I should be, or where I should be at this point, and deep within myself I want to try different types of experiences that sometimes collide with each other. I guess my point is that to some, I may live a hypocritical life, but to me, I am living these different emotional and spiritual experiences. Let's be realistic for a second... not something people would say I am.

If I believe there is no afterlife, or heaven, or hell, then this is my true gift. I need to cherish every single day's experience the best way in the moment. Let's just say, I never get the chance to dive with sharks, hang out with Ellen DeGeneres, climb Mount Everest, model Versace, or become president of anything. At least I can say I lived with passion, gratitude, adventure, and that I created magical memories with all kinds of people, from all walks of life with some risk and reward. Then fuck yeah... I lived the life worth living. I'm not saying it's all above water taking the glory road straight toward happiness every day. All roads in this life take risk, some sacrifice, and some take mad desire to keep moving toward what we eagerly anticipate.

It's not always the feel-good, kick-ass high road in this pursuit of happiness. There are pockets where I find myself completely alone and angry. For instance, the road can be super awesome and then bam...trip, fall on your face onto resentment. That evil bitch!

SCROLLING THROUGH ONLINE dating feels so yesterday and it's exhausting. Not as fun as it used to be. Plus, I'm still in this unfulfilling relationship with Mark. Why do I do this to myself over and over again?! Am I the biggest idiot? Why can't I be like all of these strong women who write books about being badass bitches and getting the fuck out of dumb, wasted relationships and finding their best friend-lovers for life right after? Ugh! I mean, am I ever going to find that? Or am I someone who really should just accept this is how it is because even if I did get out of this relationship, based on my history, I'm pretty sure I will just end up in another dull relationship.

Omg! I am beating myself up so bad right now. I'm getting so angry! Agh!!! Wait... Am I about to start my period? I want to cry, I'm so frustrated, and alone! I'm going to die unhappy, alone and depressed and... and... fuck I need to stop this. Breathe. Shut my eyes and take a deep breath. In. Out. In. Out. Just like I teach in yoga. Breathe. Relax. Slow down. It's going to be okay. The me inside starts to weep, but no tears come out of my eyes. I'm too exhausted from a long work day.

THE INTRODUCTION TO... My three heads:

The Demon: Angry, self-destructive, don't give a fuck, devious, hurtful, manic, and suffocating.
The Warrior: Strategic, bold, badass, enchanting, ambitious, protective, executing, and seducing.
The Healer: High on life, energized, healthy, vibrant, positive, giving, fun, compassionate, wise, loving, and believing.

The demon is the worst. I often feel as if there are voices in my head or as if I can't control the buildup of a volcano about to explode. If it weren't for the warrior within, I may have killed myself many times over by now. The demon often creates suicidal thoughts of unworthiness in my head. I have battled my demon my whole life. I don't remember a time without the demon.

I've researched many avenues to find out if there was something wrong with me. Was I really manic? Am I suffering when I don't have too? Do I need medication? Could I really harm myself? NO! I won't have it! My healer rushes in like a mother rescuing and holding her faint child. I believe I can weather the storm and my healer carries me through every single time.

My demon, warrior, and healer are part of my everyday life. My Great Spirit within me and all around me is aware of the three. We are one. This is the buildup of my biology, emotions, perceptions, and interactions with my internal and external world.

I have an uncle who is schizophrenic; he is my favorite uncle. I grew up watching him weave in and out of his head. Some days he was fine, talking and spoiling me and my cousins with candy and cookies from the liquor store. Other times when he was living with us, I would wake up in the middle of the night and see him laughing and talking to voices in his head. I never thought it was weird but just wondered who he was talking too.

Who were these mystery people in his head? Maybe to a child it was normal, since many kids have imaginary friends, but when I got into my teens, I still held onto this belief. Who was he talking too? I wondered what he imagined about these entities. Since I can remember, the idea of other entities living in people's heads intrigued me. Were they real? Were they faking it? Had they lost their minds? Or did other beings really exist within their minds? The brain has always fascinated me.

I never liked sharing my own battles with my demon for fear of people saying I was too negative. It wasn't until I met Dotty's best friend, Charlene, that I began to feel I could open up more about this.

When Charlene openly discussed her own battles with bipolar and its severity, I felt safe to share my own struggles. She became someone I could call on when I was literally caving and needed something uplifting or just someone to allow me to express the heavy internal pain. Charlene's opinions about pharmaceutical medications and my beliefs about it never came between us but only helped us understand and learn about our different ways of coping with our demons.

We decided to help and encourage each other to work out and eat better. We both knew food and exercise were one of the biggest, if not the biggest, healers for reducing the demons in our heads. Even though I didn't like the label, I learned from opening up about it to Charlene, Veronica and others, different ways to help myself when I was struggling.

My warrior within has been with me since I can remember too. Taking risks to get ahead, feeling the fear, doing things I really wanted to do anyways, and standing up for myself when I knew it would make me look like a bitch – yeah... I applaud my gangsta warrior within for all of that! The warrior is responsible for a lot of my seduction too. Something about her is mysteriously feminine in all saucy ways. It's as if she is the bridge between the demon and healer, conversing with both to safely balance me out through this life.

I write a list of things that make me smile when I'm down:

- ✪ *Hearing my son's voice*
- ✪ *Dancing*
- ✪ *Laughing uncontrollably with my friends*
- ✪ *Drinking wine on a mountain and making it back down safely*
- ✪ *Not drinking. Being sober, healthy, and fit*
- ✪ *Okay drinking wine, One glass. Maybe more...*
- ✪ *Maybe a lot more*
- ✪ *Giving gifts*

☆ *Orgasming on top. THE BEST!*

☆ *Orgasming period. THE BESTESS!*

☆ *Smoking some ganja and looking up at the stars*

☆ *Flirting with sexy men*

☆ *Sexy men flirting back*

☆ *Traveling to new places*

☆ *Hip hop and pole dance class*

☆ *Yoga and learning new yoga shit*

☆ *Walking into my room and seeing the bed made! YASSS!*

☆ *Realizing I am more flexible than I used to be doing yoga*

☆ *Romantic comedies*

☆ *Seeing other people laugh and smile*

☆ *Small children curious about life*

☆ *FLOWERS. FUCKING LOVE FLOWERS*

☆ *Oregon and my sisters*

☆ *Mom's awesomeness*

☆ *Puppies. Damnit, they get me every time*

☆ *Women sharing and caring for one another*

☆ *My bank account full of money*

✫ *A car that runs, bout time I got a good car*

✫ *Barnes and Nobles with lots of new books*

✫ *Raw cheesecake*

✫ *Any cheesecake*

✫ *A really good long and deep kiss*

Ups, downs, and round and round we go; the story of my emotions. I hide my demons from many people. No one sees the struggles as I weather my storms daily. I know the demon storm will pass and I believe my warrior and healer are always on standby to see me through. I believe in natural medicine and honestly believe food and thoughts can and will change the chemistry of the body. I may still have my demons, but who doesn't have to deal with her own worst enemy from within. Most days are pretty easy for me to remain happy and successful without depressed or unhappy feelings. Then there are those days when it can get really scary. The journey is not easy, and I can't promise anyone that I will be fine and have it more together in the next few years. Although, what I can promise is to do my best to weather the storms in the internal and external world.

This brings me to my healer, my light through the dark unknown streets of hell on Earth. My healer within believes in the magic of many realms; the one who leads me up the woo-woo tree. The healer is like an angel in glitter clothes that prances on fluffy clouds of dandelion flowers, carrying a firework and drawing sparkly signs in the sky that read, THIS WAY. Every direction my healer guides me, is beautiful and happy. I trust her.

Somehow, I believe we are all made up of thousands of different beliefs from the ancestors before, and the people around us, but I think we all have three leading spirits in our minds. I could be wrong. Maybe I think that because this is my story and I suppose everyone may feel this way. Or maybe, just maybe, I am right? Do we have full control of our own minds or do other entities? One day, I will have full control of my demons. Wait and see. I should have been a neuroscientist... Maybe I once was.

Chapter 36

Insane MasterGasms

"Most all of my orgasms get ratings."

I ONLY THINK IT appropriate to acknowledge something near and dear to my sacral chakra... fuck it...

Let's Go There:

ORGASMS. #NUFFSAID.

NOW, I DON'T FULLY understand the science behind them, although I have read a few books about the science behind sex and orgasms for women. I also have listened to many sex educational podcasts and still can't explain the impact of orgasms in a thoroughly scientific way. However, that doesn't mean I can't explain my opinion and feelings about orgasms.

Just as Bubba had to explain to Forrest all of the way shrimp could be prepared to one's liking, this is the way I must start this fun and furious chapter. Masturbation - a word that has the oddest sound. Almost like someone is locking up the master in a bation tank. Which almost makes sense, because masturbation literally takes our minds into fantasy fire dimensions. For most women I've spoken with it is agreed that we can have multiple orgasms in one session. This includes masturbation, foreplay, and visual stimulation, sitting on a washer or dryer, and using utensils: toys, spoons, foods, and even massages. Orgasms are like invisible wild beasts that only come out when the hunter drives them out of the wilderness. The hunter can be anything or anyone.

"Uhhhh-uhhhh," I moan.

"Yeah, baby, you like this dick don't chu?"

"Ooooh yeah, daddy. I like your big..." Is big too cliché? Maybe I should say, 'hard cock' instead, "... hard cock inside of me." Yep! That worked. I think he just got harder. I really need to work on my verbal seduction. I'm pretty sure he is going to cum any minute. I better get my mind back in it.

381

"Yeah, give it to me, pound this pussy." Tacos sound soo good right now. There he goes, he's hitting the spot now. Damn I feel so fucking sexy. It's my boobs. He's totally turned on by my boobs flopping around. Yeah, he's totally into me. He's cumming! Me too!

"Uhhh... Yess!" Holy shit. Five stars... that was a good one!

Most all of my orgasms get ratings. Five stars, two stars, and some get ratings so off the chart there are no words. That's how I know God truly exists. Orgasms are a mystery of the world and probably one of the greatest blessings from the Universe. I couldn't resist spilling the beans on the top list of orgasms worth trying:

- **Spank you very much-gasms**: These orgasms end with "Thank you" and are best done pressed up against the wall or bent over.

- **Mamma got a brand new tude-gasms**: When you had a quickie in the other room and your kids ask you for ice cream before dinner and you say "Sure, whatever you kids want."

- **I said no but I really meant yes-gasms**: When your hunter treats you like a beast and feasts on your meat and you love it.

℘ **Snail mail-gasms**: When you open an email and your lover sent you a dirty pic or video that turns you on so much you orgasm.

℘ **More bounce to the ounce-gasms**: When your booty is bouncing so hard that your moan turns into a gold record.

℘ **Chef boy are D-gasms**: When a man has cooked for you, cleaned for you, and eats the pussy real good to an orgasm.

℘ **Rock it don't stop it-gasms**:
The orgasms every girl imagines; hard rock, hard cock, and a hard body taking her to the moon and back all night long.

℘ **Insane in the Membrane-gasms**: Shit so good - your eyes roll back, and you feel like your heart is going to explode, unbelievably   strong orgasms.

℘ **Beenie-Babie-gasms**: So tiny, so short, but something better than nothing.

℘ **Choke a bitch-gasms**: When he chokes you and you like it and it makes you dirty bitches cum.

🌀 **Happy-go-lucky-gasms**:
Random orgasms you give yourself
throughout the day in random places.

🌀 **Energizer Bunny-gasms**: When your
orgasms just keep going and going and
going.

🌀 **Baskin Robbins-gasms**: When you
have multiple partners in one day and
achieve different—flavored orgasms
from each one.

🌀 **Cha-ching-gasms**: When you score an
orgasm at the same time as your
partner.

🌀 **Cha-ching-ching-gasms**: When you
score an orgasm from someone you have
been after for a really long time.

🌀 **WTF-gasms**: When you get off on
something totally weird and you have
no idea how to explain it. Never
mention this to anyone.

🌀 **I'm in love with the photo-gasms**:
When you have searched and searched
and finally found the porn video that is

going to get you off.

℘ **He's fucking amazing-gasms**: When you boast to your friends about your new lovers ability to eat it, beat it, and treat it the way you like kind of orgasm.

℘ **Levitation Equation-gasms**: When the orgasm lifts your body up and you feel like you are seriously floating in Earth space.

℘ **Religious Quotes-gasms**: Orgasm so intense, prayers, quotes, and shout outs to God are often screamed out loud.

℘ **Dry mouth-gasms**: Right after the orgasm you are gasping and dying for some water. Often sounds like, "I'm so thirsty" or "I need water." Or even, "Do you have anything to drink?"

℘ **Coma-gasms**: Orgasms so knarly they knock you the fuck out, like right after. Nothing left to give, so you sleep.

℘ **It's not you it's me-gasms**: When you are with him but your fantasies are what really take you to the moon. Wink!

℘ **I'm in a stare-gasms**: When you are

staring into each other's eyes, making love or just fucking and the orgasm is pretty intense.

I remember the first time I had an orgasm. I was on the bottom and he was on top. The funny part is, as I was having the orgasm I thought "this must be what fireworks feel like." Orgasms definitely release some major chemicals in the brain and because I'm not a scientist or someone who is a professional in this area, I'm not going to try and act like I can preach about what happens. However, I will tell you what the body feels, because I'm a woman who has had way more than a thousand orgasms in my lifetime. Now if you do the math with the partners I've had, obviously this doesn't make sense since I've not been with a thousand partners... but like I said before, I can have multiple orgasms.

"Veronica, I think I need to stop masturbating."

"Aw no, what happened?" She giggles.

"Dude, honestly, I think because I do it so much that I can't have a regular orgasm with a man. Like, if I do cum, it takes me forrrreverrrrr. When I masturbate, I cum like eleven times." I laugh.

"Whaaaat! Eleven times!" She's hysterical... "Yeah, that may be a good idea to tone it down, Helen."

"I'm like addicted to my vibrator! I may have to go to Vibrator Anonymous."

She laughs, "Or maybe you need to call the masturbation police to come pick up your vibrator." Veronica turns on her police voice, "Excuse me, Ma'am, we are going to have to confiscate your vibrator and take it down for questioning. There seems to be complaints against your vagina for taking too long to orgasm and its making your man feel small." We laugh outrageously as we hike up the mountain.

Orgasms can be described in various ways. Below is a list of different ways I have described the feelings of having an orgasm:

☆ Like a high carrying the body to another dimension with a higher high.

☆ Body goes into convulsions and the mind goes into the body.

☆ Like the body, mind, and spirit have been given a secret language.

☆ A release of toxins from the world's bullshit.

☆ Answers to questions that you had about your partner.

☆ Like a plug into another galaxy.

☆ A connection to another human being unlike any other connection on the planet.

☆ Fireworks shooting off in the sky and exploding into beautiful portraits.

☆ Weird faces but who gives a fuck, no one cares when it's that good.

☆ Harmony with nature.

☆ So good that the buildup to the orgasm cramps up my leg or foot, both pain and pleasure.

These are my best descriptions. I couldn't imagine not ever having an orgasm again. It's a portal into another world. Who doesn't want to get out of this fucking world and visit other worlds from time to time?

Masturbation is insanely amazing but the gift of giving orgasms and receiving orgasms from another human is invaluable. The idea of sharing the high, sharing the desire, or sharing the life experience is, in my eyes, a form of human love. This is one of the reasons I do believe in marriage and monogamy. If there are multiple people to share it with it becomes like a flower receiving honey from many bees. It's fucking beautiful. This is why I also believe in multiple lovers.

The body is an incredible piece of art. Take a look at your hand and just stare at it. You don't even have to get high for this; just take in all that you are made of. Look at the lines below the lines. Recognize the veins and blood flow underneath the pigment of your color. My mind is blown every time I think of how my body is designed. I'm built with such divine mechanics to think, feel, look, and breathe. It's insane!

By definition, Orgasm originates from the Greek language, also known as Orgasmos. Um, hello! ORGASMOS! The euphoric feeling during an orgasm taking us out of this world and into cosmic galaxies totally makes sense now.

When I first lost my virginity, it was all about exploring and trying out different ways to achieve the orgasm high again. When I got into my early twenties, my libido ramped and Goddess Orgasmos was preparing to make her historical debut. Goddess Orgasmos did make her debut in my late twenties. Masturbation, sexual pleasure and multiple flames ran the show of life; orgasms were flying like fireworks all day long every day. In my early thirties I had over-exhausted my libido, took it in for rest and rejuvenation, and orgasms slowed down. Now in my late thirties, orgasms are a precious jewel and firework shows are more meaningful occasions.

The idea of anorgasmia (sexual dysfunction) for women post menopause really scares the shit out of me. As my libido slows down and my craving for multiple orgasms decreases, it's easy to wonder if I'm "losing myself" or a part of myself that I so dearly love. I often question if it is my partner who is fucking up the orgasmic beast flow. LOL - maybe it is, (that fucker must go) or maybe it is the way of life (not acceptable). Either way, I choose to cherish my orgasms and the roller coaster ride they take me on.

There are times when I want to orgasm all day long, and some days when I want to hold off for a few weeks and build the anticipation. I'm at a point in life where it's fun to play and communicate the different options of pleasure. I'm finally listening to my body and getting to know more about her. When my body feels healthy, active, alive, and happy, Goddess Orgasmos is extremely pleased.

It is my hope that every woman cherishes Goddess Orgasmos, and has the chance to experience all the different flavors of orgasms in this lifetime, because it's a cosmic road worth traveling.

Chapter 37

Nerves and Shit

*"Am I nervous or am I
playing a role of cute girl
with the giggles?"*

UGH! I FEEL *SO* NERVOUS RIGHT NOW. Why do
I feel nervous? I never feel nervous. I've done
this many times. Why am I nervous?!

"Hi, Helen?" To my surprise he looks
exactly like his pics. A few inches taller than
me, about 5'10", not too thin and not too buff;
he's well built for a 5'10" tall man. His top
teeth are straight with a hint of off-white color.
(Off-white sounds gross, but not bad.) His
bottom teeth are not all aligned; however,
neither are my bottom teeth, so that gives him
a free pass. He's a mixture of Native Indian,
Philipino, and Caucasian. He has black hair,
pale skin, and dimples when he smiles.

"Hi, Yes. Samuel?" I stand up quickly and

reach out my hand. I can tell he's pleased with whom he gazes his eyes upon.

"Are you nervous?" I blurt out.

"No, I'm not nervous. Are you?" he replies with such certainty.

I have about a millisecond to think about the question. Am I nervous or am I playing a role of cute girl with the giggles? I've done this before and I'm not about to play this game again.

"No, I'm not nervous either." The moment I hear the words outside of my mouth I feel put together. I remember the reason I sought out a date in the first place. I was purposely seeking a man's attention. I didn't want just any kind of manly attention, No. This was an intentional desire I sought out.

After some time passed, my journey with Mark has come to a final close. I take some time to rethink my whole approach and beliefs regarding men. I am deeply saddened about my final breakup with Mark. During our three-year relationship we shared our love for the fantasy of each other. His family was my family, his house was my house, and his future he wanted so desperately to be my future. I lived in his world and yet, he knew nothing about my world. His disinterest in my dreams, adventures, and the ones I loved resulted in a one-way relationship. I nearly became okay and content with the whole situation. I loved him and was very open about my desire for him despite his disinterest.

Not only did I have to pull my hopeless naïve persona away from an unworthy relationship, but I also had to soothe the fierce tigress within me who cunningly wanted to take charge with a man—hating motivation. One part of me was blind and the other too destructive. My heart was broken from another failed relationship, as I saw it at the time. Although the idea of my alter ego taking charge excited me, I knew this wasn't a good time for her. I had allowed someone else's actions, or should I say non—actions, to destroy a large part of my confidence and belief in myself. I needed healing and happiness again from the inside out.

Even though I felt like I was losing myself, I knew I was in there somewhere. It was Her that said, "We came, we saw, we did not conquer and that's okay. It's time to move on." In my relationship with Mark I spent most of our time alone, even the time I spent right next to him.

During our last six months together, I realized I was technically more single than in a relationship. All I was doing was allowing a man to fuck me every now and then. There was no chemistry. I started to consider it as an offering of my appreciation for free rent and a beautiful house. Sounds fucked up, doesn't it?

Yeah, I know but this is me being honest. This book is the most honest I've ever been in my life and it feels like true freedom.

For the record, I loved Mark and let him fuck me in my ass when I clearly didn't like it at all. I also never complained when he actually orgasmed and didn't give two shits to think about turning around to return the favor. Sexually, he was a selfish bastard. I'm just saying. Repeat after me, "Good men can be selfish bastards too." Doesn't make them bad men but it does make them bad lovers. It makes me sad thinking about how much we loved each other, tried for three years to birth the sexual chemistry we weren't blessed with, and held on, broke up, made up, went round and round for so long — even though both of us knew we weren't happy.

After three years, I became oblivious to my own sexual needs. I stopped masturbating for weeks and then when I would masturbate, I cried after because my body felt so neglected from touch. I told myself, "Look self, you are Woman. You desire to be touched and gazed upon as a beautiful mysterious gem. Let's make that happen."

I have to remind myself what the purpose of seeking out dates is for during this moment of restoration. I want to understand men more. I start thinking about what an odd species we are and how much men and women are different and alike. I reflect on all the men I had previously dated and turn the attention on myself. What am I looking for that I have thought I found in these men? Am I who I say I am? Are they who they say they are? Mark and I were amazing lovers and conversationalists over the phone but in person we didn't fit and often forced the fit. Kyle and I were madly in love the first three months of the honeymoon stage but like Mark, he wasn't able to sexually satisfy me. Ross has always been my "go-to" guy for sexual needs, yet Ross has always been the twenty-something in a thirty-something's body. Ross also has major anger issues and lashes out with tantrums when the shit hits the fan. It eventually scared me away and I never wanted to return to a relationship with him.

Pause for a Thought

SO, THERE THEY ARE, my last three big relationships, my last three men I've loved and here I am stepping back in awe at the rolling hills I've painted with my life. I'm alone, but not alone. I could have anyone at any time. I could have sex with anyone I want, probably any man from my past. Minus Raymond. He's a totally different animal. LOL ... Good sex,

395

bad sex, no sex, fuck it's wild how many ratios one person can get when she adds one plus one equals SURPRISE when it comes to chemistry. Maybe it's because in chemistry, it's not just numbers but fucking alphabet letters too. Fuck me! I'm either really smart or really stupid for just figuring this out. Hahaha! Totally going off on a rant right now. I only had two puffs of the herb at Veronica's before writing this. So here I am, again, except this time I'm taking it slow I'm not jumping into the fantasy again as quickly as I used to. No more "falling in love" after a month or two of meeting someone. Uh-uh, nope! Not happening! No more drizzling in drool like a bitch in heat over a third date or checking my phone all day long to see if I got a text or missed phone call from a potential. No more chasing after a man who I am clearly more into than he is into me.

OMG! No more fantasizing what could be and adding more to the story than is realistically there after one date. No more making excuses for a man who lacks a good head on his shoulders, a man who doesn't have a financial plan, and a man who has no spiritual connection. No more high expectations either. A man is simple, he is doing the best he can with what he has just like everyone else. No more laughing at a man I clearly don't find funny. No more apologizing for being authentic and especially no more hoping that a man likes me while dating. Mutha fuckers are lucky I've given them the time and attention to get to know them. I'm a boss! A diamond in the rough! A Queen of Queens and I do dare say this, a magical and mysterious mermacorn. I'm just saying.

I figure with a record like this, I may find joy in life being single with many lovers. It may be this way until I finally get a pet of some sort but definitely not a cat. I love cats, but unfortunately, I will not be a cat lady. I know this for sure because almost everyone I know is allergic to cats. Bums me out a bit because I love cats and would probably prefer having a pet cat over a dog. How this is possible that almost everyone I know is allergic to cats, is beyond me.

Some people have recommended being polyamorous. "Helen, why don't you just become polyamorous?" They ask over and over. "It sounds like something you do anyway and probably would be more your type of relationship."

"Your type of relationship." Excuse me! My alter ego has much to say about that.

According to my core beliefs I don't believe in types, labels, and tags. Being polyamorous would not work for me. It's great for those who want to do it, but I won't share my men with anyone and I don't want a man who wants to share me. My alter ego loves the game, the chase, and all the buildup of the scheme. My naïve heart loves the fantasy, the idea of true love, and the work towards building something with someone else.

The conscious me is more of a skeptic lover. I like to learn from my mistakes and try different approaches to see if I can produce different results. It's my conscious self that has finally taken over my love life and I couldn't be more at ease about it.

I give my head a tiny shake to bring my thoughts back to the man sitting in front of me.

ॐ

"WOULD YOU LIKE SOMETHING TO DRINK?" Samuel waves the waiter over.

"Sure!" I hesitate, unsure of how this first date will go. I don't have a backup plan and none of my girlfriends know I'm out on a date. No one can save me if this shit goes south.

"You look like your pictures online." I assure him. "Yeah, so do you." He chuckles.

I stare into Samuel's eyes, trying to figure him out and remind myself to check out the rest of him as well. He stares back into my eyes as he speaks about his resume of a life. I have to keep prompting myself to listen and not stray off into fantasy land. He has a cute smile with a dimple. Ahh, not the dimple! The smile dimples get me excited every time and all I want to do is fantasize about sex with this man. Focus, Helen! I remind myself that it's easy to fall for a man in the beginning when he's hot, nice, and sweet, but then after the honeymoon phase he can become an asshole. There's a reason this man is single. I kick myself back into Goddess Warrior mind.

"Wow, Helen! Seems we have a lot in common," he proudly states.

I squint and slightly smile, "Do we? Because I can tell you right now, something tells me we are very different, even in our commonalities."

He laughs and sips his cold ice tea. "Hmmmm, okay! Tell me how we are different."

"Oh, I didn't mean to make it sound like we aren't the same in some areas." Why am I cowering? Ugh! No! Helen you better start growing some fucking nuts. It's not your fault, or his fault that you're a woman of substance.

"No, please I'd like to know your perspective," he insists.

"Well, I was just meaning that we have things in common, but I'm a woman and you're a man - therefore even what we have in common may be viewed differently. For instance, we both like to travel, but you mentioned you haven't traveled outside of the

U.S. Your perspective on travel may be a lot different than my idea of traveling. I'm just stating this because I've dated men who said the same thing, and turned out that my idea of traveling annoyed them, and they viewed me as a dreamer with my head up my ass. So that is all the point I'm making."

I could feel heat moving through my body. Did I fuck up this date by saying this? Omg, I want to run! I sounded like an ass! Stop this, Helen! Own it! Don't you dare start to apologize for being you. Remember what Veronica told you,

"You're not trying to find out if he likes you. It's about if you like him." Breathe.

"You are exactly right. I'm pretty blown away right now." I could see the fire in his eyes start to burn for me. He was clearly turned on. One point for me! Boom! Drop the mic. Got the cat in the bag. Of course, this is about me...Veronica is right and I need to remember that shit. Dude has to impress me, not the other way around. I wonder why I was so nervous in the first place.

The next day I can't wait to tell the girls at work about my date.

"Are you going to put it in the book?" they all eagerly ask.

"Fuck yeah! I'm going to put it in the book," I laugh. T-Money, J Daddy, and Yana are standing there waiting for me to finish telling my dating story when something else comes to mind.

"Speaking of the book... what do you girls think about my marketing plan? I want to have some kind of product alongside my books. What do you girls think about shirts?"

"Like what kind of shirts?" they laugh.

"Like dirty whore shirts that you can wear in a yoga studio." I laugh. "No just kidding. Okay, I'm kidding about the part of wearing them in the yoga studio."

"Okay then I totally love the idea! I would wear a whore shirt any day!" T-Money pokes, "but now I kinda want to only wear it in a yoga studio because I like to break rules." She always has a way of making dry humor sound so wet and juicy.

"I'm serious. I'm going to write this book and travel around the world creating magic in the minds of women," I announce.

"And you're going to wear dirty whore yoga shirts doing it?" T-Money raises an eyebrow.

We all look at each other and hysterically laugh.

"Yes. Yes, I am, T-Money. And my shirt is going to say, 'I cheated and I'm not sorry.' Sign off by my warrior bitch." I sarcastically defend my idea and throw up the deuces.

"How about, 'I will squirt all over your face.'" J-Daddy offers.

"Ewww...there is no such thing as

squirting!" I say.

"Yes there is! I've squirted. You just have to have the right person." J-Daddy proclaims.

"Are you sure you didn't pee-squirt?" T-Money asks. "No, you guys, I swear I squirted and he was just playing with me with his fingers. He just got me so hot and bothered that I did it."

"Yeah, she's telling the truth because I've squirted before too," Yana admits.

"Okay, well I haven't squirted but I do have periods in my life when shit gets bloody. I'm just sayin'." I laugh. Everyone laughs. We give high fives all around.

We bullshit and laugh some more until tears come out. I know then, that all of these ideas, dreams, hopes and visions I foresee for myself are true because of all the laughter and acceptance I bring to women around me. I am meant to work with women from all over. Even if it's to work with women in the very moment by connecting with them in that moment in time. I am someone women can come to, relate to, and tell their secrets to. I get it. I understand and have most likely had similar emotional experiences that can connect us. All of these relationships with men are for a bigger reason. It's bigger in so many ways that I don't clearly understand, but I know in this moment that one day I will understand and it's going to be fucking incredible.

And I can't wait to see what the future unfolds for me.

Chapter 38

The Sum of Life

"I'm cheerz-ing to accomplishment."

INCOMING TEXT:
HEY HUN. IT'S ME ROSS. I HAVEN'T SEEN YOU IN A FEW
WEEKS. CAN WE MEET FOR DINNER?

Eleven years later, Ross still calls me
endearing names like Hun and Baby even
though our sexual relationship ended two years
ago. We have become the best of friends and
still show affection and call each other often to
plan dinner and catch up periodically.

Outgoing Text:
HEY! YEAH. MEET YOU TOMORROW AFTER WORK AT
THAT SUSHI JOINT WE LIKE BY YOUR PLACE. I HAVE
SOMETHING TO TELL YOU. LET'S CELEBRATE.

Incoming Text:
WHAT IS IT?!

Outgoing Text:
TELL YOU TOMORROW.

I WALK INTO THE RESTAURANT where the lights are dim and I can see Ross smiling as I walk in.

"You look great, babe! You always look great!"

"So do you, Ross. Great to see you!" I hug.

We order from our fancy sushi restaurant in the heart of Phoenix. This guy never gives up on me. I truly care for him and know we will always be lifelong friends. I couldn't wait to give him the news first.

We order our drinks and lift our Moscow mules up. "I'm cheerz-ing to accomplishment. I was chosen for a promotion at work and... I've paid off my last debt too!" I shout!

"Oh no way, hun! That's awesome! Wow. Cheers!" he enthusiastically praises.

"I know right! This is it, Ross! This is how I will be able to financially back my plans for a property in Oregon. It is totally going to happen. I just know it!"

"I can't believe you paid off your debt!" I see the look of shock on his face.

"I totally did. I listened to Dave Ramsey and other financial YouTube videos every day, started being more disciplined with my money, paid myself first, and finally got my shit together!"

I hurry to gulp and lift my glass once more,

"And, here's another cheers…"

"What! Another cheers?!" Ross laughs.

"… Yes, another cheers to finishing my first book draft." We cheers again.

"I can't believe you are writing a book!" He laughs. "Sometimes I can't believe it either. I've got a dope ass marketing plan for it too." I wink. "Wow you've been busy!"

"Yeeeah buddy! I mean wouldn't it be cool to have two houses, one in Oregon and one here in Arizona? I'm just going for it Ross!"

"Well damn boo, cheers!"

"It doesn't stop there, mi amigo!"

The look on his face tho… we lift our glasses once more, "I got my ancestry DNA testing back too! Turns out I am a compilation from DNA's from all over the world. Mostly Native American but also Spanish, Africa, Asia, Italy, European Jewish, OMG! It's incredible! I'm a sum total of everyone and everything."

"Wow!" We both laugh and he stops and stares at me for what seems like a minute.

"What! Is there something in my teeth?"
"No." He smiles.

"What is it then?"

"You really are incredible, Helen. You know, I'm not just saying this to just say it but I'm glad you were born."

"Why thank you. I'm glad I was born too."

"No I mean, the way you were born. If your

406

Mom and your real-blood Dad never had the affairs they had, you would have never been born. Look, I'm trying to say, I know a lot of people look down at others for something like cheating or having affairs, but if your Mom had never stepped out, I would have never met you and you're the best person I have ever met in this life."

Ross has me stumped. I've never heard anyone ever say that to me. It never crossed my mind to look at my whole life like that. I mean, there were times when I joked around, professing that cheating runs in my blood or that I was a product of an affair, but I am moved and speechless.

Memories of all the beautiful faces of everyone I care about quickly comes to mind. Adventures, magical connections, the birth of my son, and all of the *I love you's'* flood my heart. Without me this would not be. Without her, I surely would not be.

My heart melts instantly, "Thank you Ross, that is the kindest and deepest compliment I have ever received." I hold back my tears.

We laugh and cheer some more that night. I never will forget his words or his friendship through all of these years. He sees right through me and that is why he is one of my best friends till this day. His words alone remind me that without my Mother's risk to step out on my abusive Dad and fall to her desire for another man, I would have never had the chance to experience this one beautiful and crazy wild life today the way I have, with the people I have, in this lifetime.

"Thank you Mom, for choosing you. And choosing me."

Chapter 39

One Hell of a Journey

"She believed in the wild heart!"

THE SKY IS DARK and lit up with sparkles of eyes staring back at me. The medicinal spirit has already taken control of my body and mind, releasing all worries and stress from the world. I can see my Great Spirit dancing in the smoke as I exhale and fill me with devout oneness as I inhale. I lie there lost in the Earth's arms from the grass underneath me. The sparkling eyes whisper sweet chords of truth unto my ears."I see you."

I smile in harmony, whispering back, "I see you too."

All my life I have been on the move. I have struggled to find my way and my own voice. I spent my whole life comparing and competing for attention with my siblings, with the school kids, friends, other people, other women, and all sorts of different types of communities.

I've been to many different countries, met thousands of different faces, learned of a ton of different beliefs, had many different kinds of lovers, and have danced to all kinds of different beats.

I lie here, looking up at the many sparkling eyes staring back at me. I listen to the Earth's noise coming from the forest. The trees dark and tall standing firm around like warriors protecting me from deep forest predators; they stand guard.

I've done it. I have returned to the glorious area of Oregon. I am loving every moment of this. I left the circle of lovers, the player's playground, and returned to my natural state of luxury -Mother Earth. I relish the quiet stillness of the forest, reflecting on my past city life.

I stand up and sway side to side. Memories of my childhood flood my mind. "Mmm, I'm a magical angel with magical witch powers." I giggle. I look up to the Universe and slowly spin around, "Yesssss! I made it!" I shout aloud.

The feeling of being a free true woman is what is magical and powerful. Free from the comparison of others. Free from the judgments of the corporate world. Free from the overwhelming towers of food in the city supermarkets. Free from the ridiculous amount of negativity from the media. And Yes, free from the desire to cheat and lie to my lovers. Free! Free at last!

I stop and look over to my right where the large cabin-like house sits staring at me. "Hello, my beautiful castle. Thank you." I smile back at the forest house. I finally purchased the property I had dreamt about. I had first imagined it to be only one of my homes. I had always imagined living in the green, but had not really understood where I was best being and calling home. This is not only my home, but I have manifested a retreat center unlike any other to be home to many wild and bold women. There she is, the castle of the wild women. Glorious. Everything I envisioned stands all around me.

I kneel down and bow in honor, raising my head back up as the sounds of my Great Spirit release the howl of my animalistic gratitude toward the moon. I can feel the souls of my mother, my father, and all of my great ancestors before me releasing their honor and gratitude within me too. Praising me for my efforts on the journey and the bravery it took every step of the way. "I did it and I'm good at it! I love teaching women from all over the world and soon many will come here to get their mojo back as I once did years ago. Thank you, Universe Juice!"

I laugh, smile and jump around as I listen to the drums of nature play within my soul. I stop, smile, think about the grand opening date, what it will be like, and what beautiful faces will show up. "It's going to be grand. I just know it." I whisper. I lie back down reflecting on the memories of past conversations and actions that inspired me to this point.

***

"I'm worried about Mom. She's still unhappy and unmotivated. It makes me so sad to hear her talk the way she does." I wait for Grazelda to say something back over the phone.

"I know. I know. It makes me sad too, but she's fine."

That is it! Is no one else as worried as I am?

"No but I mean, she is too young to be talking the way she is. There are 70 -year-olds who would gladly change places with her in a heartbeat. She is not even 65 yet and she is acting like her life is already coming to an end. She is not motivated to work out or get back into things she once loved to do. I feel like we should help her," I announce.

"I mean, if she wants to do something, Mom will do it.

She's fine, Helen. She's just always been like that."

I am shocked to hear my sister say such things. Then again, she is four years younger than me. There were years which she never understood our mother the way I had. When my mother was my age, she was a wild sexy beast. She believed in the wild heart! When my mother would go to work, my eldest sister and I would sneak in my mom's closet and try on all of her erotic clothes. We would pretend we were just as desirable as our mother. She was the ultimate Goddess in our world and we envied her ability to travel on a whim and work just as hard as a man. Mom would always tell the four of us girls,

"Don't let any man tell you, 'You can't.' A man needs a woman and we don't always need the man. We are the mothers and we can also be the fathers."

My mother came from such a cruel world of men who had raped and abused her. She was a single mother of five kids and a go-getter of many dreams. It hurt to hear my mother was unhappy and had lost her desire to be desired. She had given up after no affection for years with my step dad. I often wondered why such a high spirited wild woman would allow one man to come into her life, after all that she had been through years before, and tame her. How is this possible? I was a teenager when my stepdad came into our lives. He's a good, godly, and faithful man. I am truly thankful for him, but his lack of affection for my mother has dulled her once-dancing-in-flames spirit I so secretly admire. So why has she stayed with him, knowing very well, the part of herself that makes her happiest is being diminished? She stayed and continues to stay for... us. Her kids.

I'm no idiot and I know she wouldn't want to make it sound like it's our fault she is unhappy. A mother wolf will do anything to protect and feed her pups. My step dad makes great money and was willing to love her and take care of her children. Mom was reaching forty and realized she wouldn't be young and beautiful forever, so he may be her one and only chance to make a good future for herself and kids.

Seventeen years later, my mother and stepdad are so used to each other I can never imagine them apart. There is love between them socially but not physically or spiritually. I love my step dad and he is well-respected within our family. My siblings and I are truly thankful for his care for our family throughout the years, especially for him caring for my mother. She spent many years staying home tending the yard and gardens. She has lived the last seventeen years very blessed to be with a man who provides for her.

I see so much of myself in my mother. Like her, I stayed with a man, Mark, for such a great deal of time because he was a good man who provides and honors his family and home. There are not many men left like this. Most are on social media speaking to women on the side, can't keep their minds straight, just all over the place... like myself. My mom can't leave my step dad now that all the kids are grown and gone out of the house, because she puts his happiness above her own; it was the same for me and my feelings when I was dating Mark.

The thought of Mom leaving this lifetime unfulfilled brings tears to my spirit. I must do something. I research retreats to send her on or maybe we can do together. She needs to be around women who can reach into her soul and pull life back to her. I search online everywhere.

I see $1,795 to $2,999 for women's retreats in all different countries. Hmm, anything closer? I can't afford to put Mom on a plane right now. I find one that says $985 for a weekend in Oregon. "No Spots Left." Sigh.

Why don't I create a retreat myself? I used to speak in shelters for four years, I've traveled all over, I have taught women to empower and be bold, I'm a mutha fuckin' yoga teacher for Christ sake! Why don't I create a retreat for women for reals? The idea swirls in my mind, planting a seed. Hmmm. Okay I will, but in the meantime, I need to find something for her now.

Seeing myself starting to walk in the same path with the same kind of mate forced me to take a long hard look at my future. I love my Mom and respect her for her decisions and honor her for her sacrifices. I just cannot see myself ending up like her in the future, unhappy, untouched, and lonely. I need to do something for her and for all women around the world. I need to do something for my own self too!

What would I stand for? Why would women listen to me? I am a cheater, a player of the game, a wild and uncertain woman. Am I good enough to preach empowerment and self-life to women? I question my abilities. I fight with my inner demons. Everyday I return to the cubicles in corporate life, I become the dreamer again, seeing myself in front of thousands of women, speaking and standing strong. In my dreams and visions, I do not fear the judgment of women. I do not cower in the presence of faithful and honorable women, because I too feel faithful and honorable to my own natural practices and beliefs. I stand alongside many great and bold women with an evolution of self-life, self-love, and love-life-self wisdom offerings. Tongue twister! Whew!

So I am not a Godly woman. I am not a believer in all that is good or all that is bad. I am not a perfect mother. I am not a faithful woman to many lovers. Therefore, how can I be a trusted and an advisable soul to offer advice? Am I under my own illusion that I can be someone of high value? Am I under a spell of false empowerment? I can hear the warrior within me swoop to my rescue.

I am better than good enough for a high priestess position to advise other women! I do not and will not fear the judgment of neither man nor woman. We are all trying to figure this world out. Who is to say my words are not as fruitful in wisdom as those who escape from struggle just as much as my own journey? I feel my inner warrior carry me through my sea of self-doubt and self-harsh judgment to the resolution of strength and promise that I am capable of advising women to achieve great things.

Am I not a warrior? Am I not a woman just as much as any other woman, dealing with the same strong emotions and self-criticism? Why then do I compare myself to the media of great women when I'm great in ways that many women are seeking as well? Have I forgotten none of us need to compare ourselves; we all have issues! I have to make a choice: Press onward towards creating a reality for these visions or stand down to self-doubt. Fuck! I'd rather eat soup for the rest of my life than stand down to my own self-doubt. (Note: There is no way I would live on soup alone for the rest of my life when chocolate and wine exist.) The decision is made.

I had already been teaching Yoga for a year and half when a special Yogini had suggested that I take a look into Buti Yoga, some sort of tribal dance, power-type of Yoga. I felt uneasy about it because I was already turned off by the Yoga community and its marketing of Yoga pants and enlightened quotes on T-shirts. I was originally drawn to Yoga by the community, but after taking the 200 hour Yoga certification back in 2015, I was captivated by the life energy, Zen meditation, and the spiritual aspect of it. It was unlike any other workout and self-improvement combo pack I had ever come across.

The idea of Buti Yoga, and all its power dance hype, mixing with my honor of the Yogic way, kinda turned me off. I didn't think of Buti Yoga again for a year until later in 2016 while searching to find something to compliment my certification of Yoga. Yoga is peaceful, and I love it, but I need some wild and raunchy shit in my life, too, that can offer financial success. I can't work in a cubic box for the rest of my life! I don't want too!

Again, Buti Yoga magically appears everywhere, online, in convos with friends, and

I often find myself interested for some odd reason. I finally open up to it and watch a YouTube video. As soon as I'm done watching I realize, "*This is totally me!*" I tribal dance all over my fucking house! This is how I do my Yoga sometimes too. "*I'm doing it!*" The Buti Yoga certification course does not come easily. I resist every part of it. I almost walk out during the program but keep asking myself, "*Why am I so resistant to this? Why am I doubting myself so harshly?*" I tend to be very hard on myself especially when I want something so badly.

It's as if I want something to happen and I go for it, but at the same time if it is a challenge to achieve, I beat myself down for not obtaining it faster. Does this make sense? I find reasons to bail from things that are harder than I expect. As much as I want to give up, my body pushes through because of my competitive edge. If there is one thing I really dislike, it's giving up on myself. Hell to the Nah! Ain't happening! I will cry in the bathroom and sulk under the blankets, but I will eventually pull my shit together like a gangster warrior and move forward. And this is what I do... I become a badass Buti Yoga instructor - which is perfect for the balance of my Zen side and my '*I like to move it, move it*' side.

After Buti Yoga, I decide to keep going. I

am going to learn about nutrition and physical fitness. I have a craving like never before. I want to find out everything there is to learn about the body and how to get the healthy results I had longed for over years of "trying." The more I learn and apply what I learn to my life and help others apply to their lives, I begin to see my self-love grow.

I can't say I have always loved myself. I can only admit that I have weaved in and out of love for myself. I have always seemed to love others sometimes more than myself, but have had a true desire to turn that love inwards. Before I thought that was being selfish, because that's a blueprint idea I learned at a very young age — which, in my eyes now, is untrue. By learning more about health, fitness, and nutrition, my body feels at its best; therefore, my mind feels at its best. And when my mind is at its best, my emotions are stabilized, and my thoughts are clear.

There is no time for foolish games with men right now. Cheating has taken a backseat in my life. So far back, I don't even see it anymore. Sex is not dominating my libido anymore. I know I'm sexy as fuck, and that fact is no longer based on what I look like on the outside but how authentically beautiful and badass I feel on the inside.

I've spent my whole life justifying a way of life and now there is no more justifying to do, because frankly, for the first time ever I'm not emotionally relying on anyone to make me feel... anything. I like who I am, who I am becoming and it's more powerful than I have ever felt before.

I convinced my siblings to come in on gifting the retreat for Mom for her birthday. It always made Mom the happiest getting a conference call from all five of her kids. "Mom, we have a surprise for you," we gush. "What is it?"

"The five of us all pitched in and got you a ticket to a four day women's retreat," pause. "Oh, you kids did?" Not sure if she's really interested. Can't tell over the phone.

"So yeah, we bought you a ticket and you are going because it's going to be awesome for you. You need this Mom."

She's okay with it and that is all we want her to be. Mom goes on that retreat and when she returns, she is extremely happy and renewed. It's glorious to see my majestic mother shine through her skin once more. Her wild spirit returns to her and she joins a women's bike club. Ha! I know right then that Mom is going to be a part of my team of women who help run my future retreat. A few weeks later Mom phones me to catch up.

"When are you going to start speaking again, Helen? Like you used to do in the shelters?"

"Well I kind of already speak now except in prisons."

"Oh yeah, I forgot you do that, Helen. How is that working out for you?"

"It's definitely had an impact on my life and my perceptions."

"How so mija?"

A memory races into my mind from my last visit at the jail. I'm sitting in my car outside of the juvenile boys' jail. Me and another Yoga teacher had just finished teaching two classes as part of the prison yoga rehabilitation program. I had signed up as a volunteer teacher to gain more experience a few months back. I had begun teaching in the adult prison and then moved on to the girls' juvenile jail. My schedule eventually pushed me toward working with the juvenile boys regularly.

I end the conversation with my mom and find myself sobbing uncontrollably. What a full circle of life this is. I call my son at once. Ring!

"Hey Mom."

"Hi my Love. How are you my son?

"Good. Just got out of work. I bought my first truck!"

"You did! I'm so proud of you! You're such an incredible person papas. Look at you, going to school, going to work, taking a college course one night a week, and you bought your first truck on your own — so proud!"

"Well, you did help me with the truck."

He laughs.

"Only half! You have a paid-in-full vehicle, papas. You are starting off great!"

"What are you doing right now, Mom?"

"I just got done teaching yoga to a group of teenage boys who are locked up."

"What is it like? Were you scared?"

"No, Keme. I was sad. They are your age and feel lost. They messed up along their own journey. Please stay aware and awake on everything around you Keme; anybody can slip up. You keep on the good path okay?"

"Okay Mom, I love you."

"I love you too." We end our call.

Working with the young boys in the jail brings a great deal of healing to my heart as a mother away from her child. It also strengthens my relationship with discipline of mind. I always make sure my mind and energy are completely purified and clean before stepping into the jail. (Unlike I ever did when I was in church) To my surprise, the program's syllabus has the Niyamas and Yamas as some of the core concepts we have to teach repeatedly. What a fucking trip!

This program is changing lives and not just the inmates. I return to the present conversation with my mother. "You know, Mom, I think I'm meant to speak and teach women and maybe teens in the future all over the world."

"Oh really, and what would you speak about, Hels?" I can feel my mother's nurturing smile over the phone.

She's my biggest fan.

"Mom, life is so short... you know. We are so divided from ourselves and one another. Everyone is judging themselves so harshly, doubting, pointing fingers at others, and talking down. It's an everyday battle for many just to get out of bed," I pause. "So basically what I would tell everyone is instead of looking at your life or looking at yourself and telling yourself nice things... see through things."

"What do you mean?"

I laugh. "I mean, everything has layers. It's heavy. Like, some people hate their jobs, because they see and feel the surface. Some people hate their bodies, because they compare or pick at what they see as a flaw. People judge and judge and judge all day long, it's all surface judging."

"Okay."

I laugh again; at least Mom is sticking with me. "Basically I am trying to say, when I'm struggling or at a crossroad, I try to 'see through things.' I try to see beneath it all. Like as if I am fast forwarding into time and seeing what situations will look like when I make a decision, or if I find myself judging someone I try to see beneath the face and body. I picture her life, sometimes her toddler age. I know—

I'm weird..." I laugh, "... I envision her laughing and crying and that is when I feel compassion towards another human. I am just saying, that I would be a great speaker for women because I am a pretty powerful influential woman, Mom, and I believe we need more compassion for ourselves and for each other these days, ya know?" I pause. "And I would also tell them to pick their sexy up off the ground and put it back on. Just sayin'...I don't know, Mom, I'm just telling you that this is something I'm passionate about and I have a plan worth going for. I mean, my plan to do this is cray-cray and non-conventional but worth a shot." I laugh.

"Mija, I believe in you no matter what. I love you." Mom giggles.

Chapter 40

Don't Give Up

*"If I stay in the game, stay with me.
Please."*

I STOOD THERE. ALONE. Looking down from the top of North mountain, I feel numb watching the sun go down. I'm back in my second home, Arizona. It's different. Breathing is different. Feeling is different. Everything is different.

My brother is dead...

"Nooooooo!!" I scream out to the city. The tears flood my face. "Why Roster, why?!" I break down uncontrollably coming to my knees on the cold rock. I cover my eyes trying to stop the tears like I always have done but I'm so heart broken-for my siblings, my family, and especially for my mom. I sob trying to wrap my head around the events that unfolded the weeks before.

Everything had been going so good for once. I was ready to release my book trailer to the world and launch my website for all to see. It

426

was a proud moment for me. I worked extremely hard for the upcoming big event. It cost me three months, two paychecks, four vacations, and a shit ton of sleep to finally show the world I was serious about my book. It was only my second time going "Live" on Facebook. This was a huge thing for me. The weather was perfect that summer evening and I had even flown Keme in to witness his mother's brave attempt at fame. I was feelin' proud. Veronica stood by my side as we made the big Facebook announcement on social media,. "Watch out world! This book is coming to rock your world soon!"

The next morning, Keme and I headed to the airport. I'll never forget his words, "Enjoy this last walk through security with me, Mom, because this is the last time. Next time we go to the airport together, I will be 18."

"Omg, you're right Keme. Wow, time has passed too quick my little chucky monkey!" We hugged goodbye.

I had planned to take a week to myself from all the side hustlin' to re-energize before making the 'big push' on pre-orders. Life seemed smooth and together. I felt unstoppable.

Later on that evening I saw a missed call from Mom. She was frantic when I returned the call. "Your brother did something stupid. He shot himself in the head."

"What?!"

My initial thought was, Roster is an idiot to make anyone think such a thing. He must have been playing with his guns while drunk and probably accidently shot himself in the leg or something. Mom was trippin'. Whoever gave her this news was trippin'. Roster isn't like that. He would never....

AS I CONTINUED to gaze down onto the city from the mountain top- vivid flashes of memories bursts through my mind in an accelerated manner. Like pieces of a movie reel coming to light: hearing my sister's weep as I delivered the news over the phone that dreadful night, looking into my mother's broken soul when I made the visit to plan the funeral, seeing my step-father cry for the first time standing at the podium, looking back at my brother's large memorial poster as the lights closed to the hall as we all left to go celebrate his life without him- an eerie feeling I'll never forget.

Flashes of my whole life surfaced through my eyes as if my heart was on display before me, I could see it all as if it were current. Childhood memories with my siblings I had forgotten, like huddling with my siblings on bunkbeds in shelters and hitchhiking in town with Mom when we were car-less and rolling down hills in huge tire tractors my siblings and I had dared each other to climb into, and the dreams we all shared over our camp fires flooded my eyesight. An overwhelming amount of thoughts and memories poured in as well as the positivity I preached so heavily throughout the years in yoga and speaking engagements. Relationships, parties, vacations, struggles, obstacles, achievements, awards, travels, smiling faces, sad faces, everything surfaced coming to light in what felt like seconds. I stood there. Numb. In total disbelief.

Three months has passed. I need to let it out. Only la montaña is strong enough to allow me to release the pain I have held in. "Grief, you awful son of a bitch, you! I forgot you exist in this world. You didn't have to take my Mom's only son." I weep shaking my head, wiping my tears.

I spent hours that night allowing myself a safe space to cry on the shoulder of my mountain. Grief is ugly. Never once had I ever experienced grief in this way. Losing a sibling from this world literally felt as if a limb had been cut or removed from my soul's body. It never stops hurting. Ever. It feels like something is missing. Forever.

I wrestled for months with denial. Roster and I shared the same angels and demons. We both were unmarried, numerous failed relationships, separated from our beloved children, shackled to the system paying child support, financially struggling, living on other people's couches, partiers, dreamers, goal-oriented, social butterflies, alcoholics, jokesters, rebels- we were the wild ones of the family. We've discussed every topic including suicide. Roster hated when I got depressed and often talked me out of my own suicidal thoughts. How could he leave me and my sisters like this! How could he do this to Mom? How could he leave his kids? He loved his kids more than anything in the world.

I wish I could say, none of it makes sense, but I would be lying to myself. Roster just got fuckin tired of it all. I get it. I get tired of it all too.

They say that there is a high rate of suicides amongst siblings when one commits the act. I can understand why now. When Roster suddenly left, the reality of death became a thousand times more realistic than when my dad died. I realized everyone I love, I will also be saying "goodbye" to, unless I die before them. No positivity or any affirmative quotes can stop the horrendous power grief and death can have over one's soul when it comes to collect.

The thought of Roster tapping out and leaving the game earlier on his own began to twist my mind. On one hand, I was angry at him for being so selfish to leave us all in pain. The other hand, I was perplexed because a small part of me wanted to join him. He had escaped the pain I still hide. While we weep in grief, Roster gets to sleep in peace. While I struggle with finances, shackled to child support, Roster is free from it all. That punk muther fucker- just tapped out. I swear, he better hope there isn't an afterlife-wait till I get ahold of him again. lol

As much as I want to tell people that I've defeated suicidal thoughts, I haven't. This book is about being truthful. The truth is, my warrior rises up when I feel my flame for life diminishing. Since the death of Roster, my warrior waged war on depression and grief, saying,

*"**DEPRESSION**, you twisted fuck! Get out of my head! You took my brother and I'll be damned if I let you take me!"*

As much as some say ego is the enemy, it's the ego of my warrior that has carried me through my family's tragedy safely. The times I felt the slightest blame or guilt come to mind, my warrior stood ground within stating, "No! You don't get to do that to yourself. Release the guilt. Now."

There were rumors that Roster had shot himself because of a woman. There was a lot of blame and anger tossed towards this woman from friends and family. I felt no blame only sadness. I felt no anger only compassion. We all have demons. Roster was a warrior who lost the battle with his demons. I wasn't about to play grief's dirty little game.

Instead, I went home, put on my knee-high boots and black leather jacket, and went out on the town. I danced, I laughed, and I saluted my brother and father's spirit within.

I'm no doctor or counselor and wouldn't dare to give professional advice when it comes to grief or suicide. However, I do dare to share how I prevent myself from self-harm and how I keep the light shining within to press onward in this life.

Weapons of my inside warrior:

☆ Keep the body moving, stay active.

☆ Podcast-ask others, 'what makes them keep going?'

☆ Hold on to dreams and goals like it's better than a heaven hereafter.

☆ Join support groups (whatever support is needed).

☆ Powerful uplifting music and affirmations.

☆ Gangsta music.

☆ Motorcycle rides with Mom and friends.

☆ Call friends and family consistently.

☆ A candle to remember.

☆ Green juices and supplements to stay healthy minded.

☆ Medical marijuana to chillax and meditate

☆ Write it out: Journal, diary, blog, ect.

☆ Redirect anger towards activity and progress.

☆ Reminder: Don't take life too seriously-we all have an expiration date.

☆ Enjoy the small things, like sitting in the grass, unplug from the phone.

☆ Star gaze.

☆ Let go of everyone's expectations.

☆ Create some "Fuck It" nights.

☆ Say "No More" to the toxic jobs, toxic relationships, and toxic bullshit in your life. Say, "YES" to good times with friends, family, strangers, and adventures.

- ☆ Take action on the hunch or desire to speak up.

- ☆ Forgive ALREADY.

- ☆ Cry - Allow the release of pain to seep out.

- ☆ Stand up for yourself.

- ☆ Be strong when you can and unafraid of weakness when it surfaces.

- ☆ Chillax in nature and with animals.

- ☆ Watch sunrises and sunsets.

- ☆ Observe smiles.

- ☆ Be authentic, no matter who has something to say about it. Do *you* boo. Always.

SUICIDE IS FUCKED UP, for everyone who is left behind. No one saw my brother's death coming. It was tragically unexpected without a note or any signs. He was funny, intelligent, highly social, and a lover of life. It still seems unreal as I write this. Our family was strong; we had the closeness that was often envied by others. When Roster took his own life, all beliefs about positivity, God, and hope took a back seat in my own life. Instead I felt as if a new understanding was born unto me.

The understanding of the cycle of life, survival, and desire. See, anyone can tap out at any time, but whatever it is that is greater, fighting for you to stay- keep feeding that. Keep fucking feeding it.

We envy way too many people who are traveling the world, have good relationships, hot bodies, high paying careers, adventurous jobs, and the best-behaved kids. Meanwhile, many of us are struggling, stuck in cubicles, sitting in cars in traffic, drowning in debt, crying in our sleep over relationships and bullshit. GET THE FUCK OUT! Stop lying to yourself with excuses that you don't know how to... Google it! This is life, a golden opportunity to cease glorious moments starting from the place you are in now. Start with taking the first step out and forward. I know it can be hard. I'm right there with you. Everyday. We got this!

Don't give up. Don't give in. Wake up, release your warrior and tell your demons, "Not today! Let's dance muther fuckers!" Keep fighting the good fight. Live like today is the best goddamn day of your life.

Let's Go There One Last Time

YOU KNOW, when I first started this book I wasn't writing with an intention to publish. I was writing something for my future old-lady self. I wanted my sixty-seven, - eighty- and maybe even ninety-year-old self to remember the adventures of my youth. I've noticed my memory slipping quite radically the past year, and although I've never had an MRI, I came to wonder if I could possibly one day forget who I was and all the great and wild experiences I've had with myself and others. So, I just couldn't resist the opportunity to remind myself of how fucking awesome I am right now!

I don't always see everything in life as bad or good. Every situation is a new situation and a new canvas to color. Not everyone agrees with me, or I with them. We all come from different backgrounds and experiences. I still don't think all cheating or lying is bad or wrong, and depends on certain situations that are none of our business unless it's our own or directly affects us. It's okay to be different or weird. I mean, once you strip away the jobs and titles, the clothes and the materials, even the past and the present, all you see are other human beings looking around at other human beings asking, "How did I get here? Do you know why I'm here?" Life is filled with never-ending questions

436

from the moment we are born until death. Even that is weird don't cha' think?

Do I still want to have hot passionate sex, travel with friends, dance under the moonlit skies, and stand on top of peaks with my arms spread open wide? Hells to the yeah! These are my deepest desires and my magic carpet to many places and experiences in life. However, I've also learned that I have another deep desire to influence transformation. I humbly accept this calling too. I will go the distance until I can't go the distance anymore. A true seeker's life!

One's life tends to drift by very quickly — especially with all of the stuff we have on our lists from day to day. One day you are here and the next you are gone. It is that simple. We will all say goodbye to someone we know or love and the same is true for everyone else. Getting up the courage to be who you truly are, doing what you feel will make you happier and healthier and taking risks that you've always wanted to take, will give you wings that your friends will want to take selfies with all day long! I'm crazy blessed to have been dealt a wild card in life. While writing this whole book I was inspired by music. Music is my DMT! I'm a lover of all music: Rap, tribal, rock, country, classical, Spanish music, jazz, world music, dubstep, Christian music, R & B, oldies — you name it and I can learn to appreciate it!

I HOPE I HAVE inspired or enlightened you as the reader to become a more evolved version of "openness" for yourself. There are many situations that can fuck up our day at any given moment. How we decide to react or respond to every situation is the key that unlocks the door to everything we desire. Wow, that was like a mouthful of wisdom. Am I a saint now? Yes. Am I still a player in the game? Depending on which game we are talking about... then yes. My hope is that you will see that we are all different but very much alike. Let's stop pointing fingers and experiencing the paranoia of 'he said, she said'. Let's **LIVE** the best fucking life we can before we are too old to remember it or too buried to come back to it!

With Gratitude,
Helen